The Courage Book of
Great Sporting Teams

THE COURAGE BOOK OF GREAT SPORTING TEAMS

Compiled and edited by Chris Rhys

SELECTION PANEL

Bill Beaumont · Bobby Charlton · Denis Compton · Henry Cooper · David Hemery

Stanley Paul

London Melbourne Sydney Auckland Johannesburg

ACKNOWLEDGEMENTS

The panel and their guests have been a great help with their selection and constructive advice. I would also like to thank Ian Morrison and Andy Smith for their contributions.

I owe a great debt to Roddy Bloomfield, Marion Paull and Gabrielle Allen of Stanley Paul for their patience and guidance: and especially to Mike Reynolds of Courage Ltd. and Rodney Lucas for their sponsorship.

Additional research: Ian Morrison

PHOTOGRAPHIC ACKNOWLEDGEMENTS

The author and publishers would like to thank the following for allowing the use of copyright photographs:

All-Sport, Associated Press, BBC Hulton Picture Library, Colorsport, *Daily Record*, Robert Gate, MCC, Jim Meads, The Photo Source, Press Association, Sport & General, Syndication International, *Yorkshire Post*.

Stanley Paul & Co. Ltd

An imprint of Century Hutchinson Ltd

Brookmount House, 62–65 Chandos Place, London WC2N 4NW

Century Hutchinson Publishing Group (Australia) Pty Ltd
16–22 Church Street, Hawthorn, Melbourne, Victoria 3122

Century Hutchinson Group (NZ) Ltd
32–34 View Road, PO Box 40-086, Glenfield, Auckland 10

Century Hutchinson Group (SA) Pty Ltd
PO Box 337, Bergvlei 2012, South Africa

First published 1985
© Chris Rhys 1985

Set in Linotron Palatino by The Castlefield Press, Northampton

Printed and bound in Great Britain
by Butler & Tanner Ltd, Frome and London

The Courage book of great sporting teams.
   1. Teamwork—(Sports)—History
  I. Rhys, Chris
  796'.09   GV576

ISBN 0 09 162371 5

Contents

Preface 6
Introduction 7
Preston North End Football Club, 1888–89 8
Huddersfield Rugby League Club, 1911–20 10
The All Blacks, 1924–25 13
The Four Musketeers, 1924–34 16
Arsenal Football Club, 1925–34 18
The Wembley Wizards, 1928 21
England Cricket Team, 1932–33 23
Great Britain Davis Cup Team, 1933–36 27
Great Britain Ice Hockey Team, 1936 29
Great Britain 4 × 400-Metres Relay Team,
    1936 31
The Springboks, 1937 33
Harry Llewellyn and Foxhunter, 1948–53 35
Australia Cricket Team, 1948 37
Jamaica 4 × 400-Metres Olympic Relay Team,
    1948 and 1952 42
West Indies Cricket Team, 1950 44
The Springboks, 1951–52 49
Surrey County Cricket Team, 1952–58 52
Hungary, 1953 56
Real Madrid, 1955–60 58
Manchester United Football Club, 1956–68 61
Great Britain Ryder Cup Team, 1957 64
St Helens Rugby League Club, 1958–59 67
Tottenham Hotspur Football Club, 1960–61 70
Arkle and Pat Taaffe, 1962–66 73

Lyudmilla Belousova and Oleg Protopopov, 1962–69 75
Tony Nash and Robin Dixon, 1963–68 77
Celtic Football Club, 1965–74 78
England World Cup Team, 1966 80
Brian Clough and Peter Taylor, 1968–82 82
United States 4 × 400-Metres Olympic Relay Team,
    1968 84
South Africa Cricket Team, 1969–70 86
Nijinsky, Lester Piggott and Vincent O'Brien,
    1969–70 89
Brazil World Cup Team, 1970 91
The British Lions, 1971 93
Princess Anne and Doublet, 1971 97
Liverpool Football Club, 1973–84 99
Red Rum, Don McCain and Noel Le Mare, 1973–77 104
The British Lions, 1974 106
United States 4 × 100-Metres Medley Relay Team,
    1976 109
Oxford Boat Race Crews, 1976–85 110
East Germany 4 × 100-Metres Medley Relay Team,
    1976 113
United States Ice Hockey Team, 1980 115
Jayne Torvill and Christopher Dean, 1981–85 117
Martina Navratilova and Pam Shriver, 1981–85 119
Australia Rugby League Team, 1982 120
Australia II, 1983 122
McLaren, 1984 124
West Indies Cricket Team, 1984 127

Preface

Sporting success is often seen in the context of head to head tussles between talented individuals. Such contests do indeed stir the imagination, but many of the great sporting moments of this century have arisen from the triumphs not of great individuals but of great teams.

Indeed, a great sporting team working together in perfect harmony excites the spectators in a special way. The power of an All Blacks scrum, the raw enthusiasm of a West Indies cricket team, the arrogant skills of the Brazilian footballers . . . these, and many more, arouse our memories.

The Courage Book of Great Sporting Teams captures such memories in print with all the background details included. The memories live again . . . and so do the teams.

Courage is delighted to give its support to this fine publishing venture and to enable so many sporting highlights to be recalled.

Mike Reynolds,
Director of Publicity and Sponsorship,
Courage Limited

Introduction

On 4 February 1985 the selection panel sat to deliberate what was, to all intents and purposes, an impossible task – to select the sixty greatest teams in sporting history. They were aided by radio and television commentators and the top men in Fleet Street, including Ken Jones, the chief sports writer of the *Sunday Mirror*, Ian Robertson, the BBC's rugby correspondent, John Goodbody, Reg Gutteridge and Reg Hayter. Arguments on the merits of football, cricket and rugby teams, even of local skittles teams, are part of life. This meeting was no different.

The selections were made in the following way. Relevant information was collected from the national sporting bodies as to the number of people actively playing various sports and those who spectated. When those lists were collated, other factors were taken into account – whether the sport had worldwide appeal and whether it was a national sport in Britain. Viewing and listening figures for radio and television were also taken into account.

The information, as with *The Courage Book of Sporting Heroes*, was graded and fed into a small computer for analysis. The panel and guests then followed this popularity guideline when making their decisions.

1 Football and cricket
2 Rugby Union, Rugby League, tennis
3 Other major sports where teams are involved, i.e. athletics relay squads, swimming relay squads, Ryder Cup golf teams, and so on.
4 Teams which may on the surface be described as 'unusual': for example, Torvill and Dean; the team of Nijinsky, Piggott and O'Brien; Harry Llewellyn and Foxhunter.

The panel also took into account several other factors when making their selections:

(a) whether a team was unbeaten
(b) whether a team was world and Olympic champions
(c) that club sides should be represented
(d) whether a team was the first to achieve a feat, although not necessarily unbeaten
(e) that due credit be given to teams from the past
(f) that women's sports should be represented
(g) charisma

Finally, the opinion of each member of the panel about his own sport was taken into account.

There were far more than sixty nominations. Whether the views of the panel and their distinguished guests agree with those of other enthusiasts is obviously open to debate. However, one point was proven. There have been, over the last century, enough outstanding teams to fill a book. The result is *The Courage Book of Great Sporting Teams*.

There were several teams not included which the panel considered worthy of discussion, among them Arsenal's 'Double' team of 1971; the 1905 and 1978 All Blacks; France and Wales Grand Slam XVs of the 1970s; England's cricket team with Hurst and Rhodes at the turn of the century, and Hammond's team in the late 1920s; Yorkshire cricket; Ajax and Bayern Munich, with their European Cup triumphs; Widnes Rugby League Club in the late 1970s; Britain's Olympic coxed four gold medallists; John McEnroe and Peter Fleming; Billie Jean King and Rosie Casals; John Newcombe and Tony Roche; Marion Mould and Stroller; Diane Ford and Bernard Towler; Rodnina and Zaitzev; the East German women's 4 × 400-metres relay squad; the Wanderers; Huddersfield Town in the 1920s; the West Indies cricket team of 1966; the Russian Olympic gymnastic team in 1972; Lester Piggott and Noel Murless; France's football team in 1984; the Wallabies Rugby Union team in 1984. So many variables were possible that Hillary and Tensing, who conquered Everest, were also considered. Not everyone will agree with the panel, but their process of selection has been thorough and constructive.

STOP PRESS: As this book goes to press, Tony Jacklin and his European Ryder Cup team are celebrating their first victory over the Americans for twenty-eight years – a priority entry for the next edition!

Preston North End Football Club, 1888–89

Preston North End were the first outstanding football team. In the 1888–89 season they won the League without losing a match then completed the 'Double' by winning the FA Cup without conceding a goal. Those bare facts won them the early nicknames of 'Proud Preston' and the 'Invincibles'.

Comparison with today's teams is pointless. The FA Cup was the prime tournament but was only in its eighteenth year, the League was having its inaugural airing, and Europe was at least three days away on the stagecoach.

The League was basically the idea of William McGregor of Aston Villa. He was fed up with Villa having to cancel fixtures with teams because of FA Cup replays, and was also becoming increasingly frustrated with easy pickings against local teams. He arranged a preliminary meeting at Anderton's Hotel, Fleet Street, on Thursday, 22 March 1888, just before that year's Cup final, and the formal meeting took place at the Royal Hotel, Piccadilly, Manchester, on 17 April. The concept was for a set programme of twenty-two matches between the twelve founder members – Accrington, Aston Villa, Blackburn Rovers, Bolton Wanderers, Burnley, Derby County, Everton, Notts County, Preston North End, Stoke, West Bromwich Albion and Wolverhampton Wanderers. The rest, as they say, is history.

Preston won that first League championship by 11 points from the pioneers, Aston Villa. One of their key figures was their manager and president, Major William Sudell. It was he who had been responsible for the legalization of the professional game in England four years earlier.

The FA Cup finals were, in those days, held at Kennington Oval, then not only a football stadium but a cricket and a rugby ground, a nineteenth-century 'national stadium', which staged the first FA Cup final, the first home Test match, and the first England home rugby international. The original decree was that all FA Cup matches were to be played there, but as crowd attendances increased, the Surrey County Cricket Club suggested the FA find somewhere else after the 1892 final.

Preston's headquarters for the Cup final was the Covent Garden Hotel, from where they took the short journey to what is the Oval cricket ground today and beat Wolverhampton Wanderers 3–0. Preston led 2–0 at half-time, thanks to goals by Dewhurst after fifteen minutes and Ross after twenty-five, with Thompson adding a third after seventy minutes. The referee was Major Francis Mandarin, the president of the FA, who appeared in two finals with the Royal Engineers, including the first of all in 1872, and refereed a further eight. The linesmen were Lord Kinnaird, who had appeared as a player or official at practically every final, and Mr J.C. Clegg, who had not.

On the Monday after the final Preston continued their 'tour'. They played Sussex at the Preston Park, Brighton, and were entertained by their hosts at a smoking concert at the Imperial Hotel. It was said that the extra game and banquet were to appease Preston North End, who had to wait until 4 p.m. for the kick-off in the Cup final. It was rumoured that the officials – Mandarin, Clegg and Lord Kinnaird – were at the Boat Race.

THE TEAM

Dr R.H. Mills-Roberts

Goalkeeper. He was registered at St Thomas' Hospital, and came in as a replacement for the Welsh international James Trainor (twenty caps). Mills-Roberts, also a Welshman, appeared eight times for his country.

R. Howarth

Right back. An England international with five caps between 1887 and 1894.

R. Holmes

Left back. An England international with eight caps between 1888 and 1895.

Drummond

Right half. He replaced the injured Robertson.

Russell

Centre half.

Graham

Left half.

J. Gordon

Right wing.

J. Ross

Inside right. He scored all seven goals in the 7–0 win against Stoke on 6 October 1888, a feat which put him into the record books. The Division 1 record has never been beaten, only equalled by Ted Drake.

J. Goodall

Centre forward, and the best in the land. John Goodall came from Little Lever FC near Bolton, and played fourteen times for England. His parents were Scottish, and his brother Archie, born in Belfast, played for Northern Ireland.

F. Dewhurst

Inside right and captain. Fred Dewhurst won nine caps for England between 1886 and 1889.

S. Thompson

Left wing.

The only other absentee was Nick Ross, another full back, who missed the final but played in most of the League games.

The League

Home

8 September *v.* Burnley	won 5–2
22 September *v.* Bolton Wanderers	won 3–1
6 October *v.* Stoke City	won 7–0
13 October *v.* West Bromwich Albion	won 3–0
22 October *v.* Everton	won 3–0
27 October *v.* Wolves	won 5–2
10 November *v.* Aston Villa	drew 1–1
17 November *v.* Accrington	won 2–0
8 December *v.* Derby County	won 5–0
29 December *v.* Blackburn Rovers	won 1–0
5 January *v.* Notts County	won 4–1

Away

15 September *v.* Wolves	won 4–0
29 September *v.* Derby County	won 3–2
15 October *v.* Burnley	drew 2–2
20 October *v.* Accrington	drew 0–0
3 November *v.* Notts County	won 7–0
12 November *v.* Stoke City	won 3–0
24 November *v.* Bolton Wanderers	won 5–2
26 December *v.* West Bromwich Albion	won 5–0
12 January *v.* Blackburn Rovers	drew 2–2
19 January *v.* Everton	won 2–0
9 February *v.* Aston Villa	won 2–0

Top League Positions

		P	W	D	L	F	A	Pts
1	Preston North End	22	18	4	0	74	15	40
2	Aston Villa	22	12	5	5	61	43	29
3	Wolves	22	12	4	6	50	37	28
4	Blackburn Rovers	22	10	6	6	66	45	26

The FA Cup

Round 1 *v.* Bootle (a)	won 3–0
Round 2 *v.* Grimsby Town (a)	won 2–0
Round 3 *v.* Birmingham St George's (h)	won 2–0
Semi final *v.* West Bromwich Albion (Bramall Lane)	won 1–0
Final *v.* Wolverhampton Wanderers (The Oval)	won 3–0

Preston North End, the first 'double' winners, 1888–89. Back row (left to right): Mills-Roberts, Graham, Holmes, Russell, Howarth, Drummond; front row – Thompson, Dewhurst, Goodall, Ross, Gordon

Huddersfield Rugby League Club, 1911–20

In the period just before and for a little while after the First World War, Huddersfield, a few miles south of the Leeds-Manchester main road on the eastern slopes of the Pennines, was a sort of sporting capital of the country. Their Rugby League team was the outstanding team of the era, Yorkshire cricketers flourished there and, when the Rugby League team began to fade, the footballers started to blossom into a team which was to win the championship three years in a row. Times were different then. There was less of today's variety. The major sports were the only ones that mattered.

On 26 August 1895 the Northern Rugby Football Union (Rugby League) was founded with twenty-one clubs, who wanted to pay their players to compensate them for loss of wages when they took time off work to play. Six months later, 5 March 1896, the clubs agreed to 'sudden death' matches, the forerunner of the Challenge Cup. Both inaugural meetings were held at the George Hotel, Huddersfield. It is fitting, therefore, that the first (and possibly finest) Rugby League team should come from the town where it all started. At Fartown, Huddersfield created a fine XIII. And, although Lancastrians may disagree, they built the best club team in Rugby League history.

Just before the First World War Huddersfield were known as the 'Team with all the talents'. Their record backs up the boast. Equally impressive was their ability to reorganize directly after the cessation of hostilities. Perhaps their best season was the last before the war itself, 1914–15, when Huddersfield emulated Hunslet by winning all four trophies in a season, the Yorkshire League, the League play-off, the Yorkshire Cup and the Challenge Cup. The threequarter line of Albert Rosenfeld, Harold Wagstaff, Stan Moorhouse and Tom Gleeson were legends. In that season they scored 165 tries between them, tries created and finished in the proper manner.

Today Rugby League is still entrenched at Fartown, a far cry from the pilgrimages to Wembley for the Challenge Cup final. Crowds are rarely into four figures. Most people could not tell you the names of the thirteen players who took the field against Batley on 30 March 1985. But they remember the 1915 side. The names have been passed down through the generations.

HUDDERSFIELD RUGBY LEAGUE FOOTBALL CLUB

	Championship	Challenge Cup	Yorkshire League	Yorkshire Cup
1909–10				Winners
1910–11				Runners-up
1911–12	Winners		Winners	Winners
1912–13	Winners	Winners	Winners	
1913–14	Runners-up		Winners	Winners
1914–15	Winners	Winners	Winners	Winners
1918–19				Winners
1919–20	Runners-up	Winners	Winners	Winners

Club Records in a Season

Tries	80	A. Rosenfeld	1913–14
Goals	147	B. Gronow	1919–20
Points	330	B. Gronow	1919–20

In 1984, Huddersfield changed their name to Huddersfield Barracudas and the name of their famous Fartown ground to Arena '84, in the hope of rekindling past glories.

THEIR RECORD

1911–12

League champions – beat Wigan 13–5 in the championship play-off final – lost 2–0 to Oldham in the quarter final of the Challenge Cup (or Northern Cup as it was then called) – beat Hull Kingston Rovers 22–10 in the Yorkshire Cup final – Albert Rosenfeld set a new league record with 78 tries in the season – Stan Moorhouse also beat the old record, with 55 – Harold Wagstaff and Edgar Wrigley were fourth and fifth in the try-scoring list.

1912–13

League champions – beat Wigan 29–2 in the championship play-off – beat Warrington 9–5 to win the Northern Cup – Albert Rosenfeld was again the League's top try scorer.

1913–14

League champions – lost 5–3 to Salford in the championship play-off – lost to Hull in the semi final of the Northern Cup – beat Bradford Northern to win the Yorkshire Cup – Rosenfeld set a new league record with 80 tries – Major Holland set a new league goals record with 131 – Holland and Rosenfeld were first and second in the season's leading points-scoring list.

1914–15

League champions – beat Leeds 35–2 to win the Championship play-off – beat St Helens 37–3 to win the Northern Cup – beat Hull 31–0 to win the Yorkshire Cup – won the Yorkshire League – in semi final of the Yorkshire Cup they beat Hunslet 64–3, the biggest scoreline ever in a major semi final – six of their players scored 25 or more tries in the season – Ben Gronow set new league goals and points records: 136 and 284 respectively.

1918–19

The league and the Northern Cup were not contested but the Yorkshire Cup was, Huddersfield beating Dewsbury 14–8 in the final.

1919–20

Won the league – were runners-up in the championship play-off to Hull – beat Wigan 21–10 to win the Northern Cup – won the Yorkshire Cup – Stan Moorhouse was the league's top scorer – Ben Gronow was the league's leading kicker and points scorer with 147 and 330 respectively – both new records.

SOME HUDDERSFIELD RECORDS STILL STANDING TODAY

In the 1913 Cup final Stan Moorhouse scored three tries – a record shared by just two other men. His total of four tries in Cup finals (two) also still stands, shared by four men.

The record for the most tries in a Yorkshire Cup final is four. Two men share this record and both were Huddersfield players: G. Todd (1913, v. Bradford) and Stan Moorhouse (1920, v. Leeds).

Major Holland's five goals in the 1914 Yorkshire Cup final against Hull was the only occasion, up to 1950, that anybody had kicked five goals in the final. Although since equalled, the tally has still not been beaten.

Douglas Clark holds the record for the most appearances in a Yorkshire Cup final: ten, between 1909 and 1926. Stan Moorhouse holds the record for the most tries in aggregate in Yorkshire Cup finals with six – he jointly shares the record.

The record score in a senior Rugby League game was established on 28 February 1914 when Huddersfield beat Swinton Park Rangers 119–2. In the same game Major Holland kicked eighteen goals – still a club record and the second best of all time (it was a British record at the time). His 39 points is also still a club record.

In the 1919–20 season Ben Gronow kicked the current club record of 147 goals in a season. His points tally of 330 is also still a club record.

Between 1909 and 1929 Douglas Clark created the club record for the most appearances – 459.

THE PLAYERS

Douglas Clark

From Cumberland, he joined Huddersfield in 1909 for just £30. Classed as a 'Giant among Giants', he was a loose forward. He spent sixteen years at Fartown. He was also a renowned wrestler in his day.

Tom Gleeson

An Australian, he joined Huddersfield on 9 November 1912 for a fee of £200, plus £4 per match for a win, £3 for a draw and £2 for a loss. Shortly after his signing, the transfer ban on overseas players was reimposed.

Ben Gronow

A Welshman, and prolific goal kicker.

Major Holland

Full back and goal kicker. After excellent service at Fartown he was granted a free transfer in the 1921–22 season and joined Bramley.

Stan Moorhouse

Wagstaff's centre partner, he spent eleven seasons at Huddersfield before going to Bradford Northern as player-coach.

Huddersfield's best ever team. In 1914–15 they won all four trophies in a season

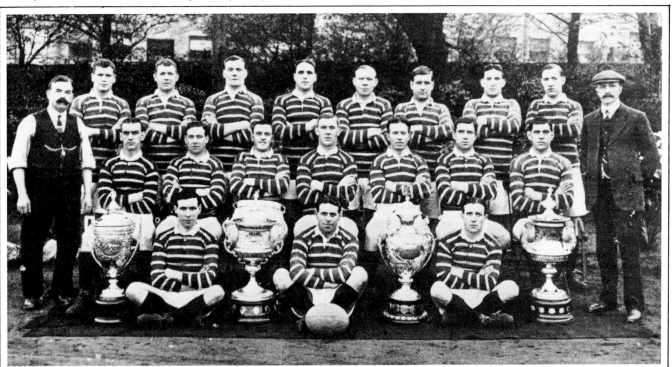

1914   HUDDERSFIELD NORTHERN UNION F.C.   1915.

A. Lee.   J. W. Higson.   H. Banks.   E. Jones.   E. Heyes.   F. Longstaff.   D. Clark.   A. Swinden.
A. Bennett (Trainer.)   R. Habron.   M. Holland.   S. Moorhouse.   H. Wagstaff (Capt).   T. Gleeson.   G. Todd.   B. Gronow.   H. Bennett (Assist. Trainer.
Y. L. Cup.   W. H. Ganley.   N. R. L. Cup.   A. A. Rosenfeld.   N. U. C. Cup.   J. H. Rogers.   Y. C. Cup.

John Henry Rogers

One of the finest Welsh players to play for the club. He had never seen a Northern Union game until making his debut on St David's Day, 1913. He cost £100. He was 5 feet 4 inches tall and weighed 10st 9lb. He twice toured Down Under. He moved to Wakefield for £300 in 1925.

Albert Rosenfeld

A prolific try scorer. When he retired in 1924 he had scored a then British record of 392 tries. He is still the holder of the most tries in one season – eighty – and in 1911 he became the third player to score eight tries in one game. Huddersfield's star of the 1950s, Lionel Cooper, also emulated this feat (twice). In the four consecutive seasons, 1911–12, 1912–13, 1913–14, 1914–15, Rosenfeld scored over fifty tries each season. Between October and December 1913 he scored tries in fourteen consecutive games, a Rugby League record only bettered by E. Harris of Leeds, who scored in seventeen. After leaving Huddersfield, Rosenfeld played for Wakefield Trinity and Bradford Northern.

Herbert (Clon) Sherwood

Ex-Hull Kingston Rovers and Castleford, he joined Huddersfield in 1908. His younger brother Arthur later joined him at Fartown.

Harold Wagstaff

The 'Prince of Centres', he was only fifteen when he made his Huddersfield debut; he was also one of the youngest ever Great Britain players. His Huddersfield debut was against Bramley in 1906. He was the club's captain throughout their glory days. He also captained Great Britain on two tours Down Under. After leading Huddersfield he coached at Halifax and Broughton Rangers. He died at the age of forty-eight.

Edgar Wrigley

A New Zealander, he was the first overseas player bought by Huddersfield, for a then club record of £200. In the 1911–12 season he and Rosenfeld were responsible for 376 points. He went to Hunslet for £500 in 1914 and then to Bradford Northern and Hull as coach. He returned to Fartown in 1935 as coach.

Huddersfield's trainer during their successful years was Arthur Bennett. He had been with the club since their Rugby Union days. He retired in 1916.

In 1920, two Huddersfield members were appointed to senior positions within the sport. Harold Wagstaff became chairman of the newly formed Northern Union Players' Union, and W. Fillan succeeded J.H. Smith as chairman of the Northern Union itself.

Gronow, Wagstaff, Rogers, Thomas and Clark – Huddersfield players selected for the Great Britain team to tour Australia in 1920

The All Blacks, 1924–25

The 1924 All Blacks, known as the Invincibles, were probably the most famous of all teams to leave New Zealand. Their own annuals and reference books suggest this. They played thirty matches in Britain and France and won them all. In the days of the 3 point try they amassed 721 points and conceded just 112. In Britain alone they scored 156 tries to sixteen. They had one desperately close struggle with Newport before winning 13–10, and were put under some pressure by Cambridge University, Llanelly (later changed to Llanelli), Somerset, Gloucestershire and by Ireland in the first of the internationals. That was all.

These tourists were the first to arrive from New Zealand for twenty years. The 1905 team had also beaten everyone in sight except Wales. The second All Blacks side were inevitably subjected to critical analysis, especially when they struggled for cohesion in the West Country during the early part of the tour. But matches in the Midlands and the North brought painful reminiscences of the past and clear evidence that the tourists had settled down.

Already the outstanding quality of some of the players had become evident – evident enough to overcome the burden of the loss of the captain, Porter, through injury and a resultant lack of fitness. George Nepia, at nineteen the youngest in the party, played in all thirty matches. The shrewd tactical kicking and generalship of Mark Nicholls at five eighth was a calming influence, and the forwards were steeped in the typical All Black tradition. Parker, Richardson and the Brownlie brothers were particularly impressive, with Parker, listed as the wing forward, fast enough to be regarded as quicker than his formidable wingers.

Four internationals were played (the All Blacks did not visit Scotland on their tour) and the first, against Ireland at Lansdowne Road, proved to be the closest of the four. The positional listing of the forwards has since proved a statistical nightmare. The All Blacks played two hookers, three in the second row, two in the back row and a loose forward. Ireland, delightfully, announced that they would pack 3-2-3 with no set positions. The first three to arrive went into the front row and so on. A try from 'Snowy' Svenson was the only time the try line was breached, and a Nicholls penalty gave the All Blacks an uncomfortable victory.

The next international was at Swansea where crowds had to be turned away. New Zealand fielded three new caps and were intent on revenge for their only defeat on the 1905 tour, when an equalizing try had been turned down; the subsequent disputes turned the incident into folklore. However, the Welsh team were in such poor shape that the 'avenging of Cardiff' turned out to be rather a hollow triumph. The All Blacks won by 19–0, scoring tries through Maurice Brownlie (two), Irvine and Svenson, with Nicholls converting two and kicking a penalty.

The All Blacks cleared the path to Twickenham and the final game of the British part of the tour against England with their now customary efficiency. A record crowd was left drifting haplessly away unable to get in. England, in rugby terms, were Britain's last hope. New Zealand won by 17 points to 11, largely because they were the fitter and better balanced side. They needed to be fitter because they were a forward short for most of the game.

The incidents which led to the sending off of Cyril Brownlie can now be fairly disregarded, indeed consigned to a chapter of well-forgotten events. Albert Freethy, from Llanelly, dismissed Brownlie after just eight minutes, when matters became certainly heated but never out of control. It spoke volumes for the All Blacks that they recovered from such a disastrous start for the seven forwards to create tries for the wings, Steel and Svenson. A half-time score of 9–3 soon became 17–3 when Maurice Brownlie, reportedly intent on salvaging the family name and playing like a man inspired, scored the third try, with Parker adding the fourth. England's late recovery owed much to the extra man in the closing stages.

George Nepia who played in every match on the tour

The All Blacks caught in uncharacteristic disarray during the International with Wales at Swansea

Over to France and two easy victories, with eight tries in the international at Toulouse, finished the tour in style. The All Blacks had maintained an unbeaten record. Two New Zealand touring teams had now been to Britain and France – they had played a total sixty-six games, won sixty-five and lost one. In Britain alone they had scored 361 tries and conceded just twenty-three.

With far fewer internationals than in the modern era, several fine players made their only test appearances on the tour. Despite fixtures with South Africa in 1921 and 1928, New Zealand played only fourteen internationals during the decade.

George Nepia turned to Rugby League and played for Streatham and Mitcham; Bert Cooke was another who turned to the thirteen-a-side game. Both were later reinstated as Union players, Nepia as a referee.

The popularity of the Invincibles can be illustrated by events at Toulouse. Max Boyce, much later, wrote poems about spectators who would dress up as ambulancemen and bandsmen to sneak into Cardiff Arms Park. In Toulouse, they all became journalists – three from New Zealand, forty-five from the British Isles, 120 from Paris and 180 from the rest of France!

THE TOUR PARTY

Full Back
G. Nepia (Hawkes Bay)

Threequarters
H.W. Brown (Taranaki), A.H. Hart (Taranaki), F.W. Lucas (Auckland), A.C.C. Robilliard (Canterbury), J. Steel (West Coast), K.S. Svenson (Wellington), C.E.O. Baddeley (Auckland), A.E. Cooke (Auckland), N.P. McGregor (Canterbury)

Half Backs
W.C. Dalley (Canterbury), M.F. Nicholls (Wellington), L. Paewei (Hawkes Bay), J.J. Mill (Hawkes Bay)

Forwards
C.J. Brownlie (Hawkes Bay), M.J. Brownlie (Hawkes Bay), L.F. Cupples (Bay of Plenty), Q. Donald (Wairarapa), I.H. Harvey (Wairarapa), W.R. Irvine (Hawkes Bay), R.R. Masters (Canterbury), B.V. McCleary (Canterbury), H.G. Munro (Otago), J.A. Parker (Canterbury), C.G. Porter (Wellington), J. Richardson (Southland), R.T. Stewart (South Canterbury), A.H. West (Taranaki), A. White (Southland)
Captain: C.G. Porter
Manager: S.M.M. Dean

THE ALL BLACKS IN EUROPE, 1924–25

	Ireland	Wales	England	France
Porter				F (1T)
Nepia	FB	FB	FB	FB
Svenson	RW (1T)	LW (1T)	LW (1T)	LW (1T)
Cooke	C	C	C	C (2T)
Lucas	C			C
Hart	LW			
Nicholls	FH (1PG)	C (2C, 1PG)	C (1C, 1PG)	FH (3C)
Dalley	SH			
Parker	F*	F	F (1T)	
Cupples	F	F		
White	F		F	F (1T)
Masters	F	F	F	F
Richardson	F	F	F	F (1T)
M.J. Brownlie	F	F (1T)	F (1T)	F
Donald	F	F	F	F
Irvine	F	F (2T)	F	F (1T)
McGregor		FH	FH	
C.J. Brownlie		F	F	F
Mill		SH	SH	SH
Steel		RW	RW (1T)	RW (1T)
Score:	6–0	19–0	17–11	30–6

* F = Forward – the New Zealand scrum packed 2–3–2–1.

All Black possession from a line-out during the victory over France at the Colombes Stadium, Paris

Leading Tour Appearances (all matches)
Nepia   30
Irvine   27
M.J. Brownlie   24
Cooke, Richardson   23
Masters   22
Svenson, White   21
McGregor   20

Chief Scorers (British Isles only)
Nicholls   97
Nepia   66

Leading Try Scorers (British Isles only)
Hart   18
Cooke, Steel   16
Svenson, Parker   15

TOUR RECORD

Opponent	Venue	Result
Devon	Devonport	won 11–0
Cornwall	Camborne	won 29–0
Somerset	Weston	won 6–0
Gloucestershire	Gloucester	won 6–0
Swansea	Swansea	won 39–3
Newport	Newport	won 13–10
Leicester	Leicester	won 27–10
North Midlands	Aston Villa F.C.	won 40–3
Cheshire	Birkenhead	won 18–5
Durham	Sunderland	won 43–7
Yorkshire	Bradford	won 42–4
Lancashire	Manchester	won 23–0
Cumberland	Carlisle	won 41–0
Ireland	Dublin	won 6–0
Ulster	Belfast	won 28–6
Northumberland	Newcastle	won 27–4
Cambridge University	Cambridge	won 5–0
London Counties	Twickenham	won 31–6
Oxford University	Oxford	won 33–15
Cardiff	Cardiff	won 16–8
Wales	Swansea	won 19–0
Llanelly	Llanelly	won 8–3
East Midlands	Northampton	won 31–7
Warwickshire	Coventry	won 20–0
Combined Services	Twickenham	won 25–3
Hampshire	Portsmouth	won 22–0
London	Blackheath	won 18–3
England	Twickenham	won 17–11
French XV	Paris	won 37–8
France	Toulouse	won 30–6

The Four Musketeers, 1924–34

With the exception of the United States, and possibly Australia, where strength in depth is common on the tennis circuits, most countries, especially in Europe, tend to throw up the occasional world-class individual or a harmonious doubles pairing. But between the wars France, in the shape of the 'Four Musketeers' – Borotra, Cochet, Lacoste and Brugnon – contrived to produce four of the world's top players.

Pierre Gillou, the coach, found team selection straightforward. At least two of the players represented France in the Davis Cup every year from 1922 to 1934; between 1927 and 1932 Gillou avoided controversy and selected all four. The first occasion when the team was assembled was against Denmark in 1922 when Cochet and Borotra played together; all four were selected for the first time against the luckless Irish in 1923; and Borotra and Brugnon brought the era to a close when they paired up against Australia in 1934.

As individuals, however, they were very different. Jean Borotra, known as 'the Bounding Basque', came from Pouy, near Biarritz; he was a fine volleyer and, for some unaccountable reason, always played in a beret. Jean René Lacoste came from Marseille; he became the most efficient baseliner in the world. He had brilliant ground strokes and was a master defensive tactician. He kept a book in which he listed other players' weaknesses, and offered a £250 reward when it was stolen. Jacques Brugnon, from Paris, excelled in the doubles. Less talented than the others, he realized that Davis Cup points and successful pot hunting depended on teaming up with his more talented colleagues. Henri Cochet, nicknamed 'the little man from Lyons', completed the 'Musketeers'. Like Borotra, he was fast and instinctive and a fine volleyer.

Lacoste was not blessed with the best of health and, in 1926, had to take six months' rest. The other three, however, could not get the game out of their system. Borotra and Brugnon played in the veterans' doubles at Wimbledon in 1964, and Cochet reached the final of the British Hard Courts championship in his fiftieth year.

It was Borotra who seemed, as he had during their playing days, to be the spokesman for the quartet. He became one of France's most successful businessmen and voiced strong and sensible opinions on a host of tennis committees. He entered the veterans' singles at Wimbledon in 1968 and graciously admitted that, at the age of seventy, he was slowing down a little. Cochet won eight Grand Slam titles, Lacoste seven and Borotra five. But the remarkable aspect of Borotra's career is that he only played abroad where and when he could combine tennis with a business meeting.

THE PLAYERS

Jean Borotra

Born 13 August 1898, he played in thirty-two Davis Cup ties between 1922 and 1947. He was forty-nine when he played in his last tie. Out of a total of fifty-four rubbers he played, he won thirty-six. He won the Wimbledon singles in 1924 and 1926, and the doubles in 1925, 1932, and 1933; the French singles in 1924 and 1931, and the doubles in 1925, 1928, 1929, 1934 and 1936; and the Australian singles and doubles in 1928. He competed in his first Wimbledon in 1922; his last one (in the veterans' competition) was in 1968 at the age of seventy. He held a degree in engineering and law and became president of the International Lawn Tennis Federation.

Jacques Brugnon

Born 11 May 1985, he played in thirty-one Davis Cup ties between 1921 and 1934 and won twenty-six rubbers out of thirty-seven. He was a doubles specialist. He had early successes with Cochet, but then established a partnership with Borotra. When the pair of them reached the French doubles final in 1939 their combined ages were eighty-four. He won the Wimbledon doubles in 1926, 1928, 1932 and 1933, the Australian doubles in 1928 and the French doubles in 1927, 1928, 1930, 1932 and 1934, and his best Wimbledon singles was in 1926 when he reached the semi-finals. He died on 20 March 1978.

Henri Cochet

Born on 14 December 1901, he played in twenty-six Davis Cup ties between 1922 and 1933, winning forty-four of fifty-eight rubbers. He was Wimbledon singles champion in 1927 and 1929, and doubles champion in 1926 and 1928. He won the US singles title in 1928, the French singles in 1922, 1926, 1928, 1930 and 1932, and the French doubles in 1927, 1930 and 1932. He turned professional in 1933 but was reinstated as an amateur after the war. He became adviser and coach after he finished playing.

Jean René Lacoste

Born on 2 July 1904, he played in twenty-six Davis Cup ties between 1923 and 1928; he won forty of fifty-one rubbers. He won the Wimbledon singles in 1925 and 1928, and the doubles in 1925. He won the US singles in 1926 and 1927, the French singles in 1925, 1927 and 1929 and the French doubles in 1924, 1925 and 1929. He beat Tilden and Johnson in crucial singles matches to win the Davis Cup for France for the first time in 1927.

GRAND SLAM TOURNAMENTS, 1924–1933

French Championships

Men's Singles

1924	Borotra	1927	Lacoste	1930	Cochet
1925	Lacoste	1928	Cochet	1931	Borotra
1926	Cochet	1929	Lacoste	1932	Cochet

Men's Doubles
1924 Borotra/Lacoste
1925 Borotra/Lacoste
1927 Cochet/Brugnon
1928 Borotra/Brugnon
1929 Borotra/Lacoste
1930 Cochet/Brugnon
1932 Cochet/Brugnon

Mixed Doubles
1924 Borotra/Billout
1925 Brugnon/S. Lenglen
1926 Brugnon/S. Lenglen
1927 Borotra/M. Bordes
1928 Cochet/E. Bennett
1929 Cochet/E. Bennett

Wimbledon Championships

Men's Singles
1924 Borotra
1925 Lacoste
1926 Borotra
1927 Cochet
1928 Lacoste
1929 Cochet

Men's Doubles
1925 Borotra/Lacoste
1926 Cochet/Brugnon
1928 Cochet/Brugnon
1932 Borotra/Brugnon
1933 Borotra/Brugnon

Mixed Doubles
1925 Borotra/S. Lenglen

United States Championships

Men's Singles
1926 Lacoste
1927 Lacoste
1928 Cochet

Mixed Doubles
1926 Borotra/E. Ryan
1927 Cochet/E. Bennett

Australian Championships

Men's Singles
1928 Borotra

Men's Doubles
1928 Borotra/Brugnon

Mixed Doubles
1928 Borotra/D. Akhurst

Davis Cup Wins

1927–1932 inclusive

Above: *Jean Borotra's athletic backhand return watched by an airborne René Lacoste at Wimbledon in 1928*

Opposite: *Henri Cochet* (right) *and Jacques Brugnon leave the Centre Court after winning the 1926 Wimbledon doubles title*

Arsenal Football Club, 1925–34

Arsenal FC surround one of football's larger prizes!

It is a bone of contention between Arsenal supporters as to whether their team was better during the Chapman era from 1925 to 1934 or during the 'Double' season of 1970-71. With a time lapse of thirty-five years, only a few supporters were able to judge each team objectively, but those in the press and media who spanned the gap are emphatic, with due respect to the magnificent feats of Bertie Mee and Frank McLintock's team which played nearly seventy games in 1970–71, that the side built by Herbert Chapman was a team of rare talent. What impressed observers in Chapman's era was not only the style of play on the field but the innovations 'off the park', mainly instigated by Chapman himself, that are still commonplace today.

Chapman took over in 1925. He had seen Huddersfield, his previous team, win two successive League titles and left during the season in which they made it a hat trick of titles. Immediately he led Arsenal to second place behind Huddersfield.

He succeeded the unfortunate Leslie Knighton as manager at Highbury, with Arsenal a middle-of-the-road First Division team. Immediately Chapman impressed with the shrewdness of his deals in the transfer market. Arsenal desperately needed shape and discipline on the field, but with money scarce Chapman had to invest wisely.

The foundations of the 'new' Arsenal were built around Charlie Buchan, whom he brought to Highbury from Sunderland in a then controversial and unusual transfer deal –

£2000 plus £100 for every goal he scored; he scored nineteen in the League and two in the Cup, and Sunderland benefited by another £2100. With Buchan, Chapman devised the W–M style of play, which, by the end of the decade, was in use world wide.

In 1927, Chapman appointed Tom Whittaker as trainer. He then needed a solid captain and found two – Tom Parker, the right back from Southampton, and his successor Eddie Hapgood, whom Chapman bought from Kettering for just £750. Hapgood went on to captain England.

Like Shankly years later, Chapman had the knack of turning mediocre players into international class performers. George Male was one such example, from an aimless half back to England's full back, and still in the Arsenal team when they won the League in 1948.

The team building continued. Policeman Herbie Roberts was signed, from another non-League team, Oswestry, for £200; he became the first 'stopper' centre half. In 1928–29, with 'real' money to spend, Chapman made three decisive captures. David Jack came from Bolton for a League record fee of £10,340; Alex James, of the long shorts and short legs, arrived from Preston for £9000; and to Exeter City Arsenal paid a then staggering £2000 for a seventeen-year-old with only seventeen League games to his credit – Cliff Bastin is still recognized as probably England's finest left winger.

There were solid players already at the club: Bob John played a then record 421 games for the Gunners between 1922 and 1938; 'Iron Man' Wilf Copping, flying winger Joe Hulme and goalscorer Ted Drake were also part of a now unbeatable squad. Drake was to score seven goals out of eight shots at Aston Villa in 1935. The eighth hit the crossbar.

By 1930–31 Arsenal and Chapman had put the pieces together, with a record 127 goals and another record of 66 points. They were not averse to the odd 6–6 draw (*v.* Leicester in 1930). The following season they were pipped by Everton in the League, and lost in the Cup final to Newcastle in the famous 'over the line' incident. They missed Alex James, who was injured.

With another 118 goals in 1932–33, the Gunners regained the League championship. How they lost to Walsall of the Third Division in the FA Cup third round remains football's biggest mystery.

Herbert Chapman died on 6 January 1934, with Arsenal three points clear at the top of Division 1. He had led Arsenal to two championships and they were on their way to their second successive title, which later became a treble. Just as in his days at Huddersfield, Chapman was instrumental in setting up Arsenal for the treble, but didn't see it completed. His great team continued under Whittaker, and the new manager, a journalist and broadcaster, George Allison.

In November 1934, Arsenal provided a record seven members of the England team that played Italy at Highbury – Frank Moss, George Male, Eddie Hapgood, Wilf Copping, Ray Bowden, Ted Drake, and Cliff Bastin. Two years later, those seven, plus Jack Crayston, Joe Hulme, Bernard Joy – later to become football correspondent of the *London Standard* – Alf Kitchen and Herbie Roberts (all England), Alex James (Scotland) and Bob John (Wales) made a total of fourteen internationals on the club's books. The domination and impetus of Arsenal FC ended only with the advent of the Second World War.

Perhaps the greatest compliment to the style of football played by Arsenal can be found in the attendance figures for the 1931–32 season. They were responsible for setting ground records at Huddersfield, Stoke, West Bromwich and Preston. Those records still stand today.

HERBERT CHAPMAN

After an undistinguished playing career at Grimsby, Swindon, Sheppey United, Northampton, Sheffield United (the only club where he figured regularly in the first team), Notts County and Spurs, he became manager of non-League Northampton Town in 1907. Within two years they were Southern League Champions. In 1912 he took over at the ill-fated Leeds City. He was with them when they were thrown out of the League for making illegal payments in 1919. He left the game for a while to become a partner in an engineering firm. In September 1920 he was appointed Huddersfield manager. The club was heavily in debt and about to merge forces with Leeds United.

During Chapman's stay, the club's record was as follows:

The League

	P	W	D	L	F	A	Pts	Pos
1920–21	42	15	9	18	42	49	39	17
1921–22	42	15	9	18	53	54	39	14
1922–23	42	21	11	10	60	32	53	3
1923–24	42	23	11	8	60	33	57	1
1924–25	42	21	16	5	69	28	58	1

Arsenal v. *Blackpool at Highbury, Christmas 1937*

Goalkeeper Frank Moss and Herbie Roberts defend the Arsenal goal against Derby County

After leading Huddersfield to two first Division titles Chapman joined Arsenal in 1925. One of his first games in charge at Arsenal was a 7–0 defeat at Newcastle!

When he arrived at Highbury he vowed he 'was going to make Arsenal the greatest team in the world', and he did. Not only did he buy players wisely and develop young players, but he was responsible for many innovations. In 1927 he changed the club's name from *The* Arsenal to plain Arsenal.

In the 1930 Cup final it was Chapman's team that walked onto the Wembley turf alongside their opponents – the first time this had ever happened.

Chapman was responsible for floodlights at Highbury, and for the introduction of the first physiotherapists. He also suggested white balls to the FA – they thought the idea ludicrous! He suggested numbering on players' shirts; a 'gimmick' said the FA. He organized supporters' special trains and saving schemes for players. It is hardly surprising the great man's bust stands in the main entrance hall at Highbury.

Chapman was also warning colleagues about the danger of high transfer fees killing the game. He suggested a 'ceiling' on all fees. Again the FA refused. He replied in the best way he knew – he went out and paid a record fee for David Jack.

His influence stretched beyond the football field. When the underground station at Arsenal was opened, the London Transport Passenger Board were going to call it Gillespie Road. Chapman wanted it to be called Arsenal, and Arsenal it was!

On Wednesday, 3 January 1934, Chapman went to watch a third-team game at Guildford. He caught a cold and went to bed. On the morning of Saturday, 6 January at Hendon, Chapman died. That afternoon Arsenal played Sheffield Wednesday at Highbury. The game, it is reported, was played by 'weeping players, in front of a weeping crowd'.

ARSENAL'S RECORD, 1925–34

The League

	P	W	D	L	F	A	Pts	Pos
1925–26	42	22	8	12	87	63	52	2
1926–27	42	17	9	16	77	86	43	11
1927–28	42	13	15	14	82	86	41	10
1928–29	42	16	13	13	77	72	45	9
1929–30	42	14	11	17	78	66	39	14
1930–31	42	28	10	4	127	59	66	1
1931–32	42	22	10	10	90	48	54	2
1932–33	42	25	8	9	118	61	58	1
1933–34	23	14	7	2	41	20	35	1

The 1933–34 figures are up to the time of Chapman's death.

The day Chapman died, Arsenal drew at home to Sheffield Wednesday 1–1, and the top of the First Division table looked like this:

1 Arsenal	35 pts	3 Huddersfield Town	32 pts
2 Derby County	32 pts	4 Spurs	30 pts

The FA Cup

1925–26	Round 6	lost to	Swansea Town
1926–27	Final	lost to	Cardiff City
1927–28	Semi final	lost to	Blackburn Rovers
1928–29	Round 6	lost to	Aston Villa
1929–30	Final	beat	Huddersfield Town
1930–31	Round 4	lost to	Chelsea
1931–32	Final	lost to	Newcastle United
1932–33	Round 3	lost to	Walsall
1933–34	Round 6	lost to	Aston Villa

The Wembley Wizards, 1928

On 31 March 1928 Scotland beat England at Wembley by five goals to one. They won with a style and ease which embarrassed England and the 80,000 crowd. There was a period in the second half when the Scots were giving and taking passes at walking pace, trying to tease the English defence out of position. England had a problem in that Bishop, the captain and Leicester City half back, had to withdraw, but the Scots had chosen Wembley as an occasion on which to display their rich talents. For once the score matched their ability.

Most Scots remember the forward line – Jackson, Dunn, Gallacher, James and Morton – yet strangely, well as the forwards had played, observers did not award any of them what would be called today the Man of the Match award. Gibson, Bradshaw and McMullan, the half backs, won possession of the midfield, created chances, stifled the opposition half backs and disrupted any thoughts of England counter-attacks.

Within the first three minutes England came close to scoring and Scotland actually scored. The Huddersfield left wing Smith beat Harkness in the Scots goal, but the ball struck the far post and rebounded into play. A moment later Scotland were in front, James and Gallacher creating an opening for Morton to place the ball on Jackson's head. For another forty-two minutes of the first half the score remained 1–0, then James put the Scots 2–0 up, and in control, with a curling cross shot.

In the first half England had succeeded only in throwing a decent disguise over the real difference between the two teams. After sixty-two minutes Scotland extended their lead with Morton again placing the ball perfectly for Jackson to head home. James scored the fourth from a free kick by Gibson, and the fifth came from Jackson, his third, and the third created by Morton. (Later evidence suggested that Gibson had scored one of Scotland's goals, but the match report records that James twice beat Hufton in the English goal.) The proverbial consolation goal for the home side came from Kelly, from a free kick. England never looked like creating anything. The match had resolved itself into a picture of Scots playing a leisurely and elaborate passing game of possession football, with England having neither the guile nor the ability to disrupt the blue tide.

As often occurs in famous victories, the element of surprise is paramount. Before the game there had been widespread complaints that no fewer than eight of the Scottish team were drawn from Football League clubs. It was said to be a shame that, in England, clubs should have to bolster their sides with Scots. In turn Scotland were accused of allowing these raids north of the border to take place, and then having to select 'foreigners' to turn against their own team-mates for an afternoon. Purists suggested that England–Scotland games were no longer a clear and fair trial of national styles and methods.

But, sadly, the Wembley Wizards failed to win another match. Wales were champions that year and Northern Ireland came second. Scotland's win at Wembley was their only victory of that season's international championship! But at least they handed England the Wooden Spoon.

England: Hufton (West Ham); Goodall (Huddersfield), Jones (Blackburn); Edwards (Leeds), Wilson (Huddersfield), Bishop (Leicester); Hulme (Arsenal), Kelly (Huddersfield), Dean (Everton), Bradford (Birmingham), Smith (Huddersfield).

Scotland: Harkness (Queens Park); Nelson (Cardiff), Law (Chelsea); Gibson (Aston Villa), Bradshaw (Bury), McMullan (Manchester City); Jackson (Huddersfield), Dunn (Hibernian), Gallacher (Newcastle), James (Preston), Morton (Rangers).

HOME INTERNATIONAL CHAMPIONSHIP, 1928

	P	W	D	L	F	A	Pts
Wales	3	2	1	0	6	4	5
Northern Ireland	3	2	0	1	4	2	4
Scotland	3	1	1	1	7	4	3
England	3	0	0	3	2	9	0

Alex James, Preston and Arsenal legend and Wembley Wizard

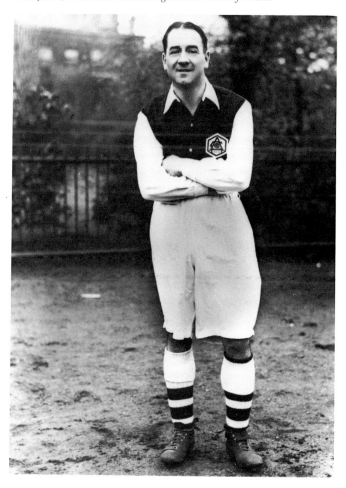

Alec Jackson beats England goalkeeper Hufton on the way to his hat-trick

THE TEAM

T. Bradshaw

He played for Bury and won his only cap as a member of the 'Wizards'.

Jimmy Dunn

He played for Hibs but moved to Everton shortly after the Wembley match. He played for Everton in the 1933 FA Cup final and scored a goal. He won six Scottish caps.

Hughie Gallacher

Although only 5 feet 6 inches tall, he was regarded by many as the best centre forward of all time. He scored 365 goals in first-class soccer and won twenty caps. Born in Belshill, he played for Raith. Hughie then went to Airdrie and to Newcastle who paid £5000 for him in 1925. Chelsea bought him for £10,000 in 1930 and then he moved to Derby County, Notts County, Grimsby and Gateshead. He scored 22 goals in his twenty Scotland games. Life was surrounded by controversies and difficulties, and he committed suicide, a lonely man, in 1957 when his body was found on a railway line.

J.D. Gibson

In 1927 he joined Aston Villa for a then British record fee of £7500. He won eight caps.

J.D. Harkness

An amateur, he played as goalkeeper for Queens Park. He won eleven caps.

Alec Jackson

He scored eight goals in his seventeen Scottish appearances. At Wembley he was the hero of the day with three goals of perfect opportunism. He was only 5 feet 7 inches tall, yet was the tallest of the Scottish forwards! Born in Renton, he started his career at Dumbarton. In the early twenties he went to the USA with his brother Wattie to play for the Bethlehem Steel team! He returned to Scotland to play for Aberdeen. Herbert Chapman took him to Huddersfield in 1925 where he spent five seasons before he had an unsuccessful season at Chelsea who paid £8500 for him. He then went into non-League soccer before taking a pub in the West End of London. In 278 League games he scored 100 goals. Four Huddersfield team-mates were in the England team at Wembley.

Alex James

The most creative of all players in the interwar years, with exceptional ball control, he was a vital member of the successful Arsenal team of the era. An inside left, he was small but well built. James joined Preston from Raith in 1926 but three years later moved to Arsenal in a £9000 deal. He played 476 League games and scored 106 goals. Born in 1902, he died in 1953. He retired in 1937 and then became a journalist. He only won eight caps!

T. Law

He played for Chelsea and made his international debut in this game. He played once more for Scotland.

Jimmy McMullan

Captain. He played for Manchester City whom he joined in 1926 from Partick Thistle. He won sixteen caps. His team talk the night before the match was: 'Go to bed and pray for rain!' The prayers were answered. He started his career at Denny Hibs before joining Partick Thistle in 1913. Two seasons with non-League Maidstone followed before going back to Partick, then joining City. He stayed at City until 1934 when he left to become manager of Aston Villa. He had subsequent spells in charge at Oldham, Notts County and Sheffield Wednesday.

Alan Morton

The 'Wee Blue Devil' – he was only 5 feet 4 inches tall – won thirty-one caps. A natural right-footed outside left, he was born in Partick. When he was a lad he used to practise by kicking a tennis ball through a hole in his garden shed. He started his career at Queens Park, joined Rangers in 1920 and went on to score 115 goals in 495 League games for them. If it was raining, he would take an umbrella on the pitch with him. He retired in 1933 and became a director of Rangers.

J. Nelson

Played for Cardiff City; he was only the second Cardiff player to appear for Scotland. He won four caps.

England Cricket Team, 1932–33

Captained by the controversial Douglas Jardine of Surrey, the England team's ambition was to regain the Ashes lost to Australia in the home series two years earlier. The 1930 series had been dominated by Don Bradman. Jardine's first thought on being appointed for Australia was to devise a plan to reduce the run machine to normal human proportions. Drawing on memories of having seen Bradman in difficulty against Harold Larwood's short-pitched express deliveries in the final Test at the Oval in 1930, he settled on 'leg theory'.

Harold Larwood of Nottinghamshire , then the fastest bowler in the world, was to spearhead the attack. Larwood's superb control and frightening pace were ideal credentials for the job. Bill Voce, Larwood's partner at Trent Bridge, was another obvious selection. Larwood, fast right arm, and Voce, awkward, quick left arm, became the classic opening bowling combination. The batting of the touring side was equally formidable. Even in the absence of the great Jack Hobbs, who had retired from the international arena two years before, there was still Wally Hammond, one the greatest cricketers of all time, the pugnacious Maurice Leyland and the solid Herbert

Sutcliffe. Les Ames, Kent's brilliant wicketkeeper–batsman, was also a fixture in the England side.

As soon as the England tour team was picked, Bradman was aware of what lay in store for him and his fellow batsmen that Australian summer. The reliance on pace (Bill Bowes of Yorkshire and Gubby Allen of Middlesex backed up Larwood and Voce) meant only one thing. As Jack Fingleton put it: 'They were after his skin . . . and Bradman knew that their general plan of skinning would not be along the lines of orthodoxy'.

Bradman did not play in the first Test of the series. He was in dispute with Australia's Board. But he had by then already had a taste of the tactics England were about to employ. Playing for an Australian XI against the MCC at Melbourne, Bradman was met by a barrage of blistering deliveries from Larwood and Bowes. Jack Hobbs, watching the game, commented that he had never seen Larwood bowl faster. Allen too, although he never bowled bodyline at any time on the tour, was impressively fast. The purpose, however, said Hobbs, of this 'demon stuff' was to 'shake Don's wonderful confidence. It seemed that this was done.' England won the First Test by 10

W.M. Woodfull ducks under a short delivery from Harold Larwood in the Fourth Test at Brisbane. The cluster of six short leg fielders graphically illustrates that England captain Douglas Jardine's policy was one of 'leg theory' and not bodyline

wickets, although not before Stan McCabe had played one of the greatest Test innings of all time – 187 not out – with only 16 runs coming on the off side, proof that leg theory could be combatted.

Bradman was back for the Second Test at Melbourne where Australia levelled the series. Bradman's first innings, however, was a disaster. All Australia expected that his reappearance in the side would signify the end of the threat of Larwood. With Woodfull out early, Bradman strode to the middle, the crowd cheering him all the way. Bowes waited for the noise to subside then began his lumbering run up. The hush of anticipation turned to the silence of disbelief as Bradman moved across his stumps, swung wildly, and deflected the ball onto the base of his leg stump. It was Bowes's only wicket of the series.

In the second innings Bradman made a century, but, according to Jack Fingleton, who played in the match, 'not like the old Bradman, for there was an absence of the spectacular'.

From then on England were in the ascendancy. Bradman began to play almost suicidally, leaving his stumps open when facing Larwood. The former Australian captain, M.A. Noble, said that suddenly Bradman had 'developed a sensational desire to score off everything'. Jardine's plan had worked: Bradman averaged only 56 in the series. 'He failed,' said Larwood after the tour. 'We knew he'd fail.' But after the Second Test the controversy boiled up into a near diplomatic incident.

In the Third Test at Adelaide, Larwood hit Bill Woodfull over the heart. The wicketkeeper Bertie Oldfield pulled a short ball onto the side of his head. Before he passed out Larwood says Oldfield murmured, 'It wasn't your fault, Harold.' Bodyline was not in operation when either batsman was hit. An Australian journalist at the match coined the expression 'bodyline' to describe the England tactics and within days it became a part of the language as telegrams were exchanged between the Australian Board and the MCC. The Australians called the tactics 'unsportsmanlike'. The MCC responded with an offer to call off the tour. Prime ministers became involved before the Australians withdrew their claim and the tour went ahead. England won the series by four matches to one and Larwood took 33 wickets at an average of 19.51. Allen took 21 wickets.

The abuse from the Australian crowds became more and more pronounced as the tour proceeded. Their main target was Jardine, in his Harlequin cap and with his silk handkerchief knotted round his throat. But Jardine never once acknowledged any comment from the crowd and, when faced by some uncompromising bowling by Australia, never flinched. Jack Fingleton considered Jardine the 'most efficient, scientific and shrewdest Test captain' he had ever come across. That England won this controversial series is history. The question that remains is would they have won without bodyline, without Larwood and without Jardine?

Bertie Oldfield reels away after being struck by Larwood in the Third Test at Adelaide

ENGLAND'S TEST RECORD, 1932–33

First Test

Sydney, 2–7 December
England won by 10 wickets
Australia
360 (S.J. McCabe 187*; H. Larwood 5–96)
164 (H. Larwood 5–28)
England
524 (H. Sutcliffe 194, W.R. Hammond 112, Nawab of Pataudi 102)
1–0

Second Test

Melbourne, 30 December–3 January
Australia won by 111 runs
Australia
228 (J.H. Fingleton 83)
191 (D.G. Bradman 103*)
England
169 (H. Sutcliffe 52; W.J. O'Reilly 5–63)
139 (W.J. O'Reilly 5–66)

Third Test

Adelaide, 13–19 January
England won by 338 runs
England
341 (M. Leyland 83, R.E.S. Wyatt 78, E. Paynter 77;
T.W. Wall 5–72)
412 (W.R. Hammond 85, L.E.G. Ames 69, D.R. Jardine 56)
Australia
222 (W.H. Ponsford 85)
193 (W.M. Woodfull 73*, D.G. Bradman 66)

Fourth Test

Brisbane, 10–16 February
England won by 6 wickets
Australia
340 (V.Y. Richardson 83, D.G Bradman 76, W.M. Woodfull 67)
175
England
356 (H. Sutcliffe 86, E. Paynter 83)
162–4 (M. Leyland 86)

Fifth Test

Sydney, 23–28 February
England won by 8 wickets
Australia
435 (L.S. Darling 85, S.J. McCabe 73, L.P. O'Brien 61,
W.A. Oldfield 52)
182 (D.G. Bradman 71, W.M. Woodfull 67; H. Verity 5–33)
England
454 (W.R. Hammond 101, H. Larwood 98, H. Sutcliffe 56,
R.E.S. Wyatt 51)
168–2 (W.R. Hammond 75*, R.E.S. Wyatt 61*)

* Not out

THE PLAYERS, 1932–33

G.O. Allen CBE (Middlesex)
(Born 31.7.02, Bellevue Hill, Sydney)

L.E.G. Ames CBE (Kent)
(Born 3.12.05, Elham, Kent)

W.E. Bowes (Yorkshire)
(Born 25.7.08, Elland, Yorkshire)

F.R. Brown MBE (Surrey)
(Born 16.12.10, Lima, Peru; died 6.6.84, Nottingham)

G. Duckworth (Lancashire)
(Born 19.5.01, Warrington; died 5.1.66, Warrington)

W.R. Hammond (Gloucestershire)
(Born 19.6.03, Dover; died 1.7.65, Durban, S.A.)

D.R. Jardine (Surrey)
(Born 23.10.00, Bombay, India; died 18.6.58, Montreux,
Switzerland)

H. Larwood (Nottinghamshire)
(Born 14.11.04, Nuncargate, Nottinghamshire)

M. Leyland (Yorkshire)
(Born 20.7.00, Harrogate; died 1.1.67, Harrogate)

T.B. Mitchell (Derbyshire)
(Born 4.9.02, Creswell, Derbyshire)

Nawab of Pataudi (Worcestershire)
(Born 16.3.10, Pataudi, India; died 5.1.52, New Delhi, India)

E. Paynter (Lancashire)
(Born 5.11.01, Oswaldtwistle; died 5.2.79, Keighley)

H. Sutcliffe (Yorkshire)
(Born 24.11.94, Harrogate; died 22.1.78, Crosshills, Yorkshire)

M.W. Tate (Sussex)
(Born 30.5.95, Brighton; died 18.5.56, Wadhurst, Sussex)

H. Verity (Yorkshire)
(Born 18.5.05, Headingley, Yorkshire; died 31.7.43, Casserta,
Italy)

W. Voce (Nottinghamshire)
(Born 8.8.09, Annesley Wodehouse, Nottinghamshire)

R.E.S. Wyatt (Warwickshire)
(Born 2.5.01, Milford, Surrey)

ENGLAND'S TOUR RESULTS, 1932–33

Played 22, won 10, drew 10, tied 1, lost 1

21–24 October	v.	Western Australia	drew
27 29 October	v.	Combined Australian XI	drew
4–8 November	v.	South Australia	won (innings and 128 runs)
11–14 November	v.	Victoria	won (innings and 83 runs)
18–22 November	v.	Australian XI	drew
25–29 November	v.	New South Wales	won (innings and 44 runs)
2–7 December	v.	Australia (First Test)	won (10 wickets)
10–12 December	v.	Southern Districts	drew
16–19 December	v.	Tasmania	won (innings and 126 runs)
23–26 December	v.	Tasmania	drew
30 December–3 January	v.	Australia (Second Test)	lost (by 111 runs)
7–9 January	v.	Victoria Country Team	drew
13–19 January	v.	Australia (Third Test)	won (by 338 runs)
21–23 January	v.	Victoria Country XIII (!)	drew
26–28 January	v.	New South Wales	won (4 wickets)
1–2 February	v.	Queensland Country XII (!)	drew
4–7 February	v.	Queensland	won (innings and 61 runs)
10–16 February	v.	Australia (Fourth Test)	won (6 wickets)
18–21 February	v.	Northern Districts	drew
23–28 February	v.	Australia (Fifth Test)	won (8 wickets)
3–7 March	v.	Victoria	tied
10–14 March	v.	South Australia	drew

Test Averages

Batting

	Matches	Innings	Not outs	Runs	Highest innings	Average
E. Paynter	3	5	2	184	83	61.33
W.R. Hammond	5	9	1	440	112	55.00
H. Sutcliffe	5	9	1	440	194	55.00
Mr. R.E.S. Wyatt	5	9	2	327	78	46.71
Nawab of Pataudi	2	3	0	122	102	40.66
M. Leyland	5	9	0	306	86	34.00
H. Verity	4	5	1	114	45	28.50
H. Larwood	5	7	1	145	98	24.16
Mr. G.O. Allen	5	7	0	163	48	23.28
Mr. D.R. Jardine	5	9	0	199	56	22.11
L.E.G. Ames	5	8	1	113	69	16.14
W. Voce	4	6	2	29	8	7.25

The following also batted: W.E. Bowes, 4* and 0*; T.B. Mitchell, 0.

Bowling

	Overs	Maidens	Runs	Wickets	Average
H. Larwood	220	42	644	33	19.51
T.B. Mitchell	21	5	60	3	20.00
H. Verity	135	54	271	11	24.63
W. Voce	133.3	23	407	15	27.13
G.O. Allen	170.6	29	593	21	28.23
W.R. Hammond	120.3	27	291	9	32.33
W.E. Bowes	23	2	70	1	70.00

Also bowled: R.E.S. Wyatt, 2–0–12–0.

Great Britain Davis Cup Team, 1933–36

The 'Four Musketeers' – Borotra, Brugnon, Cochet and Lacoste – brought France six years of supremacy in the Davis Cup from 1927. When their tenure was over, the expected domination of the Cup by the United States and Australia did not materialize. Instead, for four years, the Davis Cup remained on show at Wimbledon, brought there by the British team surprisingly but deservedly.

It is easy to dismiss the team as a one-man band. To do that would be to denigrate what was, in essence, a fine team. Certainly Fred Perry was three times Wimbledon singles champion and the first to win at all the Grand Slam venues, but the other members of the team were also proficient enough individually to reach and to win Grand Slam events. That fact is often forgotten in the mists of time.

The second-string singles player was Bunny Austin, who twice reached a singles final at Wimbledon. The key doubles player was Pat Hughes, often a finalist, and three times a doubles champion at major events. If there was a chink, it may have been H.G.N. Lee, who was replaced by Raymond Tuckey for the last two years. Tuckey and Hughes won the Wimbledon doubles title in 1936 and were runners-up the following year. The brilliance of Perry often dimmed the performance of others.

Britain's route to the Davis Cup in 1933 took them to Barcelona, where they beat Spain, and then to various locations in the South of England, beating Finland, Italy, Czechoslovakia, Australia and the USA. The Davis Cup was finally won in Paris, against the French, who, as holders, had the privilege of defending the title in their own country.

For the final, the non-playing captain, Roper Barrett, made a shrewd decision. He reckoned that Perry could win both his singles, although Cochet was world number 2 and Perry number 7, and that Britain could win by winning three of the singles. The plan worked.

It was Britain's first success for twenty-two years in the Davis Cup final and revenge for a defeat in that final in Paris two years earlier. Then Cochet was the saviour of France, beating Perry and Austin in four sets in the singles, and winning the doubles with Brugnon. Jean Borotra, eleven years older than Perry, lost to both Britons in the singles.

Of course, Fred Perry was the inspiration of the successful defence of the cup in the following years. In the four winning finals, his record in the singles was eight out of eight. In 1934 in the zonal finals the United States beat Australia, and were then beaten by Britain in the final. France had earlier disappeared to Australia. In 1935, America again won the zonal final, before being whitewashed at Wimbledon. Australia won through to the final in 1936, but, with two Perry victories, Britain retained the Cup for the fourth – and last – time.

In 1937, Perry joined the paid ranks and was replaced by C.E. Hare, who had three singles victories in six matches. But the master was naturally missed. America took the Cup and, with Australia, dominated the Davis Cup until 1974.

Just once in the intervening years did Britain reach the Davis Cup final, when the Lloyd brothers and Buster Mottram swept through on a current of national pride in 1978. However, in those victorious days of the 1930s Britain's reign was so secure that possession of the Davis Cup was almost taken for granted.

Nowadays, Fred Perry is one of the major sports-goods manufacturers in the world. In his playing days, Perry always wore long-sleeved shirts and cricket whites. The actual pioneer of casual shirts and shorts was his team-mate through the Davis Cup years – Bunny Austin.

Fred Perry (top) *beats W.J. Allison (USA) 6–1, 7–5, 6–4 in the Paris tie to decide who would challenge France in the 1933 Davis Cup final*

Bunny Austin, the first player to wear shorts, takes a refresher during his win against André Merlin in the 1933 Davis Cup final

BRITAIN'S DAVIS CUP RECORD, 1933–36

1933

Beat Spain 4–1 (Barcelona)
Beat Finland 5–0 (Queens Club)
Beat Italy 4–1 (Eastbourne)
Beat Czechoslovakia 5–0 (Eastbourne)
Beat Australia 3–2 (Wimbledon)
Beat USA 4–1 (Wimbledon)

Final (Paris)

Bunny Austin beat André Merlin 6–3, 6–4, 6–0
Fred Perry beat Henri Cochet 8–10, 6–4, 8–6, 3–6, 6–1
G.P. Hughes and H.G.N. Lee lost to Jean Borotra and Jacques Brugnon 3–6, 6–8, 2–6
Bunny Austin lost to Henri Cochet 7–5, 4–6, 6–4, 4–6, 4–6
Fred Perry beat André Merlin 4–6, 8–6, 6–2, 7–5

1934 Final

Beat USA 4–1 (Wimbledon)

1935 Final

Beat USA 5–0 (Wimbledon)

1936 Final

Beat Australia 3–2 (Wimbledon)

1937 Final

Lost to USA 1–4 (Wimbledon)

28

THE TEAM

Henry Wilfred (Bunny) Austin

Born 20 August 1906, Austin was an elegant groundstroke player and captain for Cambridge University. He was runner-up to Ellsworth Vines in the men's singles at Wimbledon in 1932 and to Donald Budge in 1938; between 1929 and 1939 he only once failed to reach the quarter finals. In 1937 he was runner-up to Henkel in the French singles. He played in twenty-four Davis Cup ties between 1929 and 1937 and won thirty-six out of forty-eight rubbers, all in singles. After his playing days he became a lecturer and organizer for Moral Rearmament.

Herbert Roper Barrett (captain)

Barrett played in the very first Davis Cup tie to be held, in 1900. He played in ten rubbers in all, and captained the side in 1900, 1919, and from 1926 to 1939. He was an Olympic gold medallist in the men's doubles in 1908 and a silver medallist in the mixed doubles in 1912.

Geoffrey Hughes

Hughes played in twenty-one Davis Cup matches between 1929 and 1936, winning fifteen rubbers out of twenty-two. He won men's doubles in the French Championships in 1933 and the Australian men's doubles in 1934, partnered by Fred Perry. With Raymond Tuckey he gained the Wimbledon title in 1936. He was twice runner-up at Wimbledon, with Perry in 1932 and with Tuckey in 1937.

H.G.N. Lee

Lee played in seven Davis Cup matches between 1930 and 1934 and won four out of eleven rubbers. Other than the Davis Cup, his best result was when he reached the semifinals of the mixed doubles at Wimbledon in 1934.

Fred Perry

Born on 18 May 1909, the son of a Stockport MP, Perry was the most successful modern British player, self-confident and with a great running forehand. He was Wimbledon singles champion in 1934, 1935 and 1936, the first man since A.F. Wilding to win in three successive years. He also won the mixed doubles at Wimbledon in 1935 and 1936. He won the US singles title in 1933, 1934 and 1935, the French singles in 1935, the doubles in 1933 and the mixed doubles in 1932, and the Australian singles and doubles in 1934. Between 1931 and 1936 he played in twenty Davis Cup matches, winning forty-five out of fifty-two rubbers, including thirty-four out of thirty-eight singles. He turned professional in 1937. He was also world table tennis singles champion in 1928 and 1929.

Raymond Tuckey

Tuckey took part in three Davis Cup ties – all finals – in 1935, 1936 and 1937, winning one of his three rubbers, with Hughes in 1935. With Hughes he also won the Wimbledon men's doubles title in 1936, and the pair were runners-up the following year. In 1932 he played in the mixed doubles at Wimbledon with his mother Agnes. She was and still is the oldest woman to compete in one of the three major events at Wimbledon.

Great Britain Ice Hockey Team, 1936

At most Olympic Games a country with no particular tradition or ability in a specific sport makes world headlines by unexpectedly winning a gold medal. Zimbabwe in women's hockey and Poland with an equestrian gold, both in the disrupted Games of 1980, are prime examples. Felipe Munoz won the 200-metres breaststroke for Mexico in 1968 and Liechtenstein won more gold medals than Norway, Switzerland and Italy at the 1980 Winter Games.

A similar surprise was the British victory in the ice hockey tournament at the 1936 Olympics at Garmisch-Partenkirchen, the Bavarian skiing centre sixty miles south of Munich. The favourites for the gold and silver were Canada (who had won the last four Olympic gold medals and were unbeaten in twenty matches at the Olympics) and the United States. Either the Czechs, Swedes or Germans, hailing from climatically more adverse conditions than the Britons, were thought likely to take the bronze.

Two significant events had taken place in Britain in the previous two years. In 1934 the Empire Pool at Wembley had begun to promote ice hockey in Britain and this had led to a chain reaction throughout halls in Brighton, Scotland and the Empress Hall at Harringay. The British Ice Hockey League was well organized and sensibly structured and, by 1935 an international club tournament comprising the Wembley Canadians, the Richmond Hawks, the Streatham Lions and Wembley Lions, all from London, and six continental teams –

Britain in play against Sweden in the opening match of the 1936 Olympic tournament at Garmisch-Partenkirchen

Berlin, Milan, Français Volants, Stade Français, Munich and Prague – had been organized.

The second factor was the influx of Canadian players. Fourteen were registered with British clubs in 1935. Their expertise helped improve the standard of the sport in Britain, but their appearance also caused a major problem. Many were past their prime and not required for their own national squad; the North American Stanley Cup and the National Hockey League catered for the selection demands of Canada and the USA. But, as members of a Commonwealth country, could they represent Britain at the Olympics?

The predictable happened. A row broke out just before the Games about the eligibility of two of the British team, goalkeeper Jimmy Foster and Sandy Archer, both of whom were Canadians, but had not been picked by their own country's selectors. The International Ice Hockey Federation voted unanimously to ban Archer and Foster from the British team. Two days later, however, the pair played for Britain in the opening match against Sweden. Other Canadian-born players were also present. The British view is that Canada, as befitted staunch supporters of the Commonwealth, withdrew their objection. The American viewpoint was that Britain blandly broke the rules and were not punished. A more likely explanation is that no one thought Britain had a chance.

Wins over Sweden, Hungary, Austria and Czechoslovakia and a draw with Germany changed the North American outlook. Britain would win a medal for certain; the question was which one.

Fourteen thousand spectators packed into the stadium to watch the Britons play Canada. Amazingly, Britain came away with a 2–1 win, a goal from Brenchley after fourteen minutes of the last period turning the final six minutes of the match into an eternity. In goal Foster held out.

Britain's final match was against the United States. Had the Americans won, then the gold would have been theirs. With Foster in remarkable form again, the motley collection of Britons and washed-up Canadians were inspired by the realization of what was at stake. The United States were continually on the offensive, but the brilliant Foster and the unflappable Dailley were impregnable. Even more remarkable was the scoreline, or lack of it. After three periods of extra time the match ended in a goalless draw.

The drama was not quite over yet. The final match of the tournament was the all-North American meeting. The United States could still take the gold.

the USA beat Canada and did not concede a goal, or if they beat the Canadians 6–1 (an unlikely situation), they would be champions.

When halfway through the first period Neville converted Farquhar's pass to score for Canada, the American dream evaporated. Canada held on to their slender lead and took the silver. The Americans, having lost their captain Garrison with an injured shoulder in the game against Britain, were rudderless and ineffective.

After the war, ice hockey declined in Britain for two reasons. Canadians, anxious to join the league of Olympic and world champions (the world title was also at stake in the coming Olympic year), swamped the British market; at one stage 90 per cent of the senior team positions were held by Canadians. Also national economic conditions were not conducive to rebuilding war-damaged stadiums and constructing new arenas. What is gratifying is that, in the last decade, sponsors and television companies have seen fit to invest in financing and screening ice hockey. They see a new future in the sport.

THE TEAM

Sandy Archer	John Davey
James Borland	Carl Erhardt (captain)
Edgar Brenchley	Jimmy Foster
Jimmy Chappell	John Kilpatrick
John Coward	Archie Stinchcombe
Gordon Dailley	Bob Wyman

THE RESULT

	P	W	D	L
Great Britain	7	5	2	0
Canada	8	7	0	1
USA	8	5	1	2
Czechoslovakia	8	5	0	3
Germany	6	3	1	2
Sweden	5	2	0	3
Austria	6	2	0	4
Hungary	6	2	0	4

Great Britain 4 x 400-Metres Relay Team, 1936

The British 4 × 400-metres gold medal team (left to right): Brown, Wolff, Rampling and Roberts. Does the 'G' on the vest stand for gold?

The key personality of this quartet was Arthur Godfrey Kilner Brown of Warwick School and Cambridge. Tall, with fair wavy hair, he looked at the world through horn-rimmed spectacles. He was a member of the Achilles Club, the haven for Oxbridge athletes, and was by far the best quarter-miler in the world in the immediate pre-war period. Like others who are not quite mortal, he ran with complete effortlessness.

It was a period when Britain was well stocked with quarter-milers. Godfrey Rampling of the Army, the reigning Empire Games champion, and Bill Roberts, a Lancastrian from Salford Harriers, were also considered medal prospects in the individual events, whilst Frederick Wolff, AAA champion in 1933, from London AC, was a useful addition to the relay squad.

From California, early in 1936, came two Americans, world record holder Archie Williams of Oakland and James Luvalle, to challenge Brown and Roberts for the individual 400-metres gold at the Berlin Olympics. Times recorded in California early in the season are bound to be better than those run in England in the spring, but it was felt that the Britons had a chance. The final comprised two Americans, two Canadians and the two Englishmen. Brown drew lane six in the final, his third lane-six placing in four races, making him a sitting target. Williams struck for home earlier than expected and, although Brown clawed back 3 metres, there are no gold medals given for distances of 401 metres. Had there been, then Godfrey Brown would have been Olympic champion. The times were 46.5 for Williams and 46.7 for Brown. Electronic timing, then un-official, gives a better guide – Williams 46.66, Brown 46.68, Luvalle 46.84 and Roberts 46.87.

Brown's disappointment was partly lifted the following day when his sister Audrey won a silver medal in the 4 x 100-metres relay, but by the final afternoon of the track and field events Britain still had not won a gold medal for athletics.

The heats and final of the relay were on the same day and the Americans, not quite at full strength, were some 10 metres faster on heat times. In the final Wolff, the lead-off man, was away well, but the tension of the race engulfed him and he 'died' 20 metres from the tape. Rampling, from Milocarian AC, had run the final leg when Britain took the silver medal in the Los Angeles Games four years earlier; it was his performance on the second leg that put the team back in contention. Roberts took over in first place after Rampling had gone from last to a clear lead, and he handed over to Brown 7 metres ahead. The composed graduate ran the last leg with the knowledge that, unless a catastrophe occurred, the gold medal lay ahead.

THE TEAM

Godfrey Brown

He won a silver medal in the 400 metres in Berlin, and a complete set of medals at the 1938 European Championships: gold in the 400 metres, silver in the 4 x 400-metres relay and bronze in the 4 x 100-metres relay. His elder brother Ralph (later to become a judge) won a bronze medal in the 440-yards hurdles at the 1934 Commonwealth Games. Godfrey was headmaster at Worcester Royal Grammar School from 1950 to 1978.

Godfrey Rampling

He was a member of the silver-medal-winning team in the 4 x 400-metres relay at the 1932 Olympics and won two golds at the 1934 Commonwealth Games – the 440 yards and 4 x 440-yards relay. He is father of Charlotte Rampling, the actress.

William Roberts

He just missed a medal in the 400 metres in Berlin. He won a silver medal in the 440 yards at the 1934 Commonwealth Games, and a gold in 1938. He also won a silver in the 4 x 440-yards relay in 1938. He was a member of the Great Britain team which won the silver in the 4 x 400-metres relay in the 1946 European Championships.

Frederick Wolff

This was Wolff's one and only major triumph.

THE RACE

Heats

One:

1	USA	3:13.0
2	Hungary	3:17.0
3	Poland	3:17.6

Two:

1	Great Britain	3:14.4
2	Sweden	3:14.6
3	France	3:15.2

Three:

1	Germany	3:15.0
2	Canada	3:15.0
3	Italy	3:16.6

Final

1	Great Britain	3:09.0
2	USA	3:11.0
3	Germany	3:11.8
4	Canada	3:11.8
5	Sweden	3:13.0
6	Hungary	3:14.8

The Springboks, 1937

This was the side known simply as 'The Greatest Springboks'. They toured New Zealand in 1937, found themselves 1–0 down in the Test series, corrected the listing ship, then, in the Third and final Test, so annihilated the All Blacks that never before or since have they been so thoroughly beaten on their own soil.

On prewar tours much more emphasis was placed on the captain and vice-captain. They were in charge of the coaching and the playing policy. In Philip Nel and Danie Craven, the Springboks had two remarkable men. They were also backed by a 'gang of five' – the Louw brothers, Gerrie Brand, Lucas Strachan and Flappie Lochner.

Behind every remarkable team is a remarkable man. In this case it was Philip Nel. Not having played rugby until he was fifteen at Maritzburg College, he then became a rugby eccentric. He farmed near Greytown in Natal. Greytown itself was a horseback ride of some 48 kilometres. From there he got a taxi to Pieter-maritzburg where he played his game – either for club or province – then set off on the return journey. He would begin his day at 4 a.m. Such dedication had its rewards. He was an outstanding lock forward, who played with distinction on the 1928 tour to New Zealand and 'retired' to club rugby after the 1933 Wallabies tour. Four years in the wilderness had whetted his appetite for internationals again. A surprise choice he may have been, but he was a wise one.

Danie Craven, a tactically astute half back, would look after the backs, and the next coup was to persuade Ben du Toit to play again. Du Toit had arrived to watch the trials and was persuaded that playing was better than watching. Then they set about organizing their henchmen. Boy and Fanie Louw were two enormous props. They were brothers who farmed at Wellington in the Border country. The family consisted of ten – five played provincial rugby, and Boy and Fanie were internationals. Mattys Michael 'Boy' Louw was a surprisingly fine tactician for a man whose strength was his strength. Gerrie Brand was the prodigious kicker. A full back, he was calm, correct and efficient, and Flappie Lochner was another good tactician. Lucas Strachan was a superb flanker.

The tour was all about the three Test matches. The Springboks had lost 17–6 in the rain and mud against New South Wales before they reached the North Island, and the early results made New Zealand clear favourites. It poured again for the First Test at Wellington. Brand, Boy Louw and Nel were all injured, Craven took the captaincy, switched himself to fly half and brought in Pierre de Villiers in his scrum-half role. Jennings had the dreadful job of replacing Louw. The match slipped gracefully away from South Africa. Badly beaten up front, they conceded two early penalties to Dave Trevathan, and although Williams managed a try, Johnny Dick raced away for another try and Trevathan added a drop goal. The Springboks eventually narrowed the margin to 13–7 with a drop goal by White. The 'gang' had chosen a bad team.

A series of impressive results against the Provinces failed to provoke any shortening of odds for the next Test despite the return of Brand, Louw and the captain Nel. Craven moved back to scrum half and Harris, a Test cricketer who was to make 60 in

Philip Nel, captain of the victorious 1937 Springboks

his Test debut against England in 1947, came in at fly half. Heavy rain again greeted the Christchurch Test and the Springbok selectors decided to omit Hofmeyr and de Villiers at the last minute. At half time the New Zealanders led 6–0 thanks to two tries from Jack Sullivan. At midpoint in the series, the Springboks had reached their nadir – one Test down and well adrift at half time in the second of three Tests. With a chance of another win and tying up the rubber, the All Blacks attacked fiercely again at the start of the second half. But gradually, for the first time, the influence of Nel and Louw began to tell.

It was Freddie Turner who raised morale. Boxed in, with three All Blacks covering, he beat Dick on the outside, then cut inside to score a memorable try. Brand's conversion had suddenly reduced the margin to a single point. The forwards became overheated and overexcited, and Brand took full advantage of a penalty award to put the Springboks ahead for the first time in the series. Bastard's late try and Brand's conversion levelled the series at 1–1.

The crowd for the Third and final Test was a record for Eden Park, Auckland. Many slept out overnight to secure a vantage place on the terraces. But they were not prepared for what happened.

The story of the match is easily told. New Zealand scored 6 points made up of two penalties by Dave Trevathan. South Africa scored 17 points, made up of five tries, with only one conversion by Brand.

The psychology started early on. Instead of opting for the line-out after an infringement, Nel said, 'We'll scrum, New Zealand'. Babrow's first try followed one such decision, and the All Black bastion fell. Babrow, who had decided that Yom Kippur was a day late because of the international date line, added another try, Bergh scored another, and the wings Turner and Williams made it a nap hand. The forwards ran riot; the backs revelled in the openings created by Craven and Harris. It was the heaviest defeat ever suffered by New Zealand (and still is). Embarrassingly, it happened in front of their own people.

Philip Nel decided that it was time to retire after the series. But he didn't exactly hang up his boots. On the way home he threw them into the Indian Ocean. At least he lasted the tour – the manager Day bought a racehorse as soon as he reached New Zealand and spent the remainder of the tour training it.

THE TOUR PARTY

Full Backs
G.H. Brand (W. Province), F.G. Turner (Transvaal)

Threequarters
D.O. Williams (W. Province), P.J. Lysks (Natal), J.A. Broodryk (Transvaal), A.D. Lawton (W. Province), L. Babrow (W. Province), J.L.A. Bester (Gardens), S.R. Hofmeyr (W. Province), J. White (Border)

Half Backs
D.F. van der Vyver (W. Province), T.A. Harris (Transvaal), D.H. Craven (E. Province), P. du P. de Villiers (W. Province)

Forwards
W.E. Bastard (Natal), W.F. Bergh (Transvaal), B.A. du Toit (Transvaal), C.B. Jennings (Border), J.W. Lotz (Transvaal), M.M. Louw (W. Province), S.C. Louw (Transvaal), H.J. Martin (Transvaal), P.J. Nel (Natal), A.R. Sheriff (Transvaal), L.C. Strachan (Transvaal), M.A. van den Berg (W. Province), G.L. Van Reenen (W. Province), H.H. Watt (W. Province)

Captain: P.J. Nel
Vice-captain: D.H. Craven
Manager: P.W. Day
Assistant manager: A. de Villiers

Gerrie Brand (left) *and Ferdie Bergh*

NEW ZEALAND v. SOUTH AFRICA, 1937

South Africa	First Test	Second Test	Third Test
F.G. Turner	FB	LW (1T)	LW (1T)
G.H. Brand		FB (2C, 1PG)	FB (1C)
D.O. Williams	RW (1T)	RW	RW (1T)
P.J. Lyster	LW		
J. White	C (1DG)	C	
L. Babrow	C	C	C (2T)
G.P. Lochmar			C
D.H. Craven	FH	SH	SH
P. du P. de Villiers	SH		
T.A. Harris		FH	FH
S.C. Louw	P	P	P
J.W. Lotz	H	H	H
C.B. Jennings	P		
M.M. Louw		P	P
W.F. Bergh	L	No. 8	No. 8 (1T)
M.A. van den Berg	L	L	L
L.C. Strachan	F	F	F
W.E. Bastard	F	F (1T)	F
G.L. Van Reenen	No. 8		
P.J. Nel		L	L
Score:	7–13	13–6	17–6

TOUR RECORD

Opponents	Result
Auckland	won 19–5
Waikato	won 6–3
Taranaki	won 17–3
Manawatu	won 39–3
Wellington	won 29–0
New Zealand	lost 7–13
Nelson, Golden Bays, Marlborough Combined XV	won 22–0
Canterbury	won 23–8
West Coast, Buller	won 31–6
South Canterbury	won 43–6
New Zealand	won 13–6
Southland	won 30–17
Otago	won 47–7
Hawkes Bay	won 21–12
Poverty Bay, Bay of Plenty, East Coast Combined XV	won 33–3
New Zealand	won 17–6
North Auckland	won 14–6

Tour Statistics

	Played	Won	Lost	Points
In Australia	9	8	1	342–65
In New Zealand	17	16	1	411–104
Total:	26	24	2	753–169

(South Africa won the Tests against Australia 9–5 and 26–17)

Harry Llewellyn and Foxhunter, 1948–53

Harry Llewellyn and Foxhunter at Wembley during the 1948 Olympics. Four years later they salvaged British reputations with a gold medal at Helsinki

If ever a team saved a nation from a complete humiliation, it was Harry Llewellyn and Foxhunter. With the exception of 1904, Britain had won a gold medal at every Olympics, and their lowest number of gold medals, apart from 1904, was three.

On 3 August 1952, at the Helsinki Olympics Britain had arrived at the final event, the team show jumping, with not a gold medal in sight. Even Iran had won more silver medals than Britain. Officials were preparing to set up facilities for the closing ceremony when the show jumping was at its climax.

The facts facing Llewellyn and Foxhunter were simple. They had to complete a clear second round and the gold medal in the team competition was theirs. Any errors, and Chile would take the prize. Chile had never won a gold at an Olympics.

As team captain Llewellyn went last for Britain. The first round had been an uncharacteristic stumble over poles which refused to stay in their sockets. History records that Harry Llewellyn and Foxhunter completed a magnificent clear second round and Britain collected a gold medal; Chile took the silver.

Five years earlier Llewellyn had bought Foxhunter and they joined the British team for the first time. At the 1948 Olympics at Wembley, the pair had won a bronze medal. The course was so difficult that only three teams – the eventual medallists – had managed to remain intact.

They were the outstanding combination in Britain. At the Horse of the Year Show they are still the only team to have won the highly prestigious King George V Gold Cup on three occasions: 1948, 1950 and 1953. Between 1947 and 1953 they won no fewer than seventy-eight international competitions.

It was at Harringay, in 1953, that the pair fell heavily, and although they continued as a team, the fall seemed to mark the end of their careers. Foxhunter was retired in 1956 and Llewellyn followed shortly afterwards.

Meanwhile Chile are still awaiting that elusive first Olympic gold medal.

THE TEAM

Foxhunter

Bred in Norfolk in 1941 by a Mr Millard, Foxhunter stood at nearly 17 hands. He was used as a hunter in Leicestershire before Llewellyn bought him in 1947. He retired from show jumping in 1956, but continued hunting. He died on 21 November 1959 after rupturing an artery leading to his kidney. His skeleton stands at the Royal College of Veterinary Surgeons in London, alongside many great classic racehorses.

Harry Llewellyn

Lieutenant Colonel Henry Morton Llewellyn – known simply as Harry – was educated at Trinity College, Cambridge. While still at university he rode Ego into second place behind Reynoldstown in the 1936 Aintree Grand National. The following year Ego and Llewellyn finished fourth. Altogether he rode sixty steeplechase winners. He was a member of the Great Britain show-jumping team for nine years, from 1947 to 1956 and was responsible for Great Britain's first postwar international success when he won the puissance in Rome on Kilgeddin in 1947. He is a former chairman and president of the British Show Jumping Association, and a former Master of the Monmouthshire Hounds. In his show-jumping career he won 152 international classes, competing in more Grands Prix des Nations than any other rider at the time.

THEIR RECORD

King George V Gold Cup
Winners in 1948, 1950, 1953

Olympic Games
1948 Team: 2nd; Individual: joint 7th
1952 Team: 1st; Individual: 15th

Olympic Games, 1952 (Helsinki)

1	*Great Britain*	
	Wilfred White, Nizefella	8.00
	Douglas Stewart, Aherlow	16.00
	Harry Llewellyn, Foxhunter	16.75
	Total:	40.75 faults
2	*Chile*	45.75
3	*USA*	52.25
4	*Brazil*	56.50
5	*France*	59.00
6	*West Germany*	60.00

Australia Cricket Team, 1948

Captained by the legendary Don Bradman, the 1948 Australian side had the most formidable batting line-up of any team to tour England and a bowling attack that probably did even more than the impressive batting to win the four Tests. Only two years earlier Bradman had walked onto the Gabba at Brisbane followed by a team in which only two other men – Barnes and Hassett – had Test experience. In that short space of time Bradman had moulded a great team, the batting based on himself, Hassett and Morris; the bowling spearheaded by Lindwall and Miller, with Bill Johnston and Ian Johnson in the wings.

By 1948, Bradman was past his best but he was still a fine batsman, good enough to score centuries at Trent Bridge (where office workers were given the day off for their last look at Bradman in a Test) and at Leeds, where in partnership with Arthur Morris, a solid opener, he added 301 as Australia raced to 404 in 345 minutes on the final day to win the match. As a captain he was tougher and more astute than his opposite number, Norman Yardley, and had the firepower at his command to make the most of those advantages.

Arthur Morris, from New South Wales, headed the averages in the Tests. Technically sound, with the ability to concentrate fully without restricting his finely balanced batting style, Morris scored three Test centuries, at Lord's, Headingley and 196 at the Oval. A left-hander, Morris had an excellent temperament for an opener, patient and cool, and could open out against spinners especially on the leg side. Ritchie Benaud called Morris 'Australia's greatest left-hander', high praise indeed when one considers that also in the 1948 side was a young and extremely talented player from Victoria – Neil Harvey.

Harvey was only nineteen when he toured England for the first time in 1948. The baby of the party came of age early when, at Headingley, after an uncharacteristically shaky start by the Australians, he hit a remarkably mature 112. When set, Harvey could destroy any bowling. Small, neat and quick on his feet, Harvey moved into position to hook, drive or cut seemingly with time to spare, a rare gift that gave him an advantage when playing on difficult pitches, especially in England. In addition to the runs Harvey scored with the bat, he saved hundreds during his test career with his brilliant fielding, developed from his experience as an exceptional baseball player.

Lindsay Hassett, small, but a brilliant batsman, backed up the middle order. Sidney Barnes, second in the averages after scoring a century at Lord's, was Morris's opening partner.

While Bradman, Harvey, Morris and Hassett formed the basis of an exceptional batting side, the heart came from the all-rounder Keith Miller and the fast bowler Ray Lindwall. Miller was not at his best on the tour, but was still an exceptional and popular player. At Trent Bridge he decided the First Test with some fine pace bowling, but injury restricted him from the rest of the series. An enigmatic character, he would cheerfully slam a century in quick time, grab the ball and bowl off whatever run he happened to fancy, a mixture of outswingers, inswingers, leg-breaks and googlies. His fielding was outstanding, especially close in and, typically, at the very time his

concentration seemed to be drifting. When the Australians ran up 721 in a day against Essex, Miller, finding the whole procedure boring, allowed himself to be out for a duck and retired to the beach. He never scored runs for the sake of it.

Top of the bowling with 27 wickets apiece were Bill Johnston, left arm medium fast, and the great Ray Lindwall. Johnston was the surprise success of the tour, bowling round or over the

England captain Norman Yardley, wandering all over the wicket, leads his team in a tribute to Don Bradman, playing in his last Test at the Oval in 1948 (below)
Eric Hollies spoils the occasion by bowling Bradman for a duck

wicket, and providing excellent support for Lindwall and Miller. Lindwall, one of the world's greatest fast bowlers, produced a remarkable spell of bowling at the Oval when he took 6 for 20 as England collapsed to 52 all out. Lindwall, inspired by watching Larwood during the 1932–33 tour, was a model for any aspiring pace bowler with a smooth run up to the wicket, gathering pace, perfectly balanced, with a fine action and follow through. He was quick, could swing the ball both ways, and had a fierce bouncer which he used as a surprise weapon.

The Australian team was the most powerful ever to appear in England, and was rivalled only in recent years by the West Indies in 1984. It was Bradman's last tour and, at the Oval in his last Test innings, the crowd rose to him as he made his way to the wicket. The England team gave him three cheers. Bradman was bowled second ball by Eric Hollies. 'I wonder,' said John Arlott, 'if he really saw the ball at all?' Nevertheless, it was a sweeping victory for the Australians in the series. A.E.R. Gilligan commented at the end of the Oval Test: 'England have lost not only the Ashes but their sackcloth as well.'

Don Tallon, the Australian wicketkeeper, catches Cyril Washbrook off the bowling of Keith Miller at Trent Bridge

AUSTRALIA'S TEST RECORD, 1948

First Test

Trent Bridge, 10–15 June
Australia won by 8 wickets

England
165 (J.C. Laker 63, W.A. Johnston 5–36)
441 (D.C.S. Compton 184, L. Hutton 74,
T.G. Evans 50)

Australia
509 (D.G. Bradman 138, A.L. Hassett 137,
S.G. Barnes 62); 98–2 (S.G. Barnes 64*)

Second Test

Lord's, 24–29 June
Australia won by 409 runs

Australia
350 (A.R. Morris 105, D. Tallon 53)
460–7 dec. (S.G. Barnes 141, D.G. Bradman 89,
K.R. Miller 74, A.R. Morris 62)

England
215 (D.C.S. Compton 53, R.R. Lindwall 5–70)
186 (E.R.H. Toshack 5–40)

Third Test

Old Trafford, 8–13 July
Match drawn

England
363 (D.C.S. Compton 145*)
174–3 dec. (C. Washbrook 85*, W.J. Edrich 53)

Australia
221 (A.R. Morris 51)
92–1 (A.R. Morris 54*)

Fourth Test

Headingley, 22–27 July
Australia won by 7 wickets

England
496 (C. Washbrook 143, W.J. Edrich 111,
L. Hutton 81, A.V. Bedser 79)
365–8 dec. (D.C.S. Compton 66,
C. Washbrook 65, L. Hutton 57, W.J. Edrich 54)

Australia
458 (R.N. Harvey 112, S.J.E. Loxton 93,
R.R. Lindwall 77, K.R. Miller 58)
404–3 (A.R. Morris 182, D.G. Bradman 173*)

Fifth Test

The Oval, 14–18 August
Australia won by an innings and 149 runs

England
52 (R.R. Lindwall 6–20)
188 (L. Hutton 64)

Australia
389 (A.R. Morris 196, S.G. Barnes 61,
W.E. Hollies 5–131)

* Not out.

AUSTRALIA'S TOUR RESULTS, 1948

Played 34, won 25, drawn 9, lost 0

28–30 April	v. Worcestershire	won (innings and 17 runs)
1–4 May	v. Leicestershire	won (innings and 171 runs)
5–6 May	v. Yorkshire	won (4 wickets)
8–11 May	v. Surrey	won (innings and 296 runs)
12–14 May	v. Cambridge University	won (innings and 51 runs)
15–17 May	v. Essex	won (innings and 451 runs)
19–21 May	v. Oxford University	won (innings and 90 runs)
22–25 May	v. MCC	won (innings and 158 runs)
26–28 May	v. Lancashire	drew
29 May–1 June	v. Nottinghamshire	drew
2–4 June	v. Hampshire	won (8 wickets)
5–7 June	v. Sussex	won (innings and 325 runs)
10–15 June	v. England (First Test)	won (8 wickets)
16–18 June	v. Northamptonshire	won (innings and 64 runs)
19–21 June	v. Yorkshire	drew
24–29 June	v. England (Second Test)	won (409 runs)
30 June–2 July	v. Surrey	won (10 wickets)
3–6 July	v. Gloucestershire	won (innings and 363 runs)
8–13 July	v. England (Third Test)	drew
17–20 July	v. Middlesex	won (10 wickets)
22–27 July	v. England (Fourth Test)	won (7 wickets)
28–30 July	v. Derbyshire	won (innings and 34 runs)
31 July–3 August	v. Glamorgan	drew
4–6 August	v. Warwickshire	won (9 wickets)
7–10 August	v. Lancashire	drew
11–12 August	v. Durham	drew
14–18 August	v. England (Fifth Test)	won (innings and 149 runs)
21–23 August	v. Kent	won (innings 186 runs)
25–27 August	v. Gentlemen	won (innings and 81 runs)
28–30 August	v. Somerset	won (innings and 374 runs)
1–3 September	v. South of England	drew
8–10 September	v. H.D.G. Leveson Gower's XI	drew
13–14 September	v. Scotland	won (innings and 40 runs)
17–18 September	v. Scotland	won (innings and 87 runs)

First-Class Averages

Batting

	Matches	Innings	Not outs	Runs	Highest Innings	Average
D. G. Bradman	23	31	4	2428	187	89.92
A. L. Hassett	22	27	6	1563	200*	74.42
A. R. Morris	21	29	2	1922	290	71.18
W. A. Brown	22	26	1	1448	200	57.92
S. J. Loxton	22	22	5	973	159*	57.23
S. G. Barnes	21	27	3	1354	176	56.41
R. N. Harvey	22	27	6	1129	126	53.76
K. R. Miller	22	26	3	1088	202*	47.30
R. A. Hamence	19	22	4	582	99	32.33
I. W. Johnson	22	22	4	543	113*	30.16
D. Tallon	14	13	2	283	53	25.72
R. R. Lindwall	22	20	3	411	77	24.17
R. A. Saggers	17	12	3	209	104*	23.22
C. L. McCool	17	18	3	306	76	20.40
W. A. Johnston	21	18	8	188	29	18.80
D. Ring	19	14	5	150	53	16.66
E. R. H. Toshack	15	12	3	78	20*	8.66

Bowling

	Overs	Maidens	Runs	Wickets	Average
R. R. Lindwall	573.1	139	1349	86	15.68
W. A. Johnston	850.1	279	1675	102	16.42
K. R. Miller	429.4	117	985	56	17.58
C. L. McCool	399.2	97	1016	57	17.82
I. W. Johnson	667.2	228	1562	85	18.37
E. R. H. Toshack	502	171	1056	50	21.12
R. A. Hamence	56.3	13	150	7	21.42
S. J. Loxton	361.2	91	695	32	21.71
D. Ring	542.4	155	1309	60	21.81
A. R. Morris	35	9	91	2	45.50
S. G. Barnes	65.4	26	121	2	60.50
A. L. Hassett	12	0	48	0	–

Also bowled: D. G. Bradman 1–0–2–0; W. A. Brown 4.1–0–16–4;
R. N. Harvey 10–3–29–1.

First-Class 100s

D. G. Bradman (11)

187	*v.* Essex at Southend
173*	*v.* England at Leeds (Fourth Test)
153	*v.* H. D. G. Leveson Gower's XI at Scarborough
150	*v.* Gentlemen of England at Lord's
146	*v.* Surrey at the Oval
143	*v.* South of England at Hastings
138	*v.* England at Nottingham (First Test)
133*	*v.* Lancashire at Manchester
128	*v.* Surrey at the Oval
109	*v.* Sussex at Hove
107	*v.* Worcestershire at Worcester

W. A. Brown (8)

200	*v.* Cambridge University at Cambridge
153	*v.* Essex at Southend
140	*v.* Derbyshire at Derby
122	*v.* Nottinghamshire at Nottingham
120	*v.* Gentlemen of England at Lord's
113	*v.* Yorkshire at Sheffield
108	*v.* Oxford University at Oxford
106	*v.* Kent at Canterbury

A. L. Hassett (7)

200*	*v.* Gentlemen of England at Lord's
151	*v.* South of England at Hastings
139	*v.* Surrey at the Oval
137	*v.* England at Nottingham (First Test)
127	*v.* Northamptonshire at Northampton
110	*v.* Surrey at the Oval
103	*v.* Somerset at Taunton

A. R. Morris (7)

290	*v.* Gloucestershire at Bristol
196	*v.* England at the Oval (Fifth Test)
184	*v.* Sussex at Hove
182	*v.* England at Leeds (Fourth Test)
138	*v.* Worcestershire at Worcester
109	*v.* Middlesex at Lord's
105	*v.* England at Lord's (Second Test)

R. N. Harvey (4)

126	*v.* Somerset at Taunton
112	*v.* England at Leeds (Fourth Test)
110	*v.* South of England at Hastings
100*	*v.* Sussex at Hove

S. G. Barnes (3)

176	*v.* Surrey at the Oval
151	*v.* H. D. G. Leveson Gower's XI at Scarborough
141	*v.* England at Lord's (Second Test)

S. J. Loxton (3)

159*	*v.* Gloucestershire at Bristol
123	*v.* Middlesex at Lord's
120	*v.* Essex at Southend

K. R. Miller (2)

202*	*v.* Leicestershire at Leicester
163	*v.* M.C.C. at Lord's

I. W. Johnson (1)

113*	*v.* Somerset at Taunton

R. A. Saggers (1)

104*	*v.* Essex at Southend

THE PLAYERS, 1948

D.G. Bradman
(Born 27.8.08, Cootamundra,
NSW)

A.L. Hassett
(Born 28.8.13, Geelong, Victoria)

A.R. Morris
(Born 19.1.22, Dungog, NSW)

W.A. Brown
(Born 31.7.12, Toowomba,
Queensland)

S.J.E. Loxton
(Born 29.3.21, Albert Park,
Victoria)

S.G. Barnes
(Born 5.6.16, Charters Towers,
Queensland)

R.N. Harvey
(Born 8.10.28, Fitzroy, Victoria)

K.R. Miller
(Born 28.11.19, Sunshine,
Victoria)

R.A. Hamence
(Born 25.11.15, Hindmarsh,
Adelaide)

I.W. Johnson
(Born 18.12.18, North
Melbourne, Victoria)

D. Tallon
(Born 17.2.16, Bundaberg,
Queensland)

R.R. Lindwall
(Born 3.10.21, Mascot, NSW)

R.A. Saggers
(Born 15.5.17, Sydenham, NSW)

C.L. McCool
(Born 9.12.15, Sydney)

W.A. Johnston
(Born 26.2.22, Beeac, Victoria)

D.T. Ring
(Born 14.10.18, Hobart,
Tasmania)

E.R.H. Toshack
(Born 15.12.14, Cobar, NSW)

Joe Hardstaff, the local player, is brilliantly caught by Keith Miller at Trent Bridge

Lindsay Hassett swivels almost full circle as he attempts a hook during the Trent Bridge Test. Godfrey Evans is the wicketkeeper

Jamaica 4 x 400-Metres Olympic Relay Team, 1948 and 1952

At the London Olympics in 1948, Jamaica were favourites with the United States for the 4 x 400-metres gold medal. Both countries were some 40 metres better than France, whose times had seemingly secured third place. On paper the Jamaicans looked the better bet. Although the Americans had three athletes in the final of the 400 metres, Jamaicans had taken the silver and the bronze. For the final of the relay on 7 August the teams lined up as follows:

USA

Arthur Harnden
Cliff Bourland   (5th in the 200 metres)
Roy Cochran   (400-metres hurdles gold medallist)
Mal Whitfield   (gold medallist in the 800 metres; bronze
                  medallist in the 400 metres)

Jamaica

George Rhoden
Leslie Laing   (6th in the 200 metres)
Arthur Wint   (gold medallist in the 400 metres; silver
                  medallist in the 800 metres)
Herb McKenley   (world 400-metres record holder; silver in
                  the 400 metres; 4th in the 200 metres)

The world record of 3 minutes 8.2 seconds had survived since 1932. On Wembley's notorious cinder track the two teams were expected to put pressure on each other and the only certainty seemed to be that there would be a new world record. With the first two men in each team as possible weak links, they were likely to cancel each other out. In fact, they did.

On the third leg the 400-metres hurdles champion Roy Cochran ran against the 400-metres flat champion Arthur Wint. Then Wint dropped out of the race with a pulled muscle, hobbling off the track in pain, anguish and disappointment. The United States anchorman Whitfield coasted home and the record remained in tact.

There was an affinity between Wint and the Wembley crowd. Bereft of any gold medals themselves, the British supported Wint. He was a Londoner, studying to become a doctor, and ran for Polytechnic Harriers at Chiswick. He won the 1946 AAA 440- and 880-yards championship and was after his second gold in his adopted city. The four Jamaicans vowed to return in four years at Helsinki. Return they did.

Apart from Whitfield, the Americans had changed personnel. Their line-up was as follows:

USA

Ollie Matson   (bronze medal in the 400 metres)
Gerald Cole
Charles Moore   (gold medallist in the 400-metres hurdles)
Mal Whitfield   (now double Olympic champion in the
                  800 metres; finalist in the 400 metres)

All that had changed in the Jamaican line-up was the running order.

Jamaica

Arthur Wint   (now double silver medallist in the
                  800 metres; finalist in the 400 metres)
Leslie Laing   (5th in the 200 metres)
Herb McKenley   (silver medallist in the 100 and the
                  400 metres)
George Rhoden   (new world record holder and gold
                  medallist in the 400 metres)

In the relay Matson confirmed the superiority which he had shown in the individual race by handing over 5 metres up on Wint, who had finished fifth in the individual final. Gerald Cole increased the lead over Laing to 12 metres after the second lap. Of the last four runners, three had just won individual golds. Yet it was the athlete who hadn't – Herb McKenley – who ran the crucial leg. Having just lost his world record to his team-mate Rhoden, and having reached five finals with three silver medals but no gold, McKenley hared off after Charley Moore. He caught Moore a metre from the change over, having run an incredible split of 44.6 seconds. Moore had recorded a useful 46.3 seconds. Rhoden set off on the last leg with the burly Whitfield on his heels. They ran their lap as though someone had tied them together. Rhoden began with a 1-metre lead and held the same margin throughout the race, finishing with that metre to spare over an athlete who had twice won gold medals at 800 metres yet had twice failed to win gold at his supposed better distance of 400 metres.

When the times were announced, the Jamaican quartet had taken 4.3 seconds off the world record set at the 1932 Olympics in Los Angeles. Their record was to last another eight years and would have won them a bronze at Moscow in 1980, and Arthur Wint, at thirty-two, became the oldest male athlete to win a track gold medal. After running his leg, he realized that the last man, Rhoden, did not have a Jamaican vest, so he gave his vest to Rhoden.

That evening the Jamaicans celebrated with whisky from a toothbrush glass in their quarters. They admitted one distinguished guest – the Duke of Edinburgh.

THE TEAM

Leslie Laing

Born 19 February 1924, his only individual Olympic event was the 200 metres. He finished sixth in 1948 and fifth in 1952.

Herb McKenley

Born 10 July 1922, he did most of his running in the USA, where he won three American 400-metres titles. In 1948 he equalled the world 400-metres record, and less than a month later the record was his outright in 45.9 seconds, making him the first man to break 46 seconds in the event. He also broke the world record for the 440 yards and the 300 metres.

Left: *Herb McKenley cruises through his 200-metres heat at the 1948 Olympics at Wembley*
Middle: *Arthur Wint wins the individual 400 metres at the 1948 Olympics from team-mate Herb McKenley (hidden)*
Right: *Leslie Laing qualifies for the final of the 200 metres at Wembley during the 1948 Olympics*

Olympic Performances

1948

4th	200 metres
Silver	400 metres (runner-up to Wint)

1952

Gold	4 x 400-metres relay
Silver	100 metres (lost in photo)
Silver	400 metres

George Rhoden

Born on 13 December 1926 in Kingston, Jamaica, he graduated from Morgan State College, Baltimore. He took the world 400-metres record off McKenley in 1950 and won the Olympic 400-metres titles in 1952, beating McKenley by 18 inches in 45.9 seconds. Between 1946 and 1954 he won a record ten medals in the Central American and Caribbean Games.

Arthur Wint

Born 25 May 1920, the son of a minister and a Scottish mother, he joined the RAF during the war and afterwards stayed in England to become a medical student at the University of London. He eventually became a surgeon. Between 1974 and 1978 he was the Jamaican High Commissioner to the United Kingdom. He was 6 feet 4 inches tall, with a stride of nearly ten feet. In 1948 he became the first Jamaican to win a track and field gold medal at the Olympics.

Olympic Performances

1948

Gold	400 metres
Silver	800 metres

1952

Gold	4 x 400-metres relay
Silver	'800 metres
5th	400 metres

1952 OLYMPIC 4 x 400-METRES RELAY FINAL

1	Jamaica	3:3.9
2	USA	3:4.0
3	Germany	3:6.6
4	Canada	3:9.3
5	Britain	3:10.0
6	France	3:10.1

West Indies Cricket Team, 1950

The West Indies came to England in 1950 determined that they would achieve their ambition of winning a series for the first time in this country. They were setting their sights high – they had not at the time even won a Test here! The West Indies had been producing truly talented players for years, but they had never forged a great side. When John Goddard assumed the captaincy in 1947, the basis of the team that was to humble England began to take shape. Frank Worrell, Clyde Walcott and Everton Weekes, that superb batting triumvirate, came together in 1947–48. The opening partnership of Allan Rae and Jeffrey Stollmeyer was introduced the following year. The spin twins Sonny Ramadhin and Alf Valentine burst on the scene in 1950.

The discourtesy of England in selecting less than their best side three years before made the West Indies even more determined to succeed, but in the first Test at Manchester England won by 202 runs on a turning pitch, a result that would have demoralized West Indies teams of the past. Individually the players performed well. Valentine's 8 for 104 in the England first innings proved his mastery of flight spin and control. Valentine was a gangling, awkward figure, casual in the extreme. He never bothered to mark out a run-up and he only discovered that he needed spectacles when he realized he could not see the scoreboard. The perfect foil for Valentine was Ramadhin. Neither of the spinners had any first-class experience before the tour. Valentine, from Jamaica, and

Jeff Stollmeyer, the West Indies opener, starts the Fourth and final Test at the Oval with an aggressive hook. The wicketkeeper is Arthur McIntyre and first slip is Trevor Bailey

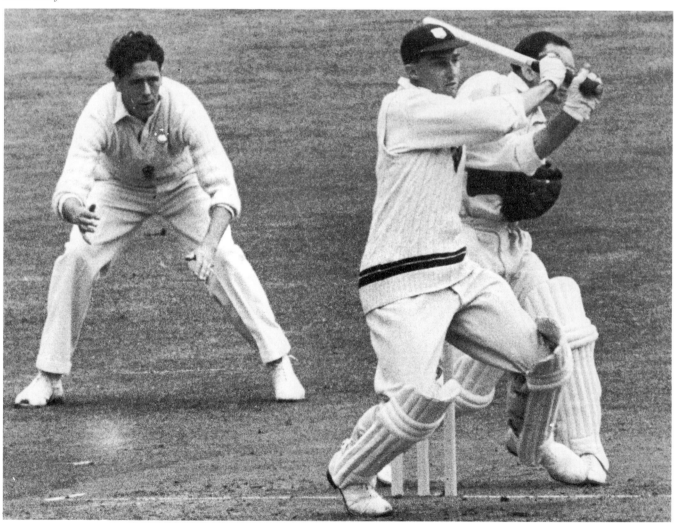

Sonny Ramadhin mesmerizes a University batsman at Fenners during the drawn match with Cambridge University

Ramadhin, a Trinidadian, were barely known in their own islands. Old Trafford changed all that. By lunch on the first day Valentine had taken the wickets of Edrich, Dollery, Yardley, Simpson and Doggart. But batting last on a wicked pitch the West Indies found Bob Berry and Eric Hollies too much for them despite Jeff Stollmeyer's 78.

History was made in the Second Test at Lord's. Allan Rae, the solid Jamaican left-hander, batted through the first day for 106. With the mystery spin of Ramadhin proving too much for England, Clyde Walcott scored a magnificent 168 not out to pave the way for Ramadhin again to demoralize England.

Ramadhin, like Valentine, was a quaint figure, but whereas Valentine was thin and awkward, Ramadhin was stocky and small, with sleeves buttoned to the wrist and always bowling in his cap. He mesmerized batsmen by turning the ball both ways without any apparent change in his action. Ramadhin was never 'found out' by the England batsmen until Edgbaston in 1957 when May and Cowdrey devised a master plan to compete, if not destroy.

Clyde Walcott's batting at Lord's had proved irresistible. Now Frank Worrell and Everton Weekes took over as the centres of attention in the next two Tests. Worrell's brilliant and graceful 261 at Nottingham laid the foundation of yet another massive victory. In partnership with Weekes, he added 283 for the fourth wicket with a display of batting described by Sir Pelham Warner as the best he had ever seen in his lifetime.

Another comprehensive victory followed at the Oval, with another century for Worrell, and for Allan Rae, and more wickets for Alf Valentine, although Len Hutton's double century for England in their first innings was true competition.

Although Worrell came from Barbados, he played most of his cricket in Jamaica; he was later to become a respected West Indies captain and statesman. Whereas Weekes and Walcott were powerful, pugnacious batsmen, Worrell gracefully persuaded the bowling to the boundary. His century at the Oval in 1950 was in an altogether different vein to the Lord Mayor's show at Trent Bridge, but courage and concentration were built into Worrell and his graft for runs against Alec Bedser, Trevor Bailey and Doug Wright was no less satisfying.

Weekes, from Barbados, a short but powerful player, was capable of destroying any attack. Particularly forceful on the off side and in front of the wicket he received no basic coaching until after he had made his debut in first-class cricket.

Walcott was taller than Weekes but just as powerful, as befits an all-round athlete. He could also keep wicket amazingly well for a tall man and at Old Trafford in 1950 he even opened the bowling, not with the effortless grace of Worrell, but enthusiastically none the less.

While the 1950 side was based on the brilliance of the three Ws and the spin threat of Ramadhin and Valentine, the captaincy of John Goddard was a major contributory factor to their series win, although the cares of leadership seemed to detract from his playing capabilities. The opening partnership of Stollmeyer and Rae (the most successful and best known openers in West Indies cricket until Greenidge and Haynes) fulfilled a major role. The West Indies came to England determined to win. Many sides have that ambition; few achieve it with such style, charm and power.

Everton Weekes hooks a ball to the boundary on his way to an unbeaten 304 against the University at Cambridge

THE 1950 TEST SERIES

First Test

Old Trafford, 8–12 June
England won by 202 runs

England
312 (T. G. Evans 104, T. E. Bailey 82*; A. L. Valentine 8–104)
288 (W. J. Edrich 71)
West Indies
215 (E. D. Weekes 52; R. Berry 5–63)
183 (J. B. Stollmeyer 78; W. E. Hollies 5–63)

Second Test

Lord's, 24–29 June
West Indies won by 326 runs

West Indies
326 (A. F. Rae 106, E. D. Weekes 63, F. M. Worrell 52;
R. O. Jenkins 5–116)
425–6 dec. (C. L. Walcott 168*, G. E. Gomez 70,
E. D. Weekes 63)
England
151 (S. Ramadhin 5–66)
274 (C. Washbrook 114; S. Ramadhin 6–86)

Third Test

Trent Bridge, 20–25 July
West Indies won by 10 wickets

England
223
436 (C. Washbrook 102, R. T. Simpson 94, W. G. A. Parkhouse
69, T. G. Evans 63, J. G. Dewes 67; S. Ramadhin 5–135)
West Indies
558 (F. M. Worrell 261, E. D. Weekes 129, A. F. Rae 68;
A. V. Bedser 5–127)
103–0 (J. B. Stollmeyer 52*)

Fourth Test

The Oval, 12–16 August
West Indies won by an innings and 56 runs

West Indies
503 (F. M. Worrell 138, A. F. Rae 109, G. E. Gomez 74,
J. D. C. Goddard 58*; D. V. P. Wright 5–141)
England
344 (L. Hutton 202*)
103 (A. L. Valentine 6–39)

* Not out.

THE WEST INDIES TOUR, 1950

Results

Played 33, won 18, drawn 12, lost 3

6–9 May	*v.* Worcestershire	drew
10–11 May	*v.* Yorkshire	won (3 wickets)
13–16 May	*v.* Surrey	drew
17–19 May	*v.* Cambridge University	drew
20–23 May	*v.* MCC	lost (118 runs)
24–26 May	*v.* Oxford University	drew
27–30 May	*v.* Glamorgan	won (innings and 26 runs)
31 May–2 June	*v.* Somerset	won (71 runs)
3–6 June	*v.* Lancashire	won (innings and 220 runs)
8–12 June	*v.* England (First Test)	lost (202 runs)
14–15 June	*v.* Northumberland	won (innings and 8 runs)
17–20 June	*v.* Nottinghamshire	won (innings and 61 runs)
21–23 June	*v.* Sussex	won (innings and 243 runs)
24–29 June	*v.* England (Second Test)	won (326 runs)
1–4 July	*v.* Hampshire	drew
5–7 July	*v.* Lancashire	won (innings and 41 runs)
8–10 July	*v.* Northamptonshire	drew
12–14 July	*v.* Leicestershire	won (innings and 249 runs)
15–18 July	*v.* Derbyshire	drew
20–25 July	*v.* England (Third Test)	won (10 wickets)
26–27 July	*v.* Durham	drew
29–31 July	*v.* Yorkshire	won (35 runs)
2–4 August	*v.* Surrey	won (innings and 69 runs)
5–8 August	*v.* Glamorgan	drew
9–11 August	*v.* Warwickshire	lost (3 wickets)
12–16 August	*v.* England (Fourth Test)	won (innings and 56 runs)
19–21 August	*v.* Gloucestershire	won (innings and 105 runs)
23–25 August	*v.* Essex	won (7 wickets)
26–29 August	*v.* Middlesex	drew
30–31 August	*v.* Kent	won (222 runs)
2–5 September	*v.* South of England	drew
6–8 September	*v.* Minor Counties	won (innings and 7 runs)
9–12 September	*v.* H. D. G. Leveson Gower's XI	drew

First-Class Averages

Batting

	Matches	Innings	Not outs	Runs	Highest Innings	Average
E. Weekes	23	33	4	2310	304*	79.65
F.M. Worrell	22	31	5	1775	261	68.26
C.L. Walcott	25	36	6	1674	168*	55.80
R.J. Christiani	24	34	10	1094	131*	45.58
G.E. Gomez	27	30	4	1116	149	42.92
R.E. Marshall	20	28	0	1117	188	39.89
A.F. Rae	26	38	4	1330	179	39.11
J.B. Stollmeyer	25	37	1	1334	198	37.05
K.B. Trestrail	19	28	5	629	94	27.34
J.D. Goddard	22	21	5	309	58*	19.31
H.H. Johnson	17	16	4	184	39*	15.33
C.B. Williams	20	18	4	152	33*	10.85
P.E. Jones	17	16	4	83	20	6.91
S. Ramadhin	21	15	8	36	7*	5.14
A.L. Valentine	21	19	3	49	9*	3.06
L.R. Pierre	12	7	1	2	1	0.33

Alf Valentine (left) *and Sonny Ramadhin* (above) – *the spin attack about whom a song was written*

A classical cover drive from Frank Worrell against Cambridge

First-Class Averages

Bowling

	Overs	Maidens	Runs	Wickets	Average
S. Ramadhin	1043.4	398	2009	135	14.88
A.L. Valentine	1185.2	475	2207	123	17.94
J.D. Goddard	295.2	96	618	33	18.72
L.R. Pierre	204	39	557	24	23.20
F.M. Worrell	480.1	170	970	39	24.87
G.E. Gomez	680.3	221	1407	55	25.58
C.B. Williams	301.2	57	856	31	27.61
H.H. Johnson	435.5	102	954	34	28.05
P.E. Jones	388.3	82	980	33	29.69
R.E. Marshall	120.5	36	336	7	48.00
J.B. Stollmeyer	27	3	117	2	58.50

Also bowled: K.B. Trestrail 3–0–17–0;
C.L. Walcott 12–6–22–0;
E. Weekes 9–0–41–2.

THE PLAYERS

R. J. Christiani
(Born 19.7.20, Georgetown)

J. D. Goddard
(Born 21.4.19, Bridgetown)

G. E. Gomez
(Born 10.10.19, Port of Spain)

H. H. Johnson
(Born 13.7.10, Kingston)

P. E. Jones
(Born 6.6.17, Prince's Town, Trinidad)

R. E. Marshall
(Born 25.4.30, St Thomas, Barbados)

L. R. Pierre
(Born 5.6.21, Woodbrook, Port of Spain)

A. F. Rae
(Born 30.9.22, Kingston)

S. Ramadhin
(Born 1.5.29, Esperance Village, Trinidad)

J. F. Stollmeyer
(Born 11.4.21, Santa Cruz, Trinidad)

K. B. Trestrail
(Born 26.11.27, Trinidad)

A. L. Valentine
(Born 29.4.30, Kingston)

C. L. Walcott
(Born 17.1.26, Bridgetown)

E. Weekes
(Born 26.2.25, Bridgetown)

C. B. Williams
(Born 8.3.26, Bridgetown)

M. Worrell
(Born 1.8.24, Bridgetown)

The Springboks, 1951–52

The fourth Springboks touring team arrived in Britain under what almost amounted to a cloud of suspicion that they were going to remain invincible and that safety-first tactics were the order of the day. They were described in their own country as not being of the same pedigree as other Springbok teams and the propaganda had soon spread to Britain. But a touring side, living and training together, has many advantages, and to their infinite credit the Springboks set out to justify themselves as sportsmen and players of open, as well as close, tactical rugby. They so succeeded in achieving their ideals, after losing their captain early in the tour, that they left the legacy of a world record at Murrayfield by beating Scotland 44–0 – a record that survives the penalty-dominated scoresheets of the present day, to say nothing of the increased value of the try.

The fulcrum of the side was removed early on. Basil Kenyon, the tour captain, was injured at Pontypool and, after only five games, decided to stand down from the playing side after the match at Gosforth to receive medical attention for his injured eye. Hennie Muller, the other No. 8 in the party, took over the captaincy. It was through Muller, an outstandingly quick and mobile player, that the manager Frank Mellish – Blackheath, England and South Africa – imparted his intimate knowledge of the British game, whilst the coach, Danie Craven, former Springbok captain and scrum half, attended, supervised and drew up the tactical concepts.

It would have been interesting to know when the Springboks settled upon their international side. As it was, twelve men – six backs and six forwards – played in all five internationals, and two others played in four.

The backs played en bloc – twenty-one-year-old Johnny Buchler, Chum Ochse, Ryk Van Schoor, Tjol Lategan, Paul Johnstone, Hansie Brewis and Fonnie du Toit – with the exception of Buks Marais for Ochse in the Scotland match (it is not often a player gets dropped after a 44–0 win). The forwards used the 3–4–1 formation. Okey Geffin played three internationals at prop and was then replaced by Jaap Bekker, and William Barnard played once at lock in place of Ernst Dinkelmann. The remainder – Hennie Muller, Salty du Rand, Stephen Fry, Basie Van Wyk, Chris Koch and William Delport – held their places unchallenged. These were mighty men, fit and with physical presence. Koch was christened 'Sledge Mawr – the great sledgehammer' – by the Welsh.

The support XV were the usual back-up of stalwarts, characters and walking wounded. Two of the backs, Des Sinclair and Hansie Oelofse, were badly injured and were seriously handicapped throughout the tour, while players like Dennis Fry, brother of the flanker Stephen, Martin Saunders, Basie Viviers, Jan Pickard, and the 'Iron Man' Gert Dannhauser would have been welcome recruits to any of the other international teams they faced.

The first two games were notable because the Springboks used entirely different teams on grounds where League football is played. Pontypool Park was the venue for the first of three or four 'tight' matches that each touring side experiences, with a late penalty from Viviers deciding the issue. The very next

Chris Koch tows the Scottish defence towards the try line during the Springboks record 44–0 win at Murrayfield

game at Cardiff, who beat the 1906 side 17–0, was similar, with Ochse's last-minute try salvaging the unbeaten record and Cardiff failing to accept two scoring chances, then presenting their opponents with two tries. Llanelly proved an equally difficult foe.

If any modern touring team complains about tortuous itineraries, then the Springboks next few fixtures before the international in Edinburgh were a classic case of crass bad planning. The games were hard, the venues seemed to have been picked by blindfolded organizers with a direction pin stuck willy-nilly into a map. The Springboks formulated their international team, learned how to use an AA map, and were beaten – by London Counties at Twickenham. The tourists led 9–8, but the Counties stiffened their defence to such effect that the Springboks could not score again. Then a huge penalty from the Harlequins lock Grimsdell, one of ten players from the county champions Middlesex, after the Springboks had infringed in the line-out proved decisive. The narrow defeat probably did the tourists more good than harm.

Scotland would certainly agree. Their rout by 44–0 is

equivalent to 53–0 in modern values. The tourists scored nine tries, seven of which Geffin converted, and a dropped goal. After a scoreless first quarter of an hour, the Springboks led 19–0 at half-time and scored five more tries in the second period.

A fortnight later, Ireland held a 5–3 lead going into the last quarter, and they were only 4 points adrift with four minutes left. Irish resistance buckled to two late tries, one by Van Schoor who had earlier been carried off unconscious.

The critical stage in any tour is the build-up before the international with Wales, especially if the Welsh have never beaten a touring side. At Swansea the Springboks again scored two late tries after the locals, at 3–3, had parked themselves on the Springboks line with seven minutes remaining.

There were just three scores in the international at Cardiff. Ochse scored a try for South Africa in the first half, Brewis added a drop goal just after the interval, and in a sustained but unavailing Welsh rally, a try by Bleddyn Williams was deserved. The brief statistics serve as an indication of the tense atmosphere and drama. The Springboks sensed that they had climbed their mountain.

Two more internationals followed. Acting vice-captain du Toit scored his side's only try at Twickenham in an awful game against England and Muller added a conversion and a penalty after he and his selection committee had decided to axe the recognized kicker, Geffin. The fifth international, in bitterly cold weather with the going treacherous after snow in Paris, was even at half-time. In the second half the Springboks added another five tries to the one they had scored earlier. The tour, which had started on 10 October, finished thirty-one games later on 16 February.

Three characters epitomized the 'bone' in this side. Fonnie du Toit, the scrum half, played against France with a temperature after he had originally dropped out to give a first cap to Oelofse.

When the unfortunate Oelofse was forced to withdraw with a recurring thigh injury, du Toit played with German measles. Van Schoor, who had returned after being knocked unconscious against Ireland, was then sent to bed for forty-eight hours. And Doctor Ernst Dinkelmann, the team medic, pronounced Salty du Rand fit for the international with Wales. Had du Rand not been fit, then Dinkelmann himself would have played.

THE TOUR PARTY

Full Back

J. Buchler (Transvaal), A. C. Keevy (E. Transvaal)

Threequarters

S. B. Viviers (Orange Free State), J. K. Ochse (W. Province), F. Marais (Boland), M. J. Saunders (Border), P. A. Johnstone (W. Province), M. T. Lategan (W. Province), R. Van Schoor (Rhodesia), D. J. Sinclair (Transvaal)

Half Backs

J. D. Brewis (N. Transvaal), D. J. Fry (W. Province), J. Oelofse (Transvaal), P. A. du Toit (N. Transvaal)

Forwards

P. Wessels (Orange Free State), W. Delport (E. Province), A. C. Koch (Boland), A. Geffin (Transvaal), H. J. Bekker (N. Transvaal), F. E. van der Ryst (Transvaal), E. Dinkelmann (N. Transvaal), J. Pickard (W. Province), G. Dannhauser (Transvaal), W. H. M. Barnard (Griqualand), S. P. Fry (W. Province), J. du Rand (Rhodesia), C. J. van Wyk (E. Transvaal), B. Myburgh (E. Transvaal), B. Kenyon (Border), H. Muller (Transvaal)
Captain: B. Kenyon
Vice-captain: H. Muller

THE SPRINGBOKS IN EUROPE, 1951–52

	Scotland	Ireland	Wales	England	France
Buchler	FB	FB	FB	FB	FB
Marais	RW				
Ochse		RW (1T)	RW (1T)	RW	RW
Van Schoor	C (1T)	C (1T)	C	C	C
Lategan	C (1T)	C	C	C	C
Johnstone	LW	LW	LW	LW	LW (2T, 1PG, 1C)
Brewis	FH (1DG)	FH (1DG)	FH (1DG)	FH	FH
Du Toit	SH	SH	SH	SH (1T)	SH
Koch	P (2T)	P	P	P	P
Delport	H (1T)	H	H	H	H (1T)
Geffin	P (7C)	P (1C)	P		
Bekker				P	P
Dinkelmann	L (1T)	L		L	L (1T)
Barnard			L		
Du Rand	L (1T)	L	L	L	L
Van Wyk	F (1T)	F (2T)	F	F	F (1T)
S. Fry	F	F	F	F	F
Muller	No. 8 (1T)	No. 8	No. 8	No. 8 (1C, 1PG)	No. 8 (1T, 1C)
Score:	44–0	17–5	6–3	8–3	27–3

Hennie Muller, who took over the tour captaincy from Basil Kenyon, leads his team out against Scotland. Okey Geffin follows him
Left: *The triumphant South African team pose with the crew of the* Caernarvon Castle *on their way home*

TOUR RECORD

Opponents	Venue	Result
Southeast Counties	Bournemouth	won 31–6
Southwest Counties	Plymouth	won 17–8
Pontypool–Newbridge	Pontypool	won 15–6
Cardiff	Cardiff	won 11–9
Llanelly	Llanelly	won 20–11
Northwest Counties	Birkenhead Park	won 16–9
Glasgow–Edinburgh	Glasgow	won 43–11
Northeast Counties	Gosforth	won 19–8
Cambridge University	Cambridge	won 30–0
London Counties	Twickenham	lost 9–11
Oxford University	Oxford	won 24–3
Aberavon–Neath	Aberavon	won 22–0
Scotland	Murrayfield	won 44–0
North of Scotland	Aberdeen	won 14–3
Ulster	Belfast	won 27–5
Ireland	Dublin	won 17–5
Munster	Limerick	won 11–6
Swansea	Swansea	won 11–3
Wales	Cardiff	won 6–3
Combined Services	Twickenham	won 24–8
Midland Counties	Leicester	won 3–0
England	Twickenham	won 8–3
Newport	Newport	won 12–6
Western Counties	Bristol	won 16–5
Midland Counties	Coventry	won 19–8
South of Scotland	Hawick	won 13–3
Barbarians	Cardiff	won 17–3
Southeast France	Lyon	won 9–3
Southwest France	Bordeaux	won 20–12
France 'B'	Toulouse	won 9–6
France	Paris	won 25–3

Played 31, won 30, drawn 0, lost 1, points 562–167

Surrey County Cricket Team, 1952–58

Between 1952 and 1958 Surrey won the County Championship every year – a record unequalled and, given the current evening-up of standards in the English first-class game, likely to remain.

Surrey's win in 1952 under their new captain Stuart Surridge was their first outright win since 1914 (although they had shared the title with Lancashire in 1950). Surridge's philosophy of captaincy was simple: 'Attack.' He believed, for example, that if fielders were prepared to stand close enough then they would pick up catches off defensive strokes. His tactics were not short of critics, particularly away from Kennington, but *Wisden*, commenting on his first successful season leading Surrey, said: 'Surridge brought to Surrey a spirit of consistent enterprise and aggression such as they had not known since the days of P. G. H. Fender 20 years previously.'

With an international-class attack comprising the pace of Peter Loader, the masterful control of Alec Bedser, and the spin and guile of Jim Laker and Tony Lock, Surridge had good reason to emphasize the value of attacking, aggressive play in the field. But Surridge himself and Bedser's twin brother Eric also weighed in with vital wickets, especially when the main strike bowlers were away playing for England.

Perhaps the contributions of the bowlers, backed by expert fielding, has been overstated in the years since Surrey's magnificent run and the contribution of the batsmen underrated. Surridge could always depend on runs scored quickly all the way down the order to number 9 and with players of the calibre of Peter May, Ken Barrington, Raman Subba Row (briefly) and, later, Micky Stewart to call upon, attractiveness and consistency were allied.

With Surrey's continued success inevitably came Test calls. In 1955 – their fourth consecutive championship year under Surridge – seven of their players were used by England: Bedser, Loader, Laker and Lock, plus May, Barrington and wicketkeeper Arthur McIntyre, who stood in for the injured Godfrey Evans. While Surrey's abundant mainstream talent provided the basis for their series of championship successes, reserve strength began to play a part as soon as international recognition was granted. Surrey's young groundstaff players were nurtured under the watchful eye of Jack Hobbs's former opening partner, Andrew Sandham, and when called upon for first-team duty were rarely out of their depth.

1956 was Surridge's last year as skipper. The nucleus of the side was the same as in 1952, the only notable departures having been Fishlock and Parker. Alec Bedser as senior professional helped mould the team's already substantial 'high skill, ruthless efficiency and matchless spirit', as *Wisden* put it, and smoothed the way for May to take over the reins. With May in charge Surrey won their sixth successive title in 1957 with nine of their twenty-one wins taking less than two days.

Surrey, on the county circuit, were the most attractive and most welcome visitors everywhere, drawing huge crowds. With a full-strength team the spectators could expect to see Alec Bedser, who had been the spearhead for England and Surrey since 1946, a bowler who R. C. Robertson-Glasgow compared with Maurice Tate: 'Both have greatness . . . Tate had the more natural genius, Bedser the more invention and variety.' There was also Jim Laker, the off-spinner *sans pareil*, who took 19 wickets for 90 against the Australians in the Old Trafford Test in 1956, then repeated the feat of taking ten wickets in an innings by taking 10 Australian wickets for Surrey at the Oval the same year. With the great Tony Lock – the first genuine slow left-arm spinner to gain a place in the Surrey team – the Surrey bowling was irresistible.

Backed by the most professional and consistent fielding unit, Surrey's close field crouching round the bat as one or other of their England bowlers reached his delivery stride is a never to be forgotten sight, especially in the last moments of an evening session after May, Barrington, Bernard Constable and the rest had destroyed the opposition bowling with a welter of strokes, always, it seemed, heeding the word of the captain: 'Attack.'

COUNTY CHAMPIONSHIP RECORD, 1952–58

Leading Positions

1952	P	W	L	D	Pts
1 Surrey	28	20	3	5	256
2 Yorkshire	28	17	2	8	224
3 Lancashire	28	12	3	11	188

1953					
1 Surrey	28	13	4	10	184
2 Sussex	28	11	3	13	168
3 Lancashire	28	10	4	10	156
4 Leicestershire	28	10	7	11	156

1954					
1 Surrey	28	15	3	8	208
2 Yorkshire	28	13	3	8	186
3 Derbyshire	28	11	6	9	168

1955					
1 Surrey	28	23	5	0	284
2 Yorkshire	28	21	5	2	268
3 Hampshire	28	16	5	6	210

1956					
1 Surrey	28	15	5	6	200
2 Lancashire	28	12	2	12	180
3 Gloucestershire	28	14	7	5	176

1957					
1 Surrey	28	21	3	3	312
2 Northamptonshire	28	15	2	10	218
3 Yorkshire	28	13	4	11	190

1958					
1 Surrey	28	14	5	8	212
2 Hampshire	28	12	6	10	186
3 Somerset	28	12	9	7	174

(NB. Where W–L–D do not balance, this is because of abandoned matches.)

Their total of 312 points in the championship in 1957 was the highest since 1950 when all counties started playing twenty-eight matches.

The following players played in each of the seven championship seasons: P. B. H. May, D. G. W. Fletcher, B. Constable, E. A. Bedser, A. V. Bedser, A. J. McIntyre, G. A. R. Lock, P. J. Loader, J. C. Laker, R. C. E. Pratt, T. H. Clark.

Peter May, with 7832, was top run scorer in county games and Tony Lock with 817 was leading wicket taker. He claimed 100 victims every season but one.

In 1957 A. V. Bedser took 109 wickets at 15.57, but was only sixth in the county bowling averages. P. B. H. May headed the batting averages every year except 1956 when T. H. Clark topped the list.

Alan Davidson falls to a fine catch by Peter May off the bowling of Jim Laker. Australia v. Surrey at the Oval, 1956

Batting

	Years	Matches	Innings	Not outs	Runs	Highest score	100s	Average
P. B. H. May	1952–8	119	188	30	7832	211*	22	49.57
R. Subba Row	1952–3	36	52	9	1553	128	3	36.12
J. F. Parker	1952	24	37	4	1109	113	1	33.60
K. F. Barrington	1953–8	125	186	33	5011	135*	10	32.75
A. F. Brazier	1952–4	14	22	4	567	92	—	31.50
D. G. W. Fletcher	1952–8	138	231	20	6531	142	8	30.95
B. Constable	1952–8	179	281	29	7536	205*	11	29.91
M. J. Stewart	1954–8	108	175	13	4839	166	9	29.87
L. B. Fishlock	1952	21	35	3	953	102*	1	29.71
T. H. Clark	1952–8	171	271	23	7324	191	7	29.53
E. A. Bedser	1952–8	160	240	34	5171	135	3	25.10
A. J. McIntyre	1952–8	159	209	32	3923	110	1	22.16
G. J. Whittaker	1952–3	28	39	3	736	68*	—	20.44
R. C. E. Pratt	1952–8	49	71	9	1214	90	—	19.58
D. F. Cox	1952–7	22	30	9	402	57	—	19.14
J. C. Laker	1952–8	135	155	27	2174	113	1	16.98
M. D. Willett	1955–8	10	13	2	184	31*	—	16.73
A. B. D. Parsons	1958	7	10	1	147	47	—	16.33
G. A. R. Lock	1952–8	140	147	32	1871	66	—	16.27
W. S. Surridge	1952–6	129	151	17	1837	70*	—	13.71
R. Swetman	1954–8	33	39	5	465	44*	—	13.68
D. Gibson	1957–8	14	13	4	110	55	—	12.22
D. Pratt	1954&56	6	8	1	52	33	—	13.14
J. W. McMahon	1952–3	17	17	11	66	23	—	11.00
A. V. Bedser	1952–8	147	153	67	883	58	—	10.27
P. J. Loader	1952–8	128	123	34	909	81	—	10.21
D. A. D. Sydenham	1957–8	8	8	6	14	8*	—	7.00
J. K. Hall	1958	3	2	1	6	4*	—	6.00
G. N. G. Kirby	1952–3	7	6	1	13	8	—	2.60
J. H. Edrich	1958	1	1	1	24	24*	—	—
R. A. E. Tindall	1956	1	1	1	19	19*	—	—
H. R. A. Kelleher	1955	3	—	—	—	—	—	—

* Not out

Bowling

	Overs	Maidens	Runs	Wickets	Average
G. A. R. Lock	5238.1	2009	10405	817	12.74
H. R. A. Kelleher	74.0	15	179	12	14.91
P. J. Loader	3484.3	837	8030	492	16.32
A. V. Bedser	4933.4	1391	10274	624	16.46
J. C. Laker	4836.4	1675	9830	576	17.07
E. A. Bedser	2851.5	968	5759	293	19.65
D. Gibson	357.4	84	885	44	20.11
D. E. Pratt	57.1	14	157	7	22.42
J. W. McMahon	581.4	204	1272	52	24.46
T. H. Clark	715.5	217	1611	64	25.17
J. K. Hall	146.3	33	406	16	25.37
D. A. D. Sydenham	213.4	42	621	23	27.00
D. F. Cox	433.3	75	1150	41	28.05
W. S. Surridge	2017.5	413	5258	187	28.12
K. F. Barrington	152.3	25	508	8	63.50
R. Subba Row	22.0	5	65	1	65.00
B. Constable	90.0	17	305	4	76.25
R. A. E. Tindall	2.0	2	—	—	—
M. D. Willett	5.0	1	11	—	—

May repeats the feat for Laker's spin partner Tony Lock with a similar catch to dismiss Neil Harvey. Australia v. Surrey, 1956

THE PLAYERS

During their successful spell between 1952 and 1958, seven Surrey players appeared for England in Test matches. Their Test career details are listed below:

	Career	M	I	No	Runs	Hs	Avge	100	Ct	Wkts	Runs	Avge	Best	5wI	10wM
K. F. Barrington (Born 24.11.30, Reading; died 14.3.81, Barbados)	1955–68	88	131	15	6806	256	58.67	20	58	29	1300	44.82	3–4	–	–
A. V. Bedser OBE (Born 4.7.18, Reading)	1946–55	51	71	15	714	79	12.75	–	26	236	5876	24.89	7–44	15	5
J. C. Laker (Born 9.2.22, Frizingham, Bradford)	1947–59	46	63	15	676	63	14.08	–	12	193	4101	21.24	10–53	9	3
P. J. Loader (Born 25.10.29, Wallington, Surrey)	1954–59	13	19	6	76	17	5.84	–	2	39	878	22.51	6–36	1	–
G. A. R. Lock (Born 5.7.29, Limpsfield, Surrey)	1952–68	49	63	9	742	89	13.74	–	59	174	4451	25.58	7–35	9	3
P. B. H. May (Born 31.12.29, Reading)	1951–61	66	106	9	4537	285*	46.77	13	42			–	–	–	–
A. J. McIntyre (Born 14.5.18, Kennington, London)	1950–55	3	6	0	19	7	3.16	–	8	–	–	–	–	–	–

The following were regarded as stalwarts of the team in the fifties and their career highlights are shown below. The only player not also included in the above section is Eric Bedser, and his date and place of birth is the same as Alec's.

K. F. Barrington	1950–63	533	831	136	31714	256	45.63	76	515	273	8907	32.62	7–40	8	0
A. V. Bedser	1939–60	485	576	181	5735	126	14.51	1	289	1924	39279	20.41	8–18	96	16
E. A. Bedser	1939–61	457	692	79	14716	163	24.00	10	236	833	20784	24.95	7–33	24	4
G. A. R. Lock	1946–71	654	812	161	10342	89	15.88	–	831	2844	54709	19.23	10–54	196	50
P. J. Loader	1951–64	371	382	110	2314	81	8.50	–	120	1326	25260	19.04	9–17	70	13
J. C. Laker	1946–64	450	548	108	7304	113	16.60	2	271	1944	35791	18.41	10–53	127	32
P. B. H. May	1950–63	388	618	77	27592	285*	51.00	85	282	0	49	–	–	–	–

Hungary, 1953

At teatime on a dark afternoon within the bowl of Wembley Stadium the inevitable had happened and 25 November 1953 had become as grey as the afternoon sky as far as British sport was concerned. To those who had seen the shadows of recent years creeping closer and closer it was no real surprise. England were at last beaten by a foreign invader. And it was a great side from Hungary. Beaten 6–3, England were undone by a mixture of their own long-ball game and exquisite short passing. Those who said that the day the continentals learned to shoot British football would have to wake up were right.

By no stretch, though, was this a bad England side. Tom Finney was missing, otherwise the team was perfectly acceptable. Critics said that it would easily beat the Scots which seemed to be the somewhat insular attitude of those days.

Within twenty-eight minutes the Hungarians were 4–1 up. Hideguti scored from 20 yards within a minute, then had another turned down as offside by the Dutch referee, Leo Horn. Sewell equalized, only for Hungary to score three in no time. It was disturbing but breathtaking. After another twenty minutes Hideguti scored again. After twenty-three minutes Puskas, receiving from the left, invited Wright's sliding tackle before rolling the ball back with his left foot and thumping it high past Merrick's left hand. The Wembley audience were amazed. The Hungarians pointed out afterwards that the skill was in their coaching handbook. Puskas, with a deflection five minutes later, took the score to 4–1, which Mortensen narrowed by a goal at half-time.

After fifty-five minutes the past was dead and buried for ever. Bozsik scored the fifth goal with a fine 20-yard drive and Hideguti completed his hat trick. Alf Ramsey's penalty on the hour rounded off the scoring, and although Grosics had to retire with an injured arm and was replaced by Geller, a Hungarian keeper was only a formal requirement.

Manager Gustav Sebes and coach Guyala Mandi had talent at their disposal, but their training methods were advanced and sophisticated. Between 1950 and 1956 Hungary – the Olympic champions – lost just one game, that being the 1954 World Cup final, a match which still embarrasses them. It broke a run of twenty-nine games without defeat. Technically Eire had been the first to win on English soil, at Goodison Park by two clear goals in 1949, but this was different. Hungary had reorganized people's view of the game. They had confused England by using Hideguti, who still managed three goals, as a deep-lying centre forward. Ramsey, Eckersley, Johnston, Mortensen, Taylor and Robb were never to wear the white shirt again. For Taylor and Robb it was their only appearance for England.

As Geoffrey Green wrote in *The Times*: 'When the ball sailed past Merrick for the first goal, it flew into the net, white and gleaming. It looked as if it could be a dove of peace. Instead it turned out to be a bird of ill omen'.

Hungarian centre forward Nandor Hideguti completes his hat-trick with the final goal

Jozef Bozsik

An attacking right half and, with Puskas, Hideguti and Kocsis, the driving force behind this great team. Born in 1925, he won exactly 100 caps, the first on 17 August 1947 in Hungary's 9–0 win over Bulgaria. He was sent off in the famous 'Battle of Berne' in 1954. He did not defect in 1956, but remained in Hungary and became a member of the House of Deputies. He briefly became the national team manager in the 1970s, but had to give it up after a heart attack, which eventually caused his death at the age of fifty-three.

Laszlo Budai II

He played thirty-nine times in the national team. A fast, tricky right winger, he was a member of the Honved team. Budai I was centre forward in the same Honved side.

Jeno Buzansky

Right back with the provincial team Dorog, a town on the Danube just north of Budapest. He gained forty-eight caps.

Zoltan Czibor

A lively, speedy outside left, he was only 5 feet 7 inches tall. Born in 1929, he joined Honved from Ferencvaros and struck up a great partnership with Puskas. When Puskas was injured in the 1954 World Cup, Czibor moved to inside left and proved his versatility. He was outstanding in the games against Uruguay in the semi final and Brazil in the quarter final. He did not return to Hungary after 1956. He tried unsuccessfully to join Roma, but eventually joined Kocsis at Barcelona and scored their first goal in the 1961 European Cup final against Benfica. Altogether he won forty-three Hungarian caps.

Gyula Grosics

A spectacular keeper, but also reliable, he won eighty-six caps. He used to come out of his area to create a 'sweeper' position. He played in the 1954, 1958 and 1962 World Cups but in between was suspended for a year and banished in disgrace from his Honved side to Second Division mining team Tatabanya. This was a result of his smuggling contraband.

Nandor Hideguti

The perfect deep-lying centre forward. Well built, he was a tireless runner, with excellent balance. Born in 1922, his first club was MTK (later Red Banner). He stayed in Hungary after the 1956 uprising and went on to manage Vasas Gyoer (one of his former clubs), Fiorentina and the national side.

Sandor Kocsis

A neat ball player and a great header of the ball, he was nicknamed 'Golden Head'. Born in 1929 his first club was KTC; it was only on joining them he owned his first pair of football boots. He then joined his favourite team Ferencvaros before going to Honved. The top scorer in the 1954 World Cup finals, he stayed out of the country after 1956 with Puskas and Czibor and eventually joined Barcelona. He played for them in the 1961 European Cup final. He scored 75 goals in sixty-eight internationals.

Michaly Lantos

Left back, he played fifty-two times for Hungary. Like many of the others, he tried his luck in management but without much success, although he did manage Bayern Munich. He played for MTK.

Gyula Lorant

Another of the Honved contingent, he was a modern day 'stopper' and played thirty-seven times for Hungary. Also played for Vasas.

Ferenc Puskas

Called the 'Galloping Major', a reference to his rank in the Hungarian Army. His Hungarian career ended with the 1956 uprising. He was in South America with Honved at the time and never returned to Hungary. He lived in Italy for a while before reviving his career with Real Madrid, where he formed a great partnership with Di Stefano. He scored 4 goals in the 1960 European Cup final against Eintracht at Hampden Park. In another final (1962) he scored a hat trick yet ended up on the losing side. Born in 1926, his first club was Kispest, which eventually merged with Honved. He won his first international cap at eighteen; in all he won eighty-four Hungarian caps, and scored 83 goals. He played four times for Spain in the 1962 World Cup. After his playing career was over he turned to management and travelled the world. He was coach to the Panathanaikos team which reached the 1971 European Cup final at Wembley. As a player he had great ball control and pace – which belied his paunchy, stocky frame. He was top scorer in Hungary four times, and also in Spain four times. Scored 324 goals in 372 games for Real Madrid.

Jozef Zakarias

A team-mate of Hideguti's at MTK, he gained thirty-five caps. He played at left half and was a forerunner of the modern 'sweeper'.

The England team that day was Merrick; Ramsey and Eckersley; Wright (captain); Johnston and Dickenson; Matthews, Taylor, Mortensen, Sewell and Robb.

HUNGARY'S TACTICS AND RECORD

Although Hideguti was claimed to be the strategist in the team, the whole side played a 4–2–4 formation with the use of many of today's tactical ploys. Below are the 4–2–4 positions, and, in brackets after the player's name, his listed position for the game at Wembley.

Grosics (G)

Buzansky (RB)   Lorant (CH)   Zakarias (LH)   Lantos (LB)

Bozsik (RH)   Hideguti (CF)

Budai (RW)   Kocsis (IR)   Puskas (IL)   Czibor (LW)

Between 1950 and 1957 Hungary played forty-eight games, won forty, drew seven and lost just one – the 1954 World Cup final 3–2 against Germany, after being 2–0 up in ten minutes – and scored 205 goals, conceding just 57.

Real Madrid, 1955–60

Normally, when evaluating the merits of great teams, two types are found. There are those teams which become outstanding over a period of a three-month tour or with successive wins in league or cup competitions. And there are those who achieve perfection on one specific evening when their performance sends those in their profession drifting away to rewrite the coaching manuals. Real Madrid, with Puskas and Di Stefano at the helm, fell into both categories.

In 1954 the progressive French sports newspaper *L'Equipe* and its subsidiary, the weekly *France Football*, decided to organize a European Cup. The champions of each country would play in a knockout competition, on a home and away basis, to decide the champions of Europe. Some nations jumped at the opportunity to take part. Others, like the Football League, refused to let their champions (Chelsea) take part. After a couple of experimental years, those who had shunned the event realized their folly.

The first competition took place in season 1955–56 and Real Madrid won the first five finals. They won with increasing authority, culminating in a demonstration at Hampden Park, Glasgow, on the evening of 18 May 1960 against the Eintracht club from Frankfurt, which qualified the ninety minutes as a candidate for the greatest match ever.

Real Madrid was founded by students in 1898. The title of Real, which means 'royal', was bestowed upon them by King Alfonso XIII in 1920. Although founder members of the Spanish League, they had, surprisingly, only twice won the title up to 1954. Then along came Santiago Bernabeu to change that image. As president he did two things in his first week. He signed Alfredo Di Stefano and he donated cash – plenty of it.

The first four finals were tinged with danger. In the very first final, against Stade Rheims, Real were given the runaround but won 4–3 thanks to Di Stefano. The Rheims winger, Raymond Kopa, by far the best French footballer until Michel Platini, gave the Real defence a nightmare evening. Real promptly went out and bought Kopa.

The following year, Real could easily have gone out in the first round to Rapid Vienna. Had the game been played in this age Real would have been eliminated on the away goals rule. But in those embryo days a replay was necessary if the scores were level. Manchester United had turned a deaf ear to the Football League and in the semi final, after two epic matches, were eliminated by Real 5–3 on aggregate. But the match had sold the European Cup to the world. As luck would have it, the final was on Real's ground.

With Di Stefano, Gento, Marquitos, Zarraga, Munoz and Rial as the fulcrum of the side, the new signings bolstered the weaker positions. After Kopa came Santamaria, a Uruguayan international centre half who had played in the 1954 World Cup. Real achieved the European hat trick in a desperately close final with AC Milan, who had put out Manchester United, devastated by the Munich tragedy, in the semi final.

Again, in 1959, Real survived in a match in which, by modern rules, they would have been eliminated. The local rivals, Athletico, had built a formidable team around the Brazilian

Zarraga, the Real captain, with the European Cup after his side's 2–0 win over Stade Rheims in the 1959 final

World Cup star Vava, and the semi final was frighteningly close.

By 1960, the team, in the eyes of Bernabeu, was complete with the arrival of Ferenc Puskas to complement the resident virtuosi. The final had the correct build-up. Eintracht Frankfurt had themselves made splendid way in the competition: their 6–1, 6–3 annihilation of Rangers in the semi final was contemptuous.

The match was a triumph for Puskas. He scored four goals. Three more came from Di Stefano, and both thrived on a string of crosses from Gento. In sustained passages in the second half, the quality of their forward play and ball control was of such finely controlled skill, of such accuracy, imagination and, indeed, impudence, as to bring thundering down around them vast waves of appreciation from Hampden's mighty crowd.

Real opened rather like elder statesmen who were a little weary of great occasions. After nineteen minutes Stein made a deep thrust on the right and Kress stole through the defence to volley home.

Eintracht were playing their part well. They had opened the scoring, looked capable of more, yet had a loose defence and a man called Stinka, who was living up to his name.

The little right winger Canario brought the holders back into the game, setting up goals for Di Stefano in the twenty-seventh and thirtieth minutes. When Puskas smashed an awesome left-foot shot past Loy, it became 3–1 to Real at half-time.

When Puskas scored a penalty after fifty-four minutes the contest dissolved into an exhibition. The fifth goal on the hour was splendid. Santamaria sending Gento on a 50-yard sprint and the short cross was headed home by Puskas. A pirouette by Puskas, belying his tubby frame, took the score to 6–1 after seventy minutes. Stein, Eintracht's centre forward brought the score to 6–2, Di Stefano thundered in Real's seventh, before Stein brought the proceedings to the ten goal mark. The standing ovation lasted thirty minutes.

It was the deadly rivals, Barcelona, who brought Real's run to an end the following season, but the trophy went, against all expectation, to Benfica from Portugal. Real reached the final in 1962, but lost 5–3; the defence, and Di Stefano, were creaking despite Puskas' hat trick. Four years later, with only Gento remaining, Real surprised Partizan Belgrade to win their sixth European Cup. But all the old names had gone.

The club, which houses a European championship-winning basketball team, and has a chapel and a swimming pool, tennis courts and an athletics track, is situated in the Chamartin district of Madrid. The Estadio Chamartin was correctly and properly renamed the Bernabeu Stadium.

Although Real have missed only one of the first thirty seasons of European football, they have naturally not been able to keep up standards. It must be a millstone.

Yet this was the club which put the concept of European club football on the map. Amazingly, when Real won their first Cup, only one paper, the *Daily Mail*, bothered to print the score from Paris. They included four lines on the final – all four on the referee, Arthur Ellis!

REAL MADRID'S MATCHES IN EUROPE, 1955–60

1955–56

Round One	Round Two	Semi final	Final (13 June 1956, Paris)
Servette 0 Real 2	Real 4 Partizan 0	Real 4 AC Milan 2	Real 4 Stade Rheims 3
Real 5 Servette 0	Partizan 3 Real 0	AC Milan 2 Real 1	

Scorers against Stade Rheims: Di Stefano, Rial (2), Marquitos. *Team:* Alonso; Atienza, Lesmes; Munoz, Marquitos, Zarraga; Joseito, Marchal, Di Stefano, Rial, Gento.

1956–57

Round One	Round Two	Semi final	Final (30 May 1957, Madrid)
Real 4 Rapid Vienna 2	Real 3 Nice 0	Real 3 Manchester United 1	Real 2 Fiorentina 0
Rapid Vienna 3 Real 1	Nice 2 Real 3	Manchester United 2 Real 2	
Real 2 Rapid Vienna 0 (if played today, Real would have lost on away goals)			

Scorers against Fiorentina: Di Stefano (pen), Gento. *Team:* Alonso; Torres, Lesmes; Munoz, Marquitos, Zarraga; Kopa, Mateos, Di Stefano, Rial, Gento.

1957–58

Round One	Round Two	Semi final	Final (28 May 1958, Brussels)
Antwerp 1 Real 2	Real 8 Seville 0	Real 4 Vasas 0	Real 3 AC Milan 2 (after extra time)
Real 6 Antwerp 0	Seville 2 Real 2	Vasas 2 Real 0	

Scorers against AC Milan: Di Stefano, Rial, Gento. *Team:* Alonso; Atienza, Lesmes; Santisteban, Santamaria, Zarraga; Kopa, Joseito, Di Stefano, Rial, Gento.

1958–59

Round One	Round Two	Semi final	Final (2 June 1959, Stuttgart)
Real 2 Besiktas Istanbul 0	Weiner SK 0 Real 0	Real 2 Athletico 1	Real 2 Stade Rheims 0
Besiktas Istanbul 1 Real 1	Real 7 Weiner SK 1	Athletico 1 Real 0	
		Real 2 Athletico 1 (if played today, Real would have lost on away goals)	

Scorers against Stade Rheims: Mateos, Di Stefano. *Team:* Dominguez; Marquitos, Zarraga; Santisteban, Santamaria, Ruiz; Kopa, Mateos, Di Stefano, Rial, Gento.

1959–60

Round One	Round Two	Semi final	Final (18 May 1960, Glasgow)
Real 7 Esch 0	Nice 3 Real 2	Real 3 Barcelona 1	Real 7 Eintracht Frankfurt 3
Esch 2 Real 5	Real 4 Nice 0	Barcelona 1 Real 3	

Scorers against Eintracht Frankfurt: Puskas (4), Di Stefano (3). *Team:* Dominguez; Marquitos, Pachin; Vidal, Santamaria, Zarraga; Canario, Del Sol, Di Stefano, Puskas, Gento.

Some of the leading players were:

Canario

A Brazilian winger, his first European Cup final was in 1960.

Luis Del Sol

He appeared in his first European Cup final in 1960 and also played in the 1962 final. Winner of sixteen caps, his first club was Seville. Went to Italy and played for Juventus and Roma.

Alfredo Di Stefano

Argentine, Columbia and Spanish international. Born in 1926 in Buenos Aires, he played for River Plate, as did his father. He went on loan to Huracan, where he became so useful that River Plate asked for him back immediately. He won his first cap in 1947. In 1949 he signed for Millionarios of Bogotá where at first he played in the reserves, the regular first-team place being held by a Scot, Bobby Flavell. When Di Stefano joined Real for £20,000 in 1953 there was a big argument involving Barcelona, who said they had paid a fee to River Plate, whereas Real paid it to Millionarios. The Spanish League ruled that Real should have him for the first season, and then he should go to Barcelona. But he played so badly in his first season that Barcelona told Real they could keep him. He played in the 1956, 1957, 1958, 1959, 1960, 1962 and 1964 European Cup finals, scoring in each of the first five. In all he played 510 games for Real and scored 428 goals. He retired in 1964 after joining Espanol Barcelona. Won thirty-one caps for Spain.

Rogello Dominguez

An Argentine international, he succeeded Alonso as goalkeeper in 1959. He also played in the 1960 final.

Francisco Lopez Gento

Born in Santander in 1933, Gento is a legend in European Cup history. An exciting left-winger, known as Paco, he played in eighty European Cup ties between 1956 and 1966 and also in the Cup Winners' Cup final against Chelsea in 1971 at the age of thirty-eight. He stands alone as the only man to score in eleven consecutive European Cup competitions. He played for Nueva Montana, Astillero and Real Santander before moving to Real in 1953. He spent eighteen years at Real, eleven of them playing alongside Di Stefano whom he succeeded as captain. Won forty-three Spanish caps. Became the youth team trainer after his retirement in 1971. His pastimes are hunting and fishing.

Raymond Kopa

He came from the mining area of Northern France, where his parents settled after leaving Poland. He played in three European Cup finals for Real and one for Rheims. He was outstanding in the 1958 World Cup, and won forty-five caps in his career.

Marquitos

He played in the 1956, 1957, 1959 and 1960 European Cup finals, scoring a goal in the first. He played twice for Spain, and his son, Marcos, is also a Spanish international.

Enrique Mateos

Capped eight times by Spain, he missed a penalty in the 1959 European Cup final but scored the first goal.

Miguel Munoz

Captain of the 1956 and 1957 teams, and coach in 1960 and 1966, he is now the Spanish team manager. He won seven caps.

Pachin

He was in the team that won trophy in 1960. He also appeared in two losing finals, 1962 and 1964 and was in the team that last won the European Cup in 1966. He played eight times for Spain.

Ferenc Puskas

He played in the 1960, 1962 and 1964 European Cup finals, scoring four goals in the 1960 final, and three in 1962 when Real lost. For further details see Hungary, 1953, p. 57.

Hector Rial

Classical inside left of the first four finals before losing his place to Puskas. He won five caps for Spain.

Antonio Ruiz

Left half in the 1959 final. He stayed on with Real to become a youth team coach.

Jose Santamaria

He played for Uruguay in the 1954 World Cup and for Spain in 1962. He joined Real from Nacional in 1958. A great header and tackler, he played in the 1958, 1959, 1960, 1962 and 1964 European Cup finals.

Vidal

He only played in one European Cup final – 1960. He won four Spanish caps.

Jose Maria Zarraga

He played in all five finals from 1956 to 1960. He was captain in the last three, after Munoz retired. He played eight times for Spain.

Manchester United Football Club, 1956–68

That Manchester United in the 1950s was a fine advertisement for all that is good in British football is in no doubt. After the appalling and tragic accident on 6 February 1958 until 29 May 1968 when United became the first English team to win the European Cup, it took ten years of hard work, reorganization and disappointment for United to reach their own particular goals.

Matt Busby was appointed manager on 15 February 1946. Old Trafford was a mass of rubble and girders, a legacy of a German bomber, aiming for the nearby docks. The office was in a coal depot and home games were played at Manchester City's ground at Maine Road. As a player, Busby had clocked up 317 League appearances for Manchester City and Liverpool and had played once for Scotland. The family roots were at Belshill, a Lanarkshire mining village.

Busby advocated gradual change. Out went, in stages, Carey, Rowley, Pearson, Chilton and Cockburn from that marvellous team which handsomely won the 1948 Cup final, and in came Byrne, Edwards, Taylor, Colman, Whelan, Viollet,

Pegg, Jones, Blanchflower and others from the youth scheme. They won the Football League in 1956 and 1957 with a side known as 'the Busby Babes'. Babes they may have been, but they were an experienced group of young players.

In the European Cup, United reached the semi finals in 1957, but lost their games with Real Madrid. Better able to cope with European pressures the following season, they were rated as favourites to overcome the ageing Real team. Then came Munich.

The previous weekend United had beaten Arsenal at Highbury in a game that was a classic. United won 5–4. The team list now reads like an obituary column: Gregg; Foulkes, Byrne; Colman, Jones, Edwards; Morgans, Charlton, Taylor, Viollet, Scanlon. On their way back from a 3–3 draw against Red Star in Belgrade in the quarter finals of the European Cup, the plane carrying the United team to Manchester crashed while taking off at Munich Airport. Byrne, Bent, Colman, Jones, Edwards, Pegg and Whelan were amongst the twenty-three who died out of a complement of forty-three passengers. The

Manchester United with the 1968 European Cup. Back row (left to right): *W. Foulkes, J. Aston, J. Rimmer, A. Stepney, A. Gowling, D. Herd; middle row – D. Sadler, A. Dunne, S. Brennan, P. Crerand, G. Best, F. Burns, J. Crompton (trainer); front row – J. Ryan, N. Stiles, D. Law, Sir Matt Busby (manager), R. Charlton, B. Kidd, J. Fitzpatrick*

survivors included Matt Busby, Berry, Blanchflower, Charlton, Foulkes, Gregg, Morgans, Scanlon, Viollet and Wood. A note in the programme for 19 February 1958 read:

Although we mourn our dead and grieve for our wounded, we believe the great days are not done for us. The sympathy and encouragement of the football world and particularly our supporters will justify and inspire us. The road back may be long and hard but with the memory of those who died at Munich, of their stirring achievements and wonderful sportsmanship ever with us, Manchester United will rise again.

The early signs were slightly hopeful. That same spring United reached the Cup final, to lose to Bolton Wanderers by two goals from Nat Lofthouse. But their position as runners-up in the League in 1958–59 gave a false impression of strength.

However, such was the deep, abiding morale of the club that the period of recuperation proved astonishingly rapid. After such a shattering blow, most clubs would have sunk with despair to the underworld. At United there was a spark of tradition handed on like an Olympic torch from one generation to the next. Within five years they were a force to be reckoned with once more.

Certainly money helped with the restoration work. Law, Quixall, Crerand, Herd, Setters, Cantwell and Dunne cost over £300,000, but there were still youthful players to count on who could develop under Busby and his assistant Jimmy Murphy.

United won the League title in 1964–65 and 1966–67. In 1966 they had lost again in the European Cup semi finals, this time to Partizan Belgrade, a team whose only talent was to live up to their name. The eventual winners were Real Madrid, but they were now on the decline.

With their 4–2–4 line up, United began the 1967–68 European Cup campaign. They dispatched Hibernians of Malta and another tough Yugoslav team, Sarajevo, before drawing a quarter-final tie against the Polish champions Gornik. It was a memorable encounter: 2–0 to United at Old Trafford, against a side defied by brilliant goalkeeping, and then 1–0 to the Poles on an arctic pitch in Silesia. It would have been even more memorable but for what happened in the semi final.

Pitched against Real Madrid, United won by a single glorious goal by George Best after fifty-five minutes at Old Trafford. It seemed hardly enough to take to the second leg in the Bernabeu.

In the first half of the return match Real had built a 3–1 lead with goals from Pirri, Gento and Amancio. United's goal came from a bobbling shot from Dunne. Now the fairy tale began to weave itself and out of nothing a magical recovery was born. After seventy-five minutes Sadler completed good work by Foulkes and Crerand, and with twelve minutes left Foulkes, an experienced warrior of sixteen seasons, following up in a moment of inspiration, turned in a cross from Best. United had won the battle.

All that remained was Wembley and the prospect of Benfica on 29 May – Derby Day. The one sadness for United was again the absence of Law, in hospital undergoing a cartilage operation. The final was remarkable. United dominated the first half, but had only a glancing header by Charlton to show for their pressure. They flagged badly in the second half when Graca equalized, but after Stepney had twice, crucially, foiled Eusebio, they fashioned victory with a three-goal burst in seven minutes in the first half of extra time. Best, Kidd – on his nineteenth birthday – and Charlton took full advantage of a unique display by Aston on the left wing. It was Charlton's night, with two goals, and it was he who went to collect the giant European trophy with his team straggling behind.

In June Matt Busby was knighted. A year later he retired, his job done. He also revealed another priceless asset – he knew when it was time to go.

MANCHESTER UNITED EUROPEAN CUP TEAM, 1968

	d.o.b.	p.o.b.	United League Apps.	Goals	Total League Apps.	Goals	Caps
John Aston (Other clubs: Luton Town, Mansfield Town, Blackburn Rovers)	28.6.47	Manchester	156	25	376	62	1 (England Under–23)
George Best (Other clubs: Stockport County, LA Aztecs, Fulham, Hibernian, Bournemouth)	22.5.46	Belfast	361	137	411	147	37 (Northern Ireland)
Shay Brennan	6.5.37	Manchester	260	3	290	3	19 (Republic of Ireland)
Bobby Charlton (Other club: Preston North End)	11.10.37	Ashington	606	198	644	206	106 (England)
Pat Crerand (Other club: Glasgow Celtic)	19.2.39	Glasgow	304	10	304	10	16 (Scotland)
Tony Dunne (Other club: Bolton Wanderers)	24.7.41	Dublin	415	2	585	2	32 (Republic of Ireland)
Bill Foulkes	5.1.32	St Helens	567	6	567	6	1 (England)
Brian Kidd (Other clubs: Arsenal, Manchester City, Everton, Bolton Wanderers)	29.5.49	Manchester	203	53	451	151	2 (England)
David Sadler (Other club: Preston North End)	5.2.46	Yalding	271	22	376	25	4 (England)
Alex Stepney (Other clubs: Millwall, Chelsea)	18.9.44	Mitcham	433	2	570	2	1 (England)
Nobby Stiles (Other clubs: Middlesbrough, Preston North End)	18.5.42	Manchester	312	18	415	21	28 (England)

Football League

	P	W	D	L	F	A	Pts	Pos.
1955–56	42	25	10	7	83	51	60	1
1956–57	42	28	8	6	103	54	64	1
1957–58	42	16	11	15	85	75	43	9
1958–59	42	24	7	11	103	66	55	2
1959–60	42	19	7	16	102	80	45	7
1960–61	42	18	9	15	88	76	45	7
1961–62	42	15	9	18	72	75	39	15
1962–63	42	12	10	20	67	81	34	19
1963–64	42	23	7	12	90	62	53	2
1964–65	42	26	9	7	89	39	61	1
1965–66	42	18	15	9	84	59	51	4
1966–67	42	24	12	6	84	45	60	1
1967–68	42	24	8	10	89	55	56	2

FA Cup

1955–56	Round 3	lost to Bristol Rovers	0–4
1956–57	Final	lost to Aston Villa	1–2
1957–58	Final	lost to Bolton Wands	0–2
1958–59	Round 3	lost to Norwich City	0–3
1959–60	Round 3	lost to Sheffield Wed	0–1
1960–61	Round 4	lost to Sheffield Wed	0–7
1961–62	Semi final	lost to Tottenham H	1–3
1962–63	Final	beat Leicester City	3–1
1963–64	Semi final	lost to West Ham	1–3
1964–65	Semi final	lost to Leeds United	0–1
1965–66	Semi final	lost to Everton	0–1
1966–67	Round 4	lost to Norwich City	1–2
1967–68	Round 3	lost to Tottenham H	0–1

League Cup

1960–61	Round 2	lost to Bradford City	1–2
1966–67	Round 2	lost to Blackpool	1–5

Europe

1956–57	European Cup	Semi final lost to Real Madrid	3–5 (agg.)
1957–58	European Cup	Semi final lost to AC Milan	2–5 (agg.)
1963–64	Cup Winners' Cup	Quarter final lost to Sporting Lisbon	4–6 (agg.)
1964–65	Fairs Cup	Semi final lost to Ferencvaros	2–1 (play off after agg. 3–3)
1965–66	European Cup	Semi final lost to Partizan	1–2 (agg.)
1967–68	European Cup	Final beat Benfica	4–1

Roll of Honour

1956	Division 1 Champions FA Youth Cup (winners) Central League Champions
1957	Division 1 Champions FA Cup (runners-up) Charity Shield (winners) FA Youth Cup (winners) Manchester FA Senior Cup (winners)
1958	FA Cup (runners-up) Charity Shield (winners)
1959	Division 1 (runners-up) Manchester FA Senior Cup (winners)
1960	Central League Champions
1963	FA Cup (winners)
1964	Division 1 (runners-up) Manchester FA Senior Cup (winners)
1965	Division 1 Champions Charity Shield (joint winners)
1967	Division 1 Champions Charity Shield (joint winners)
1968	European Cup (winners) Division 1 (runners-up) World Club Championship (runners-up)

INTERNATIONAL PLAYERS, 1956–1968

England: J. Berry, J. Bradley, W. Bradley, R. Byrne, R. Charlton, J. Connelly, D. Edwards, W. McGuinness, D. Pegg, D. Sadler, A. Stepney, N. Stiles, T. Taylor, D. Viollet, R. Wood

Scotland: P. Crerand, D. Law

Wales: G. Moore, C. Webster

Northern Ireland: G. Best, J. Blanchflower, W. R. Briggs, H. Gregg, S. McMillan, J. J. Nicholson

Eire: S. A. Brennan, N. Cantwell, J. Carolan, A. P. Dunne, P. A. G. Dunne, J. Giles, W. Whelan

Leading Scorers

1955–56	T. Taylor	25
1956–57	W. Whelan	26
1957–58	D. Viollet	17
1958–59	R. Charlton	29
1959–60	D. Viollet	32 (United record)
1960–61	R. Charlton	21
1961–62	D. Herd	14
1962–63	D. Law	23
1963–64	D. Law	30
1964–65	D. Law	28
1965–66	D. Herd	24
1966–67	D. Law	23
1967–68	G. Best	28

Great Britain Ryder Cup Team, 1957

The sports pages for Sunday, 6 October 1957, were, for the most part, entirely predictable. Football dominated the news, with an England Under-23 team which included Don Howe, Jimmy Armfield, Duncan Edwards, Jimmy Greaves and Johnny Haynes in the wars because of injuries sustained the day before in the League fixtures. Wolves and West Bromwich Albion led the First Division, Blackpool beat Sunderland 7–0, and Spurs lost at home (again) to Nottingham Forest. Liverpool were in the Second Division.

The world mile record holder, Derek Ibbotson, strolled through two races at the Birchfield Harriers' meeting at Perry Barr, and there were fears for the health and safety of one Victor Pepeder of France as he was about to climb into the ring with the Liverpool-based world featherweight champion, Hogan Kid Bassey.

But whereas these features may have had greater publicity on a normal autumn day, they were mere decorations for the centrepiece of the news: 'Ryder Cup regained after twenty-four years'; 'Rees's team magnificent in the singles'; 'Astounding US collapse'.

The match took place over two days, Friday, the 4th, and Saturday the 5th of October. After Friday's foursomes, observers could be forgiven if they thought that the same old story was about to unfold. The United States, with maximum efficiency, had won the foursomes 3–1. In those days there were no complications with fourballs, just four foursomes on the first day, and eight singles on the second and final day. Only Ken Bousfield and the captain Dai Rees prevented an American whitewash.

The singles began on a blustery morning at Lindrick Common, on the moors above Sheffield. By the middle of the day, when the totting-up of relevant scores had begun, Britain were ahead in five of the eight singles and all square in the others. The prospect of victory inspired the British; the thought of defeat communicated itself to the Americans.

Britain won six of the eight singles, and won the Ryder Cup for the first time since 1933, by seven matches to four, with one halved. In the end it was a rout. The usual counter-attack never came.

A rout is never worth describing; an attempt to find its cause is more worthwhile. The claim that the Americans were short of quality players does not stand up. Their selection principles were always the same, and if good players had not made the team, it meant that they had not accrued enough points on their own circuits to gain selection. Their stars had also come to Britain and lost in previous ties – Snead, Mangrum and Middlecoff. Of this particular collection of players, Jack Burke was held in the highest esteem, and he lost 5 and 3 to Peter Mills, who was making his Ryder Cup debut.

Some of the Americans, however, had lost form. Herbert, Fungol and Bolt had not played well in the USA, but their system, in which points are given over a two-year period, meant that a player could find himself selected after having played well in the year before the tie. Burke himself admitted that to use the small ball was a mistake. It was his decision as captain, and he took the blame.

But the real reason lay in the start to the singles. After the first five holes in each match, Britain were up in seven and all square in the eighth. This suggests that the Americans lost the Cup rather than that the British won it. This is unfair. Splendidly led by Dai Rees, who had an experienced team under his command, Britain put the United States under pressure. It was not their fault that the Americans collapsed.

The Ryder Cup was presented to the winning team by Sir Stuart Goodwin, who, in congratulating Dai Rees, modestly omitted one important fact. He himself had donated £10,000 to the Ryder Cup fund so that he could witness the day that British golfers should play so splendidly.

The controversial Harry Weetman

Peter Alliss

THE TEAM

Peter Alliss

Born in Berlin in 1931. His father, Percy Alliss, also played in the Ryder Cup, making them the only father and son to have taken part in the competition. Alliss won the British PGA in 1957, 1962 and 1966, and the Spanish, Portuguese and Italian Opens in 1958. He played in the Ryder Cup in 1953, 1957, 1959, 1961, 1963, 1965, 1967 and 1969. In 1957 he was the only one of the eight to lose his singles.

Ken Bousfield

Born in Yorkshire in 1919, he was the British Professional Matchplay champion in 1955 and won the German Open in 1955 and 1959, the Belgian and Swiss Opens in 1958, and the Portuguese Open in 1960 and 1961. He took part in the Ryder Cup in 1949, 1951, 1955, 1957, 1959 and 1961; in 1957 he and Rees were the only players to win two matches.

Harry Bradshaw

Born in County Wicklow, Eire, in 1913, Bradshaw is remembered for his British Open appearance in 1949 when he lost in the play-off to the South African, Bobby Locke. Bradshaw's ball landed in a broken bottle at the fifth in the second round and he was forced to play the shot from the bottle. This led to a subsequent change in the rules. He won the Irish Open in 1947 and 1949, was the British Open runner-up in 1949, won the Dunlop Masters in 1953 and 1955 and, with Christy O'Connor, won the World Cup in 1958. He took part in the Ryder Cup in 1953, 1955 and 1957.

Eric Brown

Born in Edinburgh, Scotland, in 1925, Brown was a railway fireman who turned professional in 1946. He won the Swiss Open in 1951, the Italian Open in 1952, the Portuguese and Irish Opens in 1953, the Dunlop Masters in 1957 and the British Professional Matchplay championships in 1960 and 1962. He took part in the Ryder Cup in 1953, 1955, 1957 and 1959 and, as

non-playing captain, in 1961 and 1971. He won all his singles in his four Ryder Cup appearances. In 1969, with Brown as non-playing captain, Great Britain tied; it was their best result since 1957.

Max Faulkner

Born in Sussex in 1916, he won the Spanish Open in 1952, 1953 and 1957, the British Professional Matchplay Championships in 1953 and the Portuguese Open in 1968 at the age of fifty-two. He took part in the Ryder Cup in 1947, 1949, 1951, 1953 and 1957. But his greatest achievement was to win the 1951 British Open.

Bernard Hunt

Born in Warwickshire in 1930, he won the French Open in 1957, and the German Open in 1961. He took part in the Ryder Cup in 1953, 1957, 1959, 1961, 1963, 1965, 1967 and 1969 and, as non-playing captain, in 1973 and 1975. His brother Geoffrey also played in the 1963 Ryder Cup. Bernard and Geoffrey contested the final of the 1953 British Assistants Championships at Hartsbourne; Bernard won 2 and 1.

Peter Mills

Born in Virginia Water, Surrey, in 1931, he won the British Professional Matchplay Championships in 1956. In 1957 he made his only Ryder Cup appearance, the youngest member and only debutant in the team, winning his singles. He was reinstated as an amateur in 1980.

Christy O'Connor

Born in Galway, Northern Ireland, in 1924. He won the Dunlop Masters in 1956 and 1959, the PGA Matchplay Championships in 1957, the World Cup (with Harry Bradshaw) in 1958, and the World Seniors Championships in 1976 and 1977; he was runner-up in the British Open in 1965. He took part in 10 Ryder Cups between 1955 and 1973, more matches than any other player, British or American. In 1955 he became the first person to win a four-figure cheque in first-prize money in Britain, and in winning the John Player Golf Classic at Hollinwell, Nottinghamshire, he became the first to win a £25,000 prize. His nephew, Christy O'Connor Jr, took part in the 1975 Ryder Cup.

David James (Dai) Rees CBE

Born in Glamorgan, Wales, in 1913, the son of a professional golfer. He served South Hertfordshire Golf Club for over twenty-five years as a professional. He won the Belgian Open in 1954, and was runner-up in the British Open in 1961, he came joint second in the British Open in 1953 and 1954. He took part in the Ryder Cup in 1937, 1947, 1949, 1951 and 1953, and as captain in 1955, 1957, 1959, 1961 and 1967. He was the oldest member of the team in 1957, winning both his matches. He was voted BBC Sports Personality of the Year in 1957. He died on 15 November 1983.

Harry Weetman

Born in Oswestry, Shropshire, in 1920, Weetman was a long hitter and big favourite with the crowds. At Croham Hurst golf course in Croydon, Surrey, he shot a round of 58, the lowest score for a course of 6000 yards or more in Britain. He was the British Professional Matchplay champion in 1951 and 1958, won the Dunlop Masters in 1952 and 1958 and the German Open in 1957. He took part in the Ryder Cup in 1951, 1953, 1955, 1957, 1959, 1961, 1963 and 1965 (as non-playing captain). He won his 1953 Ryder Cup singles against Sam Snead after being four down with six to play. He died in 1972 after a car accident.

At Lindrick, Sheffield, 4 and 5 October 1957

Foursomes

Great Britain		USA	
P. Alliss and B. J. Hunt	0	D. Ford and D. Finsterwald (2 and 1)	1
K. Bousfield and D. J. Rees (3 and 2)	1	A. Wall and F. Hawkins	0
M. Faulkner and H. Weetman	0	T. Kroll and J. Burke (4 and 3)	1
C. O'Connor and E. C. Brown	0	R. Mayer and T. Bolt (7 and 5)	1
	—		—
	1		3

Singles

Great Britain		USA	
E. C. Brown (4 and 3)	1	T. Bolt	0
R. P. Mills (5 and 3)	1	J. Burke	0
P. Alliss	0	F. Hawkins (2 and 1)	1
K. Bousfield (4 and 3)	1	L. Hebert	0
D. J. Rees (7 and 6)	1	E. Furgol	0
B. J. Hunt (6 and 5)	1	D. Ford	0
C. O'Connor (7 and 6)	1	D. Finsterwald	0
H. Bradshaw (halved)	0	R. Mayer (halved)	0
	—		—
	6		1

Grand aggregates: Great Britain, 7 matches; USA, 4 matches; 1 match halved
Captains: D. J. Rees, Great Britain, and Jack Burke, USA

Above: *Dai Rees, the Great Britain captain*

Left: *Max Faulkner*

St Helens Rugby League Club, 1958–59

St Helen's victorious 1959 Championship final team.
Back row (left to right): *V. Karalius, A. Terry, T. Van Vollenhoven, J.A. Prinsloo, P. Fearis, E. Bowden, B. Briggs, R. Huddart; front row – D. Karalius, A.G. Moses, D. Greenall, A. Murphy, H.B. Howard*

There is a saying that the best publicity for a town is for it to have a club belonging to the Football League. That guarantees free publicity – good or bad – every Saturday afternoon and a permanent place in the minds of those who dabble with the pools.

Certain places awake similar feelings in those not deeply entrenched in the traditions of Rugby League, places such as Featherstone, Leigh, Wigan, Widnes and Hunslet. Their names are brought to the attention of southerners once a year when their orderly and cheerful supporters make their way to Wembley for the Challenge Cup final, and leave an impression of courtesy that those who use the stadium afterwards rarely equal.

St Helens is one of those towns: population 104,986; market days Mondays, Fridays and Saturdays; early closing on Thursday; one AA hotel, one AA garage; industries – mining, glass and Rugby League. Liverpool is 12 miles away, Widnes 9 and Warrington 11. And in the 1958–59 season they were unquestionably the best club side in the world.

In that season St Helens topped the League, winning thirty-one and drawing one of their thirty-eight games and scoring 1005 points, the first club in the sport's history to achieve the feat in a League season. The leading clubs in the League go forward to the play-offs; St Helens won the championship play-off 44–22 against Hunslet in front of a crowd of well over 50,000. Austin Rhodes kicked 10 goals, Tom Van Vollenhoven scored three tries and Alex Murphy two. The number of points they amassed and the size of the crowds who watched them testify to their influence on the game.

The club coach at the time was the legendary Jim Sullivan, a champion goal kicker, who moved to Rochdale Hornets shortly afterwards, and then to Wigan for a second spell before being forced to retire through ill health. Sullivan had played 921 games of Rugby League – a record.

Oddly the Great Britain selectors chose to play only three of this side: Alex Murphy, Abe Terry and Vince Karalius. They would like to have picked two others, Tom Van Vollenhoven and Jan Prinsloo, but could not because they were South African. Vollenhoven created havoc against the British Lions Rugby Union side in 1955 and, as there is no League code in his homeland, decided to foresake placid Pretoria for the delights of the East Lancashire Road. He was the League's leading try scorer in 1958–59 with sixty-two, and led the try scorers for the next two seasons. His total for the three seasons was 176.

Murphy added thirty–seven tries to Van Vollenhoven's sixty–two, with Prinsloo in third place with twenty–seven.

Peter Fearis was entrusted with the kicking role. He had 165 successes, making fourth on the League lists and was the club's leading points scorer with 354.

A couple of games stand out. The proverbial 'St Valentine's Day massacre' was administered to Barrow, with Fearis collecting 29 points as the Saints won 71–15. Then, on the 29 March 1959, at Central Park, Wigan, the two clubs attracted a crowd of 47,747 – still a record crowd for a League game in Britain.

The Saints were the most successful side in the country in the 1950s and 1960s. Their list of titles during that time is impressive: League champions in 1959, 1960, 1965 and 1966; championship play–off winners in 1959 and 1966; Challenge Cup winners in 1956, 1961 and 1966; and seven wins out of ten in the decade of the 1960s.

In that marvellous winter of 1958–59 St Helens broke records in style; they attracted record crowds, they played fast, open, attacking rugby – this in an era when the Union game was struggling in comparison; except for the Lions Union international matches were painfully negative. And everyone knew which team played in white shirts with a large red 'V' on the front.

LEADING LEAGUE POSITIONS, 1958–59

	P	W	D	L	F	A	Pts
St Helens	38	31	1	6	1005	450	63
Wigan	38	29	0	9	894	491	58
Hunslet	38	27	3	8	819	493	57
Oldham	38	28	1	9	791	477	57
Wakefield	38	27	1	10	790	393	55
Swinton	38	27	1	10	691	442	55

THE LEADING PLAYERS

Austin Rhodes

He was capped four times for Great Britain. Local born, he started his career with the Saints and ended it there in the mid–sixties after spells at Leigh and Swinton. Austin still lives in the town.

Vollenhoven, backed up by Alex Murphy, chases Hunslet's winger, Walker, in the 1959 Championship final. Duggie Greenall, far right

Tom Van Vollenhoven

A legend in St Helens Rugby League history. The fast South African winger was signed on 15 October 1957 for £8000 and a crowd of 5000 turned up for his Saints debut in an 'A' team match. He was a former policeman from Northern Transvaal and could run 100 yards in 9.8 seconds. His speed led to one of the finest tries ever to be scored by a Saints player when he went past half the Hunslet team in an amazing cross–field 60–yard burst in the 1958–59 season.

On his return to his home country after finishing his career with St Helens in 1969 after scoring 381 tries in 393 games, he took up coaching and opened a tyre business. He has suffered tragedies – a rare illness nearly killed him and he came close to losing the sight of one of his eyes following an accident.

Brian McGinn

A local lad, Brian started his Rugby League career with a junior side, Holy Cross. He came through the ranks at Saints and ended up playing for the county. He worked for the local council when he played for Saints, but was forced to change jobs because of the amount of time he had to take off. His new job meant him travelling to Northern Ireland a great deal. Consequently he retired, and senior rugby lost a great talent.

Jan Prinsloo

A winger, Prinsloo joined the Saints from Transvaal in 1958 and, before returning to South Africa, had a spell at Wakefield Trinity. Jan died leaving the field while playing rugby in South Africa in the mid–seventies.

Wilf Smith

Son of Tommy Smith, a one–time player with St Helens Recs. A solid player, he was stand–off and played for Sutton St Annes before signing for the Saints when he was nineteen. The Saints was his only club.

Alex Murphy

One of the sport's great characters, Murphy played for Great Britain twenty–seven times and won most of the major honours in the game. Controversial, his skill and talent were never questioned. As a coach he has equalled the successes of his playing days. After leaving the Saints he played for Leigh and then Warrington – he played for all three in winning Cup final teams. His coaching days have seen him in charge at Leigh, Warrington, Salford and Wigan. He has recently been appointed manager of Leigh – his third spell at the club – but there is no guarantee he will stay put.

Abe Terry

An open–side prop forward, Terry was a giant weighing well over 16 stone. He only came into the team towards the end of the 1958–59 season as an eighteen year old but soon established himself there before going on to play for Great Britain. A local lad, he had an excellent side–step. After leaving the Saints he went to play for Leeds and eventually settled in Yorkshire.

Tommy McKinney

Born in Scotland, Tommy came from the Salford area. He played for Salford and Warrington before coming to the Saints, and the transfer revived his Great Britain career which had wavered. He finished his career with the Saints.

Alan Prescott

The club captain, Alan eventually succeeded Jim Sullivan as coach. He also captained Great Britain for whom he played on twenty–eight occasions. His playing for seventy–six minutes of a Test match in 1958 with a broken arm is immortalized in Rugby League lore. Alan captained the Saints to their first Challenge Cup success in 1956. After his days at St Helens he coached at Leigh and Workington with little success. He is now a publican in the St Helens area.

Brian Briggs

Another Great Britain international, he joined the Saints from Huddersfield. Jim Sullivan was impressed and signed him. A big lad, he was fearless, a great cover tackler. After leaving St Helens he went to Wakefield Trinity where he became a director. He now runs a very successful pub just outside the Yorkshire town.

Dick Huddart

A Cumbrian, Dick Huddart emerged as one of the great all–time running second–row forwards. A former Lance Todd winner, he subsequently spent a great deal of his career in Australia after taking a liking to the country following a Great Britain tour. He played for Great Britain sixteen times. His son Milton is currently starring in the Second Division with Carlisle whom he joined in 1985 from Whitehaven.

Peter Fearis

What he lacked in general skills, Peter Fearis made up for in his great goal–kicking ability. A utility back, he normally performed at full back and in the game against Barrow in February 1959 he kicked a club joint record of thirteen goals and a record 29 points. He started his career at Blackpool Borough and was, in his day, one of the 'pin–up' boys of Rugby League.

Vince Karalius

Another of the many legends to have emerged from the St Helens club over the years, Widnes–born Karalius was overlooked by his home–town and signed for the Saints in 1952. After winning most major honours with St Helens, the 'Wild Bull of the Pampas' lost his job as team captain in 1962 to Alex Murphy. Six weeks later Karalius moved to Widnes for £4500 where he went on to win further honours. He hung up his boots in the sixties, but Widnes brought him out of retirement in 1972 when he became their coach for three years. In 1976 it was the turn of Wigan to lure him out of retirement. Then, in May 1983, Widnes acquired his services again, this time as manager. He led them on to further glories, including another Challenge Cup win. A successful businessman, Vince is now based on the Isle of Wight and only makes rare appearances at Widnes even though he is still team manager.

Doug Greenall

A tough tackling centre, Doug was another Saints player who went on to play for Great Britain. His only club was St Helens, following his father's example who also played for the club. After retiring, Doug became landlord of the Talbot Hotel in the town. He subsequently moved to a pub in Derbyshire, but was homesick and returned to his home town.

Tottenham Hotspur Football Club, 1960–61

In 1960–61 Tottenham Hotspur completed the 'Double' of winning the League championship and FA Cup in the same season. The performance had been achieved twice before, but under entirely different circumstances. In 1889 Preston North End played just twenty–two League games, then competed in the FA Cup after the season had finished. In 1897 Aston Villa played thirty League games and then embarked on a successful FA Cup campaign.

Tottenham were fortunate that they were not involved in two competitions which had been recently added to the itineraries of successful teams, the League Cup and the European Cup. But they played forty–nine competitive matches and a friendly. Their players were also required by various international squads. But a myth had grown up around the Double. In the modern game there was reputedly too much football. And Arsenal, Huddersfield, Wolves and Manchester United had all built supposedly far more accomplished teams, yet failed to win the Double.

The 1960–61 season was a vintage one. Tottenham (115), Wolves (103) and Burnley (102) scored over a hundred League goals, whilst Newcastle (109) and Chelsea (100) conceded a century each. Chelsea, however, managed to score 98; Newcastle totalled 86 and were relegated. Tottenham were the guiding light. They won their first eleven League games; they played fluid, open football with all but fourteen of their League goals coming from the forwards. Their tactics and ability to vary their game made them an entertaining side.

Like most outstanding teams, they had no injury problems. Les Allen, Danny Blanchflower, Ron Henry and John White played in all forty–two League games, Peter Baker, Bill Brown and Maurice Norman missed just one, whilst Terry Dyson appeared in forty, Dave Mackay thirty–seven and Bobby Smith thirty–six. Cliff Jones suffered from knee trouble and missed thirteen, but his fellow Welsh international friend, Terry Medwin, was a suitable replacement.

The side was shrewdly managed by Bill Nicholson. Like other great managers of the era, he was a former international half back. Matt Busby and Bill Shankly were others of similar outlook and beliefs. Nicholson was born on 26 January 1919 in Scarborough, and came to Tottenham as a junior apprentice. He made 306 League appearances for Spurs and won one England cap. He was a vital member of the famous Tottenham 'push and run' side of the early 1950s. He may have thought that there would be nothing further for him to achieve after his first day as manager. After being coach for former manager Arthur Rowe, and assistant to Jimmy Anderson, he took over as

Terry Dyson (out of picture) heads Tottenham's second goal past Gordon Banks in the Cup final against Leicester City. Victory clinched the double for Spurs

manager in October 1958. In his first match Tottenham beat Everton 10–4!

Nicholson spent more money than any of his contemporaries, but he bought wisely. Bill Brown came from Dundee, Dave Mackay from Hearts and John White from Falkirk, and all became loyal Tottenham men. The combined cost for the three was not much more than £80,000. Another deal which made sense was the exchanging of the talented international Johnny Brooks, for the more pedestrian but hard–working Les Allen.

The following season (1961–62) Tottenham were victims of their own achievements the previous year. Not only might they win the Double, but why not the European Cup as well? And they had Jimmy Greaves.

In the event, Tottenham fell just short. Beaten in the League by Ipswich, who had come up from the Second Division under Alf Ramsey, and Burnley, Tottenham consoled themselves with retaining the FA Cup with a 3–1 victory against the skilled Burnley team. In the European Cup, the ailing Real Madrid had been overtaken by an unknown but equally talented Iberian club, Benfica from Lisbon, with Eusebio, Coluna and the bearded central defender Germano. European survival seemed to be brief when in their very first game Spurs went to the Silesian coalmining centre of Żabrze to play Gornik. They lost 4–2. Fortunately the Poles found London N17 even less hospitable and collapsed 8–1 in the return leg. Tottenham met Benfica in the semi final and a certain defensive frailty in Lisbon saw them returning to White Hart Lane with a 1–3 deficit. How Benfica held out to lose by only the odd goal in three in the return still defies belief. Suitably relieved, Benfica plundered Real 5–3 in the final.

In 1963 Spurs won the Cup Winners' Cup, annihilating Athletico Madrid in the final 5–1 to become the first Football League team to win a European trophy. But, as the team gradually broke up, comparisons with the Double team became invidious. They had become victims of the standards they themselves had set.

THE TEAM

Bill Brown

Goalkeeper. Born 8 October 1931 in Dundee, he played for Dundee, then joined Tottenham for £30,000 in 1959. Played 222 League games for Spurs from 1959 to 1965. He joined Northampton and played seventeen League games in 1966. He won twenty–eight caps for Scotland.

Peter Baker

Right back. Born 10 December 1931 in Hampstead, he played for Enfield, just a few miles from Spurs' training ground. He played 299 League games for his only League club. Uncapped. His Tottenham career lasted from 1953 to 1964.

Ron Henry

Left back. Born 17 August 1934 at Shoreditch, he played 247 League games for Spurs, his only League club, from 1954 to 1965. He played once for England.

Danny Blanchflower

Right half. Born 10 February 1926 in Belfast. Captain of Tottenham and Northern Ireland, and elected Footballer of the Year in 1961, having previously won the award in 1958. His first club was Glentoran, before a £6500 transfer to Barnsley (sixty–eight League games), Aston Villa (148) and finally Tottenham (337) for £30,000. He retired in 1963, after winning fifty–six caps for Northern Ireland.

Maurice Norman

Centre half. Born 8 May 1934 in Wymondham, he joined Norwich City in 1954. He played thirty–five games before joining Spurs in 1955–56, 357 League games for Spurs and won twenty–three England caps.

Dave Mackay

Left half. Born 11 April 1934 in Edinburgh, he progressed into the Hearts and Scotland teams before Bill Nicholson brought him to Tottenham. He broke his leg twice in a Spurs career of 268 League games from 1958–1967. He later went on rescue missions to Derby and Swindon, managed Derby to the League Championship and won twenty–two caps for Scotland.

Cliff Jones

Right wing. Born 7 February 1935 in Swansea, he was one of the famous Swansea schoolboys team of that era. He played 168 League games, with 46 goals for Swansea from 1952 to 1957, before joining Spurs for £30,000 in 1958. He scored 134 League goals in 318 games for Spurs before going to Fulham in 1968. He played fifty–nine times for Wales. He was recognized as the best winger in the world.

John White

Inside right. Born on 28 April 1937 in Musselburgh, White was tragically killed in July 1964 at the age of twenty–seven when sheltering from a thunderstorm at the Crew Hill golf course at Enfield. He signed for £30,000 from Falkirk in 1959–60, and played 220 League games for Tottenham. He was capped twenty–three times by Scotland.

Bobby Smith

Centre forward. Born 22 February 1933 in Langdale, Smith played for Chelsea between 1950 and 1955, scoring 23 goals in 74 games. From 1955 to 1963 he scored 176 times in 271 League games for Spurs, before moving to Brighton. He was capped on fifteen occasions by England, scoring 13 goals.

Les Allen

Inside left. Born 4 September 1937 in Dagenham, Allen played for Briggs Sports before joining Chelsea in 1956. In three seasons he played forty–four League games, scoring 11 goals, before moving, like Smith and Greaves, to Spurs, where he played 119 League games and scored 47 goals. He moved to Queens Park Rangers for another 128 League games and 54 goals. He was uncapped, but his son Clive has played for England.

Terry Dyson

Outside left. Born 29 November 1934 in Scarborough, the son of a famous jockey, he played 184 League games, scoring 42 goals for Spurs. He then moved to Fulham and Colchester. Uncapped.

Terry Medwin

Winger. Born 25 September 1932, he played for Swansea from 1951 to 1955, scoring 59 goals in 148 League games, and for Tottenham from 1956 to 1962, scoring 65 goals in 197 League games. He played thirty times for Wales.

The reserves were led by Tony Marchi, born 21 January 1933, who played 131 League games between 1949 and 1956 before moving to Juventus. He returned in 1959 for a further 101 League games between 1959 and 1964. John Smith, an England Under–23 international, played twenty–one League games from 1959 to 1963 after joining the club from West Ham. He later moved to Coventry.

The League

They equalled Arsenal's 1930–31 record of 66 First Division points

They won the most games (31) in First Division history, with the most away wins (16)

They equalled Arsenal's 1930–31 record of 33 away points in a season

They completed the Double over eleven clubs to equal the First Division record set by Manchester United (1956–57) and Wolves (1958–59)

Their eleven consecutive wins at the start of the season was a League record

They reached 50 points faster than any other club – in twenty-nine games

Their 115 goals is still a club record for one season

League Results

Home

20 August	Everton	2–0
31 August	Blackpool	3–1
3 September	Manchester United	4–1
14 September	Bolton Wanderers	3–1
24 September	Aston Villa	6–2
10 October	Manchester City	1–1
2 November	Cardiff City	3–2
5 November	Fulham	5–1
19 November	Birmingham City	6–0
3 December	Burnley	4–4
24 December	West Ham United	2–0
31 December	Blackburn Rovers	5–2
21 January	Arsenal	4–2
4 February	Leicester City	2–3
22 February	Wolves	1–1
22 March	Newcastle United	1–2
31 March	Chelsea	4–2
1 April	Preston North End	5–0
17 April	Sheffield Wednesday	2–1
26 April	Nottingham Forest	1–0
29 April	West Bromwich Albion	1–2

Away

22 August	Blackpool	3–1
27 August	Blackburn Rovers	4–1
7 September	Bolton Wanderers	2–1
10 September	Arsenal	3–2
17 September	Leicester City	2–1
1 October	Wolves	4–0
15 October	Nottingham Forest	4–0
29 October	Newcastle United	4–3
12 November	Sheffield Wednesday	1–2
26 November	West Bromwich Albion	3–1
10 December	Preston North End	1–0
17 December	Everton	3–1
26 December	West Ham United	3–0
16 January	Manchester United	0–2
11 February	Aston Villa	2–1
25 February	Manchester City	1–0
11 March	Cardiff City	2–3
25 March	Fulham	0–0
3 April	Chelsea	3–2
8 April	Birmingham City	3–2
22 April	Burnley	2–4

Leading League Scorers:

Bobby Smith	28
Les Allen	23
Cliff Jones	15
John White	13
Terry Dyson	12

Top League Positions

		P	W	D	L	F	A	Pts
1	Tottenham Hotspur	42	31	4	7	115	55	66
2	Sheffield Wednesday	42	23	12	7	78	47	58
3	Wolverhampton Wanderers	42	25	7	10	103	75	57

The FA Cup

Having assured themselves of the League, Spurs went to Wembley on 6 May having completed their League fixtures. Favourites against Leicester City they played well below their League form. Leicester were well in the game but suffered from the Wembley 'jinx' when Len Chalmers went down injured. He left the field and although he subsequently returned he was just a passenger. Spurs capitalized as Bobby Smith opened the scoring in the sixty-sixth minute with a great solo goal. Dyson added the second nine minutes later. Spurs won 2–0, and they were presented with the cup by the Duchess of Kent. The crowd was 100,000 and receipts £49,813. In the Leicester side was Frank McLintock who went on to lead Arsenal to the Double ten years later.

Spurs Path to Wembley

Round 3	v. Charlton (h)	won 3–2
Round 4	v. Crewe Alex (h)	won 5–1
Round 5	v. Aston Villa (a)	won 2–0
Round 6	v. Sunderland (a)	drew 1–1
	Sunderland (h)	won 5–0
Semi final	v. Burnley (Villa Park)	won 3–0
Final	v. Leicester City (Wembley)	won 2–0

Leading Cup Goalscorers

| Terry Dyson | 5 |
| Bobby Smith | 4 |

Arkle and Pat Taaffe, 1962–66

Arkle ran in thirty–five races, three on the flat, six over hurdles and twenty–six steeplechases. He won twenty–two of the steeplechases and, of the four defeats, one was due to an unfortunate slip, in two he had to concede a ridiculous weight advantage to his opponents, and in the fourth he finally succumbed to an injury which ended his career.

Arkle was born at Balymacoll Stud, by Archive out of Bright Cherry. In 1960 he was bought for 1150 guineas by Tom Dreaper who trained him as a three–year–old for Anne, Duchess of Westminster. Arkle was named after a mountain on the Duchess's Scottish estate in Sutherland, near to a mountain called Foinavon, the name of the controversial winner of the 1967 Grand National.

To Arkle's jockey Pat Taaffe, their first meeting was rather like the driver of a mini watching a Porsche vanishing up a motorway. Taaffe was on Arkle's stable–mate Kerford in a hurdle race at Navan. Arkle was entered after two defeats on the flat. Taaffe, who had ridden his first winner in 1947, was astounded at the ease with which Arkle passed them at the final flight. The going was heavy but Taaffe recognized quality. The pair were united for the next outing and the partnership was born. After they won the Honeybourne Chase at Cheltenham in November 1962, no other jockey rode Arkle.

Arkle, as one famous Irish trainer said, 'was extraordinarily lucky to be in the stable he was. They knew he needed time and were prepared to give it to him.' At the Kilsallaghan yard they were not concerned overmuch with hurdles, and Pat Taaffe was a jockey who brought the best out of the great horses in the yard.

When he had first arrived at Kilsallaghan Arkle was still awkward. Dreaper, who had trained twelve of the thirteen horses bred by Bright Cherry, was unconcerned that the sire, Archive, was utterly useless.

By the age of five Arkle was ready for his first steeplechase. The Cheltenham Gold Cup was the ultimate objective. Dreaper thought him ready for the English novices, and the Honeybourne Chase proved him right.

The following year – 1963 – after the horse had shown some early–season form, including the Carey's Cottage Chase over 2 miles 4 furlongs at Gowran Park, Dreaper announced that Arkle would go to Newbury to meet Mill House in the Hennessy Gold Cup. Mill House, winner of the Cheltenham Gold Cup earlier in the season, was the pride of Fulke Walwyn's Lambourn stable. He was said to be the steeplechaser of the century, unbeatable, an amalgam of all Gold Cup winners rolled into one.

Arkle, like Golden Miller, never fell in a steeplechase, but he did make the odd mistake. At the third last in the Hennessy he slipped on clearing the fence. Mill House, giving Arkle 5 lb, won by eight lengths going away. Then, frightening opponents away, Mill House won the King George at Kempton on Boxing Day 1963. On the same day, at Leopardstown, Arkle was at least having a race. Wary scribes went over to look at him.

The return match with Mill House was set for Cheltenham early in 1964 in the Gold Cup. Only four runners set out in a blizzard; Mill House was 13 to 8 on, Arkle 7 to 4. Two from home Mill House was two lengths clear. Arkle sauntered past the favourite and won by five lengths, and Pat Taaffe won a suit off Mill House's jockey.

Their paths then took different courses – Arkle stayed in Ireland for the Irish Grand National at the end of the season and the Carey's Cottage at the beginning of the next. Mill House just failed to give Dormant a whopping 42 lb in the Whitbread at Sandown.

The first big race of the 1964–65 season was, as usual, the Hennessy. Arkle did to Mill House that afternoon of 5 December 1964 what Mill House had once been expected to do. Arkle won by ten lengths from Ferry Boat, to whom he was conceding 35 lb.

Results like that can only get horses into trouble with the handicappers. The next outing saw Arkle beaten in the Massey Ferguson. He lost by one length to Flying Wild and Buona Notte. He gave the winner 32 lb and the second 26 lb.

By the time the 1965 Gold Cup came round in March, Arkle, aged eight, was splendidly mature. Pat Taaffe, a quiet, unassuming jockey, led him home twenty lengths clear of Mill

Pat Taaffe and Arkle clear the last fence to win the Cheltenham Gold Cup for the second successive year

House, no longer a rival or a contender. Arkle won the Whitbread carrying 12½ stone; Brasher in second place carried 10 stone. In his next race at Sandown, the Gallaher Gold Cup, Arkle broke the track record.

The 1965–66 season opened with a casual trot round Ascot, and his preparation for the third Cheltenham Gold Cup took in the King George at Kempton on Boxing Day.

The Gold Cup was considered to be a mere walkover for Arkle, and that was how it turned out. Mill House had developed tendon trouble and was out for the season, and only four other horses opposed Arkle. The final verdict was a thirty-lengths win from Dormant, but at the eleventh fence only a superb piece of horsemanship from Taaffe kept the pair afloat. After the race Arkle retired for the season.

His next race was in November 1966. As always he was the top handicap, but to everyone's astonishment and dismay, despite conceding 31 lb to Stalbridge Colonist, he was overhauled after the last fence. Back to form for the SGB Chase, he was then entered for the King George VI at Kempton.

The race is soon told. Trying to retain the King George he fractured a bone in his left foot and hobbled round trying to stave off Dormant, who pipped him by a length.

During his illness he became Britain's best-loved patient. Wellwishers had to be controlled by Securicor, but it soon became obvious that he was not responding to treatment as he should. The greatest of them all would not race again.

Two stories concerning Arkle emphasize the qualities of the horse. In Ireland, the handicappers adopted two sets – one when Arkle was racing, the other when he was not.

In 1985, on the morning of the Grand National – a race Arkle never bothered with – *The Times* printed the following on the chances of a horse called Last Suspect, a 50 to 1 shot. 'Comes from the same stable as Arkle, but should not be mentioned in the same breath.' Last Suspect won.

THE TEAM

Arkle

Arkle ran in thirty-five races in all. He won twenty-seven, was second twice, third on three occasions, fourth twice, and was unplaced once. His full list of victories is as follows. All wins are steeplechases unless specified:

1962

Bective Novice Hurdle, Navan
Rathconnell Handicap Hurdle, Naas
Wee County Handicap Hurdle, Dundalk
HE The President's Handicap Hurdle, Gowran Park
Honeybourne Chase, Cheltenham

1963

Milltown Chase, Leopardstown
Broadway Chase, Cheltenham
Power Gold Cup Chase, Fairyhouse
John Jameson Cup Chase, Punchestown
Donoughmore Plate (flat), Navan
Carey's Cottage Handicap Chase, Gowran Park
Christmas Handicap Chase, Leopardstown

1964

Thyestes Handicap Chase, Gowran Park
Leopardstown Handicap Chase, Leopardstown
Cheltenham Gold Cup, Cheltenham
Irish Grand National, Fairyhouse
Carey's Cottage Handicap Chase, Gowran Park
Hennessy Gold Cup, Newbury

1965

Leopardstown Handicap Chase, Leopardstown
Cheltenham Gold Cup, Cheltenham
Whitbread Gold Cup, Sandown Park
Gallaher Gold Cup Handicap Chase, Sandown Park
Hennessy Gold Cup, Newbury
King George VI Chase, Kempton Park

1966

Leopardstown Handicap Chase, Leopardstown
Cheltenham Gold Cup, Cheltenham
SGB Handicap Chase, Ascot

Pat Taaffe

Pat Taaffe was born on 12 March 1930, the second son of Tom Taaffe, a leading jump trainer. Pat was hunting by the age of eight and show jumping shortly after. His first 'major' was the 1949 King George at Kempton, and in the following year he was selected as Tom Dreaper's number one jockey. He rode the winner of the 1955 Grand National, Quare Times, and retired shortly after winning the 1970 Grand National on Gay Trip. He also won four Gold Cups, six Irish Grand Nationals and more than five hundred races, including Hennessys, Mildmays and Mackesons, a fitting rider for the greatest steeplechaser of them all.

Pat Taaffe's first professional ride, in 1950 for Tom Dreaper, was on 14 January on his new stable's mare. The horse was called Bright Cherry, who went on to win six chases and be placed eleven times with Taaffe. Bright Cherry was then retired to stud where she produced Arkle.

Lyudmilla Belousova and Oleg Protopopov, 1962–69

Oleg Protopopov and Lyudmilla Belousova were the first Soviet skaters to gain international supremacy. For a country where winter lasts from October to April, and where propaganda insists that music and art are still the basis of their culture, it seems incredible that it was not until the arrival of the Protopopovs in the early 1960s that Russia dominated the ice pairs. But, having arrived on the scene, the Protopopovs not only managed to attract international acclaim for their country, but created a new blend of technical expertise and fluency that brought a new dimension to the programme.

Oleg was born in 1932, Lyudmilla in 1935. Both became interested in the sport at a comparatively late stage. At the age of sixteen Oleg saw a Sonja Henjie film and became hooked; Lyudmilla was also sixteen when she decided to persevere with ice skating. Their first meeting, however, was a long way off. Oleg, based in Leningrad, was being given skating lessons under his mother's guidance, while Lyudmilla, from Ulyanovsk, a town halfway between Moscow and the Urals on the Volga River, was still in the Russian sports system.

Oleg joined the Navy for three years; then his mother, who was a ballet teacher, took her twenty–two–year–old son to Moscow. Also in Moscow, on another course at the same rink, was Lyudmilla Belousova. A year later they were married and set up home in Leningrad.

Five years later they were selected for their first major international event, the 1960 Olympics at Squaw Valley. Their lack of experience at the highest level was obvious, but Protopopov and Belousova (Lyudmilla always used her maiden name in competitions) finished ninth and were already exhibiting the style that was to become their hallmark. Their strength and grace were noticeable. Oleg was only 5 feet 9 inches tall, but he towered over his wife by some 7 inches. The 'death spiral' was their trademark, with Lyudmilla lying backwards, her head skimming the ice. It was so successful that everyone now includes the spiral in their routine. For three successive years, from 1962 to 1964, the pair finished second, in both the World and the European Championships.

But where more appropriate than the Olympics to achieve the breakthrough. At the 1964 Innsbruck Games, Oleg, now thirty–two, and Lyudmilla, now twenty–nine, won their first gold medal. The runners–up, Marika Kilius and Hans Jurgen Baumler of Germany, world champions for the previous two

The Protopopovs perform the famous 'death spiral' during their gold medal performance at the 1964 Olympics

years, were not only beaten into second place but subsequently lost their silver medals for taking part in a professional ice review.

During the next four years the Protopopovs won every competition that they entered. They regained their title at Grenoble in the 1968 Olympics, receiving eight 5.9s for the artistic impression and six 5.9s for technical merit (in those days 6.0 was not commonplace). They ended their amateur careers in 1969, handing over to Alexei Ulanov and Irina Rodnina after finishing third to the new Russian heroes in the European Championships and second in the World Championships. Oleg was nearly thirty–seven. They became part of a professional touring company and coached their successors.

Television had made them the best–known couple in the sporting world. They were graceful and artistic, and skated as one. At the end of their amateur career Oleg said, 'How can these skaters who are only brother and sister convey the love and emotion that exists between man and woman. We skate from the heart . . . to us it is a spiritual beauty, not a performance for which we are measured by points.'

In a later interview Oleg admitted that he had sometimes thought that he was too old to dedicate himself to the sport. 'When I joined the Russian Navy in 1951, they tried to drill this namby–pamby sport out of me. But I preferred tracing figures of eight as opposed, as you people say, to having one over the eight.'

THE PROTOPOPOVS' WORLD CHAMPIONSHIP RESULTS

1962 (Prague)

		Pts
1 Maria Jelinek/Otto Jelinek	Canada	15
2 Belousova/Protopopov	USSR	16.5
3 Margaret Gobl/Franz Ningen	West Germany	25.5

1963 (Cortina)

1 Marika Kilius/Hans Jurgen Baumler	West Germany	9
2 Belousova/Protopopov	USSR	20
3 Tatiana Zhuk/Alexandr Gavrilov	USSR	31

1964 (Dortmund)

1 Marika Kilius/Hans Jurgen Baumler	West Germany	13
2 Belousova/Protopopov	USSR	14
3 Debbi Wilkes/Guy Revell	Canada	28

1965 (Colorado Springs)

1 Belousova/Protopopov	USSR	9
2 Vivien Joseph/Ronald Joseph	USA	19
3 Tatiana Zhuk/Alexandr Gorelik	USSR	32

1966 (Davos)

1 Belousova/Protopopov	USSR	13
2 Tatiana Zhuk/Alexandr Gorelik	USSR	14
3 Cynthia Kauffmann/ Ronald Kauffmann	USA	30

1967 (Vienna)

1 Belousova/Protopopov	USSR	9
2 Margot Glockshuber/ Wolfgang Danne	West Germany	25
3 Cynthia Kauffmann/ Ronald Kauffmann	USA	27

1968 (Geneva)

1 Belousova/Protopopov	USSR	9
2 Tatiana Zhuk/Alexandr Gorelik	USSR	19
3 Cynthia Kauffmann/ Ronald Kauffmann	USA	27

1969 (Colorado Springs)

1 Irina Rodnina/Alexei Ulanov	USSR	9
2 Tamara Moskvina/Alexei Mishin	USSR	23
3 Belousova/Protopopov	USSR	26

THE PROTOPOPOV'S MEDALS

Olympic Games
1964	Gold
1968	Gold

World Championships
1962	Silver
1963	Silver
1964	Silver
1965	Gold
1966	Gold
1967	Gold
1968	Gold
1969	Bronze

European Championships
1962	Silver
1963	Silver
1964	Silver
1965	Gold
1966	Gold
1967	Gold
1968	Gold
1969	Silver

Tony Nash and Robin Dixon, 1963–68

Britain's successes in the Winter Olympics are varied and few. At the last eleven Olympic Games the Union Jack has been raised on six occasions. Figure skating has featured three times with Jeanette Altweg (1952), John Curry (1976) and Robin Cousins (1980); the incomparable Torvill and Dean won their ice dance gold in 1984 and the ice hockey team surprised the world in 1936.

Some were expected, some unforeseen, but the sixth gold medal that has come Britain's way was totally unexpected as it was in an event in which there are no facilities for practice at home. When Robin Dixon and Tony Nash won the two–man bobsleigh run at the 1964 Innsbruck Olympics, the number of bobsled runs in the United Kingdom was nil.

But the British had already set up a base abroad. The British and St Moritz bobsleigh clubs have long flourished in Switzerland, and St Moritz has become to bobsleighing what Lord's is to cricket. But the mere position and stature of St Moritz determined who can and who cannot afford either to get there or to use the facilities once in the Engadine region. There are two major courses at St Moritz, the 'town' course and the Cresta Run. The British claim to be the innovators of both.

Britain enjoyed a fine spell of international success in 1936 when our teams became world champions in the two–man and four–man bobsleigh. The four–man bob retained their title the following year.

In the late 1950s Britain again began to feature in the higher echelons of the sport. In 1959 Flight Lieutenant Colin Mitchell of the RAF became the official world champion, and Britain's number one four–man bob team also commanded much respect. Two of that team were Tony Nash and Robin Dixon.

The 1963 World Championships were held at Innsbruck to assess the suitability of the track for the following year's Olympic Games. Nash and Dixon in the two–man bob finished third behind the Italians, for whom the legendary Eugenio Monti won yet another world title. Nash and Dixon were also members of the four–man bob team which finished fourth.

The Olympic gold medal became the property of Nash and Dixon on 1 February 1964. The races are decided on times. Each two–man bob has four descents to make, and the combined times for the four runs are added together for the overall placings. Nash and Dixon triumphed by twelve hundredths of a second. While not to detract in any way from their achievement, the generosity of Eugenio Monti of Italy played a part in their success.

While waiting for the call for their second run, the British pair noticed that the axle bolt on their bob had broken. Monti was at the bottom of the course, having completed his two runs on the first day of the competition. On hearing of Nash and Dixon's predicament, he immediately removed his axle bolt and personally supervised its transport back up to the top of the mountain so that the British team could make their run. At the same time Monti was the reigning world champion with his compatriot Siorpaes. He had won the world title six times, yet had never won a coveted Olympic gold medal. The temptation to blame poor British organization must have been paramount in his mind as he searched for that elusive gold.

Tony Nash, the driver, was born on 18 March 1936, and the Honorable Robin Dixon, the brakeman, and heir to Lord Glentoran, on 21 April 1935. They became the first gold medallists (and the last so far) from a lowland nation to win the bobsleighing gold medal. Just to prove the doubters wrong, Nash and Dixon retained their world title the following year (the World Championships had been held concurrently with the Olympics in 1964).

TWO-MAN BOB OLYMPIC RECORD 1964

1964 (Innsbruck)

1	Great Britain	(Nash and Dixon)	4:21.90
2	Italy I	(Zardini and Bonagura)	4:22.02
3	Italy II	(Monti and Siorpaes)	4:22.63

Tony Nash (driver) and Robin Dixon (brakeman) hurtle down the Igls course on their way to the gold medal

Celtic Football Club, 1965–74

Before the 1960s the knowing population on the 'bob bank' on the terraces of most successful football teams would tell you that the great sides were all based around the half-back line. Then, with the advent of more sophisticated training methods and tactics, came a new partnership – the manager/captain. Not that a half-back line was no longer vital, but supporters began to talk of Moore and Ramsey, Busby and Charlton, Beckenbauer and Schoen. At Parkhead, home of Celtic Football Club, they had such a combination in Stein and McNeill. That was to be the pivot of the most successful side in Scottish football history (although Rangers fans might disagree).

The first to arrive was Billy McNeill, who made his League debut in 1958 against Clyde and played for Celtic for eighteen years. During that time he led the club to a European Cup win, nine championships, seven Scottish Cups and six League Cups. He played twenty-eight times for Scotland.

Jock Stein was a former centre half with Celtic with 128 league games to his credit when injury cut short his career in 1954. He became a coach at Parkhead, before accepting posts at Dunfermline and Hibernian. He was not first choice when Celtic advertised for a new manager in 1965. Celtic, fed up with their local rivals Rangers scooping all the trophies on the pitch and monopolizing the back page of the Glasgow sports papers, put in a bid for Alfredo Di Stefano, the legendary Real Madrid centre forward who had just ended his playing days. Perhaps Di Stefano had already heard of the dangers of possible defeat

at Partick Thistle on a wet Wednesday in February; he decided to remain in the warmer Mediterranean climes and Jock Stein was approached.

Appointed as manager on 31 January 1965, Stein could not take over until 24 April as he still had commitments to Hibs, and Celtic finished eighth in the table in 1964–65. The following season they were champions. They were to be champions for nine successive seasons, a world record only ever equalled by CSKA, the army team from Sofia which monotonously won the Bulgarian league, but they benefited from the Communist mania for military prowess and could recruit virtually any good player available in the country at the time.

By the end of the 1961–62 season Celtic had acquired three of the youngsters who were to become part of their successful team in Lisbon: Tommy Gemmell from Cotness United, Jimmy Johnstone, brilliant, talented and erratic little winger from the Celtic club of Blantyre, and Bobby Lennox from Ardeer Recreation. Stevie Chalmers, lively forward, was part of the youth policy at Parkhead, and Bertie Auld, who had left Celtic for Birmingham City, in 1961 decided to return home.

During their championship seasons Celtic also reached the final of every Scottish FA and League Cup except one. But the greatest achievement occurred in Lisbon on the warm night of 25 May 1967. Celtic beat Internationale of Milan 2–1 to become the first British team – Manchester United, Liverpool and all – to win the European Cup. Ironically, Jock Stein had studied and

Grand Slam winners 1966–67. Celtic team with the Glasgow Cup, League Championship trophy, European Cup, Scottish Cup and League Cup

admired the methods of Inter coach Helenio Herrera and based his own club set-up on Herrera's principles.

The Celtic team were competing in the European Cup for the first time. They overcame a dull and pathetically negative Inter, and played a fast, attacking, muscular game. Gemmell overlapping at full back, equalized after Inter's early penalty from Mazzola, and eight minutes from time Chalmers shrewdly deflected the ball past Sarti.

There are several stories about that night. Legend has it that, by 1985, no fewer than twenty-one Celtic supporters had still failed to return from Portugal. And of those that did, one was grateful to his friends for bringing him home in a tired, emotional state, until he realized back in Glasgow that he had left his car in Lisbon!

With the natural and gradual disbanding of the 'Lisbon Lions', Stein proved himself adept at rebuilding his fading team. Celtic did well to reach their second European final in 1970 against the Dutch champions Feyenoord, who proved more resilient and tactically adept. The rebuilding was hastened, but with no lack of success on the Scottish domestic front.

Stein and McNeill reorganized their team around a couple of old favourites, Chalmers and Lennox, who were particularly appreciated even as their skills declined. Stein also introduced a group of youngsters who called themselves the 'Quality Street Gang' after a well-known television advertisement. There was Ronnie Glavin, who came from Partick and went to Barnsley, Danny McGrain, who was loaned to Maryhill to learn his trade, and Lou Macari and David Hay, who were eventually to move into the more lucrative Football League.

A seventeen-year-old apprentice joiner was just getting into the first team. 'I spent my time shovelling shavings and hitting nails, mostly my own.' His description of himself was 'a wee, fat number 4'. His name: Kenny Dalglish.

CELTIC'S RECORD, 1965–74

Scottish League

	P	W	D	L	F	A	P	pos
1965–66	34	27	3	4	106	30	57	1
1966–67	34	26	6	2	111	33	58	1
1967–68	34	30	3	1	106	24	63	1
1968–69	34	23	8	3	89	32	54	1
1969–70	34	27	3	4	96	33	57	1
1970–71	34	25	6	3	89	23	56	1
1971–72	34	28	4	2	96	28	60	1
1972–73	34	26	5	3	93	28	57	1
1973–74	34	23	7	4	82	27	53	1

Scottish FA Cup

1965–66	Final	lost to Rangers	0–1	(after 0–0)
1966–67	Final	beat Aberdeen	2–0	
1967–68	Round 1	lost to Dunfermline	0–2	
1968–69	Final	beat Rangers	4–0	
1969–70	Final	lost to Aberdeen	1–2	
1970–71	Final	beat Rangers	2–1	(after 1–1)
1971–72	Final	beat Hibernian	6–1	
1972–73	Final	lost to Rangers	3–2	
1973–74	Final	beat Dundee Utd	3–0	

Scottish League Cup

1965–66	Final	beat Rangers	2–1
1966–67	Final	beat Rangers	1–0
1967–68	Final	beat Dundee	5–3
1968–69	Final	beat Hibernian	6–2
1969–70	Final	beat St Johnstone	1–0
1970–71	Final	lost to Rangers	0–1
1971–72	Final	lost to Partick Thistle	1–4
1972–73	Final	lost to Hibernian	1–2
1973–74	Final	lost to Dundee	0–1

1967 European Cup final – Bobby Lennox (out of picture) appeals for a penalty as Willie Wallace (left) is impeded by the Inter Milan defence

Europe

1965–66	Cup Winners' Cup	Semi final	lost to Liverpool	1–2 (agg.)
1966–67	European Cup	Final	beat Inter Milan	2–1
1967–68	European Cup	Round 1	lost to Dynamo Kiev	2–3 (agg.)
1968–69	European Cup	Quarter final	lost to AC Milan	0–1 (agg.)
1969–70	European Cup	Final	lost to Feyenoord	1–2
1970–71	European Cup	Quarter final	lost to Ajax	1–3 (agg.)
1971–72	European Cup	Semi final	lost to Inter Milan	0–0 (agg.)*
1972–73	European Cup	Round 2	lost to Ujpest Dozsa	2–4 (agg.)
1973–74	European Cup	Semi final	lost to Athletico Madrid	0–2 (agg.)

* lost on penalties

England World Cup Team, 1966

Six months before the 1966 World Cup England manager, Alf Ramsey, cornered by pressmen, stated that England would win the Cup. He had a fine footballing pedigree: a member of the Spurs 'push and run' team of 1951, a cultured full back for England, and a successful manager of Ipswich – Division 2 champions in 1961, and Division 1 champions at the very first attempt in 1962. No one doubted his sincerity, but were England better than Brazil with Pele, and Portugal with Eusebio? And England's warm-up games had not been impressive, except a 2–0 win in Spain, where Ramsey paraded a team playing 4–3–3 without wingers.

The style was criticized heavily in some quarters, but Ramsey explained, correctly, that if the quality of the wingers in the Football League was not up to standard in international terms, then there had to be a plan to emphasize the particular strengths of the best players in the country.

The 1966 World Cup was opened by the Queen, who then had to sit through a goalless opening match, in which Uruguay, with eight or nine men in defence, stifled the new England system.

Terry Paine and Martin Peters replaced Alan Ball and John Connelly for England's second game against Mexico. England beat the Mexicans 2–0 with a marvellous right-foot drive from 25 yards by Bobby Charlton past the keeper Antonio Carbajal, who was playing in his fifth World Cup tournament. Roger Hunt finished off a Jimmy Greaves shot, after Charlton's fine through ball, for the second. England then won Group 2 by inflicting a similar defeat on France, cruelly robbed of midfielder Robert Herbin, by a Stiles tackle. Hunt scored both goals, but the midfield and defence were unconvincing.

England's quarter final against Argentina was won eight minutes from the end by a glancing header from Geoff Hurst who had been recalled. Argentina had the all-round skill and ability to win, but resorted to a policy of cynical obstruction and endless petty fouling. The patient Herr Kreitlein eventually dismissed Antonio Rattin, the Argentinian captain, for dissent and Ramsey hoped that the remainder of the teams left in the tournament would not act like 'animals'.

Meanwhile a fading Brazil had gone out in the group matches on Merseyside. Pele had been badly injured and the other 'names' had run out of competitive steam. Portugal and Hungary both beat Brazil 3–1, and Morais, the Portuguese

Geoff Hurst completes his hat-trick with the fourth and final England goal. Wolfgang Overath gives unavailing chase

defender, was tarred with the tackle that put Pele out of the competition. Italy, too, had disappeared, to everyone's amazement, to the North Koreans; Pak Do Ik's goal reverberated around the world.

In the semi finals England at last found in Portugal a team willing to attack and be attacked. There were some cries of 'fix' after the game was rescheduled for Wembley but the British official on the FIFA committee, Sir Stanley Rous, actually wanted the game played at Everton. He was overruled.

Two goals, one after thirty and the other after seventy-nine minutes, both thundered in by Bobby Charlton, gave England a clear path to the final, but Eusebio, quiet under the influence of the close-marking Stiles, scored from an eighty-second minute penalty after Jack Charlton had handled a header from Torres. The last few minutes were very tense.

West Germany came through the other semi-final against the Russians by 2–1 against nine fit men and one, Chislenko, sent off. Fittingly, Beckenbauer's goal took them to Wembley for the first time in the tournament.

As everyone knows, England won a dramatic final against a side which, up to then, had yet to beat them in an international. Hunt remained in place of Greaves. An uncharacteristic error from Wilson, who headed straight into Haller's path, gave West Germany a goal in the nineteenth minute. Moore planted the ball precisely on Hurst's head for the equalizer, and Peters put England into the lead in the second half after Weber had blocked Hurst's mishit shot. But it was Weber, the Cologne midfielder, who eventually dragged Emmerich's last-minute free kick past Banks to equalize.

'You've won it once, now go and win it again' was Ramsey's blunt assessment of extra time. Ball's amazing running on the right was the platform needed. Ten minutes into extra time he forced a cross towards Hurst who pivoted and struck the underside of the bar with the ball. Bakhramov, the Russian touch judge, confirmed to referee Dienst that the ball had crossed the line – just. West Germans still dispute the decision. With people on the pitch at full time celebrating victory, Hurst made certain by lashing in the fourth from a telling clearance from Moore.

So Ramsey had been as good as his word. England were world champions, their team work deservedly giving them the Cup. They had produced good performances when it mattered none more so than Hurst and Charlton. But, in the final itself, Alan Ball, the little redhead from Blackpool, wearing the red number 7, was the hero on the day. His unfailing spirit and running emphasized and typified England's performance.

ENGLAND'S WORLD CUP RECORD, 1966

Group Matches

11 July v. Uruguay	drew 0–0
16 July v. Mexico	won 2–0 (R. Charlton, Hunt)
20 July v. France	won 2–0 (Hunt 2)

	P	W	D	L	F	A	Pts
England	3	2	1	0	4	0	5
Uruguay	3	1	2	0	2	1	4
Mexico	3	0	2	1	1	3	2
France	3	0	1	2	2	5	1

Quarter Final

| 23 July v. Argentina | won 1–0 (Hurst) |

Semi final

| 26 July v. Portugal | won 2–1 (R. Charlton 2) |

Final

| 30 July v. West Germany | won 4–2 (Hurst 3, Peters) |

Banks; Cohen, Wilson; Stiles, J. Charlton, Moore (captain); Ball, Hunt, Hurst, R. Charlton, Peters.

THE SQUAD

	Club	d.o.b.	p.o.b.	Number of matches	Caps in career
Jim Armfield	Blackpool	21.9.35	Blackpool	0	43
Alan Ball	Blackpool	12. 5.45	Farnworth	4	72
Gordon Banks	Leicester City	30.12.37	Rawmarsh	6	73
Peter Bonetti	Chelsea	27. 9.41	Putney	0	7
Gerry Byrne	Liverpool	29. 8.38	Liverpool	0	2
Ian Callaghan	Liverpool	10. 4.42	Liverpool	1	4
Jack Charlton	Leeds United	8. 5.35	Ashington	6	35
Bobby Charlton	Manchester United	11.10.37	Ashington	6	106
George Cohen	Fulham	22.10.39	Kensington	6	37
John Connelly	Manchester United	18. 7.38	St Helens	1	20
George Eastham	Arsenal	23. 9.36	Blackpool	0	19
Ron Flowers	Wolves	28. 7.34	Edlington	0	49
Jimmy Greaves	Tottenham	20. 2.40	East Ham	3	57
Roger Hunt	Liverpool	20. 7.38	Golborne	6	34
Norman Hunter	Leeds United	29.10.43	Middlesbro	0	28
Geoff Hurst	West Ham United	8.12.41	Ashton	3	49
Bobby Moore	West Ham United	12. 4.41	Barking	6	108
Terry Paine	Southampton	23. 3.39	Winchester	1	19
Martin Peters	West Ham United	8.11.43	Plaistow	5	67
Ron Springett	Sheffield Wednesday	22. 7.35	Fulham	0	33
Nobby Stiles	Manchester United	18. 5.42	Manchester	6	28
Ray Wilson	Everton	17.12.34	Shirebrook	6	63

Brian Clough and Peter Taylor, 1968–82

Brian Clough and Peter Taylor met at Middlesbrough in 1955 when Taylor arrived from Coventry to take over as first-team goalkeeper. During practice, he was impressed by a tearaway forward from the reserves. Taylor's first impression of Clough was that he was a very brash young man, but he spotted Clough's potential and spent a good deal of his spare time talking football with the young man and frequently persuading him not to ask for a transfer.

Briefly Clough flirted with the big time, two England caps, three Under-23 appearances and a handful of First Division matches after his transfer to Sunderland. But a knee injury by then threatened his playing career. At the age of twenty-nine he became the youngest manager in the game – at Fourth Division Hartlepool. He persuaded his former mentor Taylor to team up with him (Taylor was already in charge at non-league Burton Albion), and between them they laid the foundation for Hartlepool's finest hour – promotion to Division Three for the first and the only time.

By the time Hartlepool had assumed such dizzy heights Clough and Taylor's management potential had been spotted by the once great Derby County. At Hartlepool financial constraints were so severe that Clough was forced to paint the stand and drive the team bus himself. It was a thrifty attitude that appealed to the club's chairman, and Derby's Sam Longson could never have been called a spendthrift.

Clough and Taylor arrived at the Baseball Ground with Derby nearer Division Three than Division One. The new managers revitalized the spirit of the club first with bargain signings – like Dave Mackay, said to be a spent force at Tottenham, but whose sterling defensive qualities coupled with a powerful attacking style and inspirational leadership hauled Derby to the top of the Second Division – then with more ambitious and expensive

Brian Clough, for once taking the back seat, keeps an eye on Peter Taylor

acquisitions like Colin Todd, bought for £170,000 when the chairman was away on holiday.

Having won promotion from Division Two as champions in 1969, Clough set his sights on the League title. He achieved it two years later with a side built, as all their great sides were, on solid defence. Todd partnered the cultured Roy McFarland in the centre. Archie Gemmill ran tirelessly and effectively in midfield, while up front Kevin Hector poached the goals. Clough and Taylor, their job done, took the players away to Majorca on holiday at the end of the season even though their fate was to be decided on a Monday night by other sides still in with a chance of overhauling them. They failed, and Clough and Taylor had realized their first ambition.

Clough's outspoken comments, which at first endeared him to a television audience still, in those days, hooked on the game, began to grate with the Derby board and especially with the chairman. Longson asked Clough to restrict his television appearances. Clough refused and carried out what he had threatened on numerous occasions – he resigned, and took Taylor with him. The players, loyal to the pair who had brought them success, revolted against the board, organized protest meetings and sit-ins and threatened to go on strike.

Briefly Clough and Taylor were tempted to Brighton. Clough did not like the South and never moved from Derby. Taylor, determined to make his own reputation, stayed at the Goldstone when Clough slipped away for a forty-four-day spell as manager of Leeds in place of Don Revie, the newly appointed national team manager. Clough was not a success with the players he inherited from the Revie regime. Too often in the past he had criticized their attitude and style.

Out of work, Clough was eventually approached by Nottingham Forest's vice-chairman to take over from Allan Brown. Clough resisted at first, then agreed in January 1975. No sooner had he arrived at the City Ground than the revamped Derby board asked him to return to the Baseball Ground. Clough refused and set about rebuilding Forest, who were dangerously close to relegation from Division Two.

Forest finished eighth that season with a flurry of wins towards the end of the campaign. Then, in July 1976, the club completed what Clough called the best stroke of business it had ever done. Taylor resigned from his job in charge at Brighton and agreed to link up again with Clough. He admitted it had been a mistake for them to have split up.

The following season underlined that view as Forest improved to snatch promotion to Division One. Once in the First Division Taylor's job was to find the players necessary to provide the impetus of a championship challenge. He had already made decent players of Tony Woodcock and John Robertson – two men who were destined for the lower divisions before Taylor's arrival; he improved the tactical sense of Martin O'Neill; and in the early stages of the 1977–78 season he bought Peter Shilton to play in goal; he strengthened the midfield with Archie Gemmill and transformed Birmingham's striker Kenny Burns into a class defender.

The combination of average players inspired by Clough's novel methods of motivation and bullying and good players bought from other clubs who had labelled them misfits worked. Forest won the League Cup after a replay with Liverpool – the first trophy at the club for twenty-nine years and achieved with five top players absent – then rolled on to take the League championship for a remarkable double in their first season back in the First Division.

Augmented by the acquisition of Trevor Francis from Birmingham City – Britain's first £1 million footballer – the team performed as capably the following year, missing out on the League title (they were runners-up) but taking the League Cup again, and, amazingly, the European Cup at the first attempt.

Another European Cup win followed the next year. Again Peter Taylor's pattern – defensive – won the match against Hamburg in Madrid as John Robertson scored the only goal, and Forest concentrated on blunting the effectiveness of Kevin Keegan by pushing him deeper into midfield.

As players got older Clough and Taylor ruthlessly replaced them. Too ruthlessly, say some critics – O'Neill and Gemmill left before their time was really due, Woodcock sought his fortune abroad. The replacements, including the £1 million signing of Ian Wallace and Justin Fashanu, were never adequate. The Clough–Taylor partnership broke up in May 1982 with rumours of disagreements and rancour. Taylor decided to retire after thirty-six years in the game (he made a brief unhappy comeback at Derby), while Clough soldiered on at Forest.

As a managerial pair they were unmatched: Clough the motivator, Taylor the evaluator of players. They will not be forgotten at Derby or Nottingham. Ever.

THE PARTNERSHIP

Brian Clough

Born in Middlesbrough on 21 March 1935, he joined Middlesbrough FC from a local amateur side, Great Broughton, in May 1953. He made 213 League appearances for Boro, scoring 197 goals – all in the Second Division. In 1958–59 and 1959–60 he was the division's top scorer with 42 and 39 goals respectively. Hardly surprisingly, Sunderland snapped him up in July 1961 and he maintained his goalscoring form for them in the Second Division in the 1961–62 season with 29 goals. The following season he scored 24 goals. Injury forced him to retire after making just three appearances in the top flight.

Career Record

League games	274
League goals	251
Full England appearances	2 (Wales, 1959, drew 1–1; Sweden, 1959, lost 2–3)
England goals	0
England 'B' caps	1 (Scotland, 1957)
England Under-23 caps	3 (Scotland, Bulgaria, 1957; Wales, 1958)

Peter Taylor

Born in Nottingham on 2 July 1928, joined Coventry City in May 1946 and played a total of 87 League games for the Highfield Road club. In August 1955 he went to Middlesbrough, where he teamed up with Clough. Altogether he played 140 League games at Ayresome Park, before his final game, for Port Vale, in the 1960 61 season.

Career Record

League games	228

Clough and Taylor's Record

1968–69	Second Division Championship	Derby County
1971–72	First Division Championship	Derby County
1977–78	First Division Championship	Nottingham Forest
	Football League Cup winners	Nottingham Forest
1978–79	European Cup winners	Nottingham Forest
	First Division runners-up	Nottingham Forest
	Football League Cup winners	Nottingham Forest
1979–80	European Cup winners	Nottingham Forest
	European Super Cup winners	Nottingham Forest
	Football League Cup runners-up	Nottingham Forest

United States 4 x 400-Metres Relay Team, 1968

What constitutes a perfect team? The American 4 x 400-metres relay team which won the gold medal in the 1968 Olympics in a world record time which still stood in 1985 is an obvious example.

The team consisted of the athletes who had won the three medals in the individual 400-metres event – Lee Evans, Larry James and Ron Freeman. The fourth man was a former world record holder who had finished fourth in the US trials. Vince Matthews went on to win the individual gold medal in the 400 metres four years later at the Munich Olympics. In 1968 the top twelve 400-metres runners in the world were all Americans.

The final, on 20 October, saw the United States going for a world record. It was Ron Freeman's amazing second leg that was the decisive factor. His 43.2 seconds was the fastest leg ever in a 4 x 400-metres relay. Anchorman Lee Evans finished the race 30 yards clear of the second man, Charles Asati (Kenya). Their world record time of 2:56.1 was altered by the IAAF on 1 January 1981 to 2:56.16.

Sadly, the Americans did not defend their marvellous performance at Munich. They had to name a squad of six, of which any four could run. Two of the team, Vince Matthews and Wayne Collett, gold and silver medallists in the individual 400 metres, were sent home for their behaviour on the winners' rostrum. That reduced the squad to four. Then it was announced that John Smith, who was injured in the 400-metres final, had pulled a hamstring. That left three athletes, including Lee Evans, and, as a consequence, the team had to withdraw.

THE TEAM

Lee Evans

Born at Modena, California, on 25 February 1947, for seven seasons from 1966 he was the world's top 400-metres runner. Surprisingly, his style was not 'textbook' as he had a cumbersome rolling-head action. His record time of 43.86 seconds for the 400 metres at the 1968 Olympics still stood at the beginning of 1985. He also set world records in the 4 x 200 metres, the 4 x 220 yards and the 600 metres. He failed to make the 1972 Olympic team in the individual 400 metres, and after the Games he joined the Professional International Track Association, teaming up with athletes like Bob Seagren, Jim Ryun and Randy Matson. He was reinstated as amateur in 1980.

Ron Freeman

Born 12 June 1947, he was bronze medallist in the 1968 Olympic 400 metres (44.4 seconds).

Larry James

Born 6 November 1947, he set a world 400-metres record in 1968 when he finished second to Lee Evans at South Lake Tahoe. Evans ran 44.06, James 44.19, but Evans was wearing an illegal 'brush' spike shoe and consequently his time was not ratified as a new world record.

Vince Matthews

Born on 16 December 1947, he became a social worker in New York. He broke the world 400-metres record in August 1968 but lost it two weeks later to team-mate Larry James. He also beat Lee Evans twice in 1968 – the only man to beat him during the year. In 1972 he was the Olympic 400-metres champion.

THE OLYMPIC FINAL

1	United States	2:56.1*
2	Kenya	2:59.6
3	West Germany	3:00.5
4	Poland	3:00.5
5	Great Britain	3:01.2
6	Trinidad	3:04.5
7	Italy	3:04.6
8	France	3:07.5

Legs

1st	Matthews	45.0
2nd	Freeman	43.2
3rd	James	43.8
4th	Evans	44.1

*world record

Larry James (left) hands over to Lee Evans as America wins the gold medal in the 4 × 400-metres relay at the Mexico Olympics. Evans took the gold medal in the individual event with James winning the silver. In 1985 Evans still held the world record for the 400 metres, and James had clocked the second fastest time

South Africa Cricket Team, 1969–70

In the English summer 1961 a team of young South Africans, known as the Fezelas, played twenty-one matches in England, Scotland and Ireland. Under the beneficiary of one S. Murphy, a retired sugar planter, the team was captained by the Test player Roy McLean, who insisted on positive attacking cricket. Of the twenty-one games, twelve were won and the other nine drawn, mostly in favour of the touring team. These young men, fresh out of school and university, saved their outstanding performances for the matches that mattered – three first-class games. They murdered the opposition, beating Essex by six wickets and the Combined Services (then a force) and Gloucestershire by an innings and plenty. Those few spectators draped around the boundary at Chelmsford, Bristol and Portsmouth went home and told their sons of Barlow, Lindsay, Botten, Bland, Van der Merwe and Pollock.

South Africa's next Test series was against New Zealand in 1961–62. In the first Test they capped no fewer than seven new players. Four were Fezelas: the opening bat and seam bowler Eddie Barlow, Kim Elgie, the former Scottish rugby international Colin Bland, a fine middle order batsman and brilliant fielder, and Peter Pollock, the fast bowler, who won the match with fourth-innings figures of 6 for 38. The series was drawn 2–2.

For the next series, against Australia in 1963–64, three more of those Fezelas made their Test debut. Dennis Lindsay, the wicketkeeper-batsman, and Peter Van der Merwe were two of the six newcomers to Test cricket. The third was Graeme Pollock, only an 'honorary Fezela'; he had accompanied his parents to watch his elder brother Peter.

As school reports say, 'steady progress was maintained' – the series was tied in Australia 1–1, several Fezelas becoming, at a formative age, established Test cricketers. Barlow hit his maiden Test century in the First Test, Graeme Pollock, not yet twenty years of age, followed suit in the Third. In the Fourth Test Barlow (201) and Pollock (175) added 341 for the third wicket to level the series, a South African Test record for all wickets. In the final Test, the South Africans needed 176 to win, but when time ran out were 76 for no wicket just 100 runs away from winning the series. Bland, quite the best fielder in the world, made his first Test century (126), whilst Peter Pollock collected 25 wickets in the series.

The South Africans moved on to New Zealand where they drew all three matches, but at the Basin Reserve came the first inkling of sinister problems ahead. The government had added the awful word 'apartheid' to the constitution, and New Zealand protesters damaged the pitch.

The next series against England in 1964–65, was decided by an innings win for England in Durban in the First Test – the other four Tests were drawn, and England, boring England, left for home confident of a repeat success in the summer of 1965.

The three-match series in England hinged on the Trent Bridge Test and the Pollock brothers. Graeme made a quite magnificent 125 and 59, whilst Peter claimed 5 for 53 and 5 for 34. South Africa won by 94 runs. The other two Tests were drawn. Barlow, Lindsay, Bland, Van der Merwe (captain),

Peter Pollock and Botten had all been with the Fezelas four years earlier.

With the world's anger directed straight at the Parliament buildings in Cape Town and Pretoria, the South Africans played just two more series in the five years after beating England. Both series were against the Australians, both series were won by embarrassing margins, and both series proved that not only were South Africa by far and away the leading cricket nation in the world, but they were introducing young players into the solid structure of the team. When they sadly departed the international scene in 1970, the only question was

Dennis Lindsay hits John Gleeson of Australia for four during the Fourth Test at Port Elizabeth, 1970

whether they would have survived as the best in the world until Lillee and Thomson in 1975, or until the West Indies of the 1980s.

By now Barry Richards and Mike Procter had joined the fold. Ali Bacher was the new captain, but, sadly, Trevor Goddard missed the final Test match of all. He was present during the birth pains and teething troubles of a great side.

But at least South Africa had manged to squeeze in that final series against Australia in 1969–70. A year earlier the then Prime Minister B.J. Vorster had virtually closed the door by stating at the Bloemfontein National Congress that their own Basil

D'Oliveira was not welcome as part of the M.C.C. touring party. D'Oliveira, ever the diplomat, suggested that Vorster had to quell a revolt from within his own party and had to assert his authority. Cricket was that opportunity.

South Africa now struggles to overcome 'rebel teams' of fading stars, run-of-the-mill county players and those who never quite made the grade. A great future seemed ahead for them in 1970. Brian Crowley's *Cricket Exiles*, sums it up perfectly: 'All that is now left are the memories, the nostalgia, and a tremendous sadness . . . and it now all seems such a long time ago.'

SOUTH AFRICA v. AUSTRALIA, 1969–70

The 1969–70 series at home to Australia was the South Africans first Test series for three years and their last series in Test cricket.

First Test
22–27 January (Cape Town)
South Africa
382 (E. Barlow 127; A. Mallett 5–126)
232 (A.N. Connolly 5–47)
Australia
164
280
South Africa won by 170 runs
It was the first time in seven meetings that South Africa had beaten Australia at Newlands. Barry Richards made his Test debut in this match

Second Test
5–9 February (Durban)
South Africa
622–9 declared (R.G. Pollock 274, B.A. Richards 140)
Australia
157
336
South Africa won by an innings and 129 runs
Their 622 was their highest score in Test cricket and Pollock's 274 was a record for a South African batsman, and was also the highest Test score ever made in South Africa.

Third Test
19–24 February (Johannesburg)
South Africa
279
408 (E.J. Barlow 110; J.W. Gleeson 5–125)
Australia
202 (P.M. Pollock 5–39)
178
South Africa won by 307 runs

Fourth Test
5–10 March (Port Elizabeth)
South Africa
311 (A.N. Connolly 6–47)
470–8 declared (B.A. Richards 126, B.L. Irvine 102)
Australia
212
246 (M.J. Procter 6–73)
South Africa won by 323 runs
This was the last of South Africa's 172 Test matches. B.L. Irvine scored their last century. It was the first time South Africa had won all Tests in a rubber consisting of two or more matches. Richards became the first player to score 500 runs for South Africa in a Test rubber. Pollock pulled a hamstring after the first ball of his last over in Test cricket and could not complete it

South Africa's Averages, 1969–70

Batting

	Matches	Innings	Not outs	Runs	Highest Innings	Average
R.G. Pollock	4	7	0	517	274	73.85
B.A. Richards	4	7	0	508	140	72.57
E.J. Barlow	4	7	0	360	127	51.42
B.L. Irvine	4	7	0	353	102	50.42
M.J. Procter	4	7	1	209	48	34.83
A. Bacher	4	7	0	217	73	31.00
H.R. Lance	3	5	0	139	61	27.80
J.D. Lindsay	2	4	0	109	60	27.25
D. Gamsy	2	3	1	39	30*	19.50
P.M. Pollock	4	7	3	74	36*	18.50
T.L. Goddard	3	5	0	58	17	11.60
A.J. Traicos	3	4	2	8	5*	4.00

Also batted: G.A. Chevalier 0, 0*; M.A. Seymour 0, 0; P.H.J. Trimborn 0

Bowling

	Overs	Maidens	Runs	Wickets	Average
M.J. Procter	143	50	353	26	13.57
P.M. Pollock	115	39	258	15	17.20
G.A. Chevalier	42.1	11	100	5	20.00
T.L. Goddard	126.3	58	203	9	22.55
E.J. Barlow	94	27	257	11	23.36

Also bowled: H.R. Lance 30–10–77–1; R.G. Pollock 3–1–8–0; B.A. Richards 12–3–26–1; M.A. Seymour 30–8–68–2; A.J. Traicos 78.2–24–207–4; P.H.J. Trimborn 37.2–5–91–4

Graeme Pollock on his way to 274 against Australia in the Second Test, Durban, 1970

TEST AVERAGES

	Tests	Runs	Average	Wickets	Average
R.G. Pollock	23	2256	60.97	4	51.00
B.A. Richards	4	508	72.57	1	26.00
E.J. Barlow	30	2516	45.74	40	34.05
B.L. Irvine	4	353	50.42		
M.J. Procter	7	226	25.11	41	15.02
A. Bacher	12	679	32.33		
H.R. Lance	13	591	28.14	12	39.91
J.D. Lindsay	19	1130	37.66	57c 2st	
D. Gamsy	2	39	19.50		
P.M. Pollock	28	607	21.67	116	24.18
T.L. Goddard	41	2516	34.46	123	26.12
A.J. Traicos	3	8	4.00	4	51.75
G.A. Chevalier	1	0	0.00	5	20.00
M.A. Seymour	7	84	12.00	9	63.55
P.H.J. Trimborn	4	13	6.50	11	23.66

Nijinsky, Lester Piggott and Vincent O'Brien, 1969–70

The combination of Nijinsky, Lester Piggott and Vincent O'Brien – the best horse, jockey and trainer of recent times – proved outstanding in 1970 when Nijinsky became the first horse since Bahram in 1935 to win the Triple Crown of the 2000 Guineas, the Derby and the St Leger.

Lester Piggott, who holds the record for a jockey of twenty-nine classic wins, says that Nijinsky was the greatest horse he ever rode. Vincent O'Brien, the leading English trainer in 1966 and 1977 and with sixteen classic wins between 1953 and 1984, says that Nijinsky was the greatest horse he ever trained. The credentials of both jockey and trainer give authority to their assessment of the horse.

Nijinsky was born in 1967, bred in Ontario, by Northern Dancer out of Flaming Page. A bay, he stood at 16.3 hands when fully grown. He was bought by Mr Charles Engelhard on the advice of Vincent O'Brien for $84,000 and made his debut as a two-year-old in the Erne Maiden Stakes which he won at odds of 11 to 4 on. His jockey was Liam Ward who rode him to three more victories that season. His first win with Piggott was the Dewhurst Stakes in the same year.

In 1970, as a three-year-old, Nijinsky won the Gladness Stakes at the Curragh, again with Ward, and then with Piggott ran in his first classic, the 2000 Guineas. He became sweated up in the parade ring before the race, but nevertheless he won.

In the Derby Nijinsky beat the more fancied Gyr, the son of the great Sea Bird, despite suffering an attack of colic twenty-four hours before the race. After the Derby he went on to win the Irish Derby (with Ward riding), and then, with Piggott, produced a magnificent performance to beat Blakeney, the 1969 Derby winner, in the King George VI and Queen Elizabeth II Diamond Stakes.

In his third classic of the season, the St Leger, Nijinsky romped to the treble, winning by a length from Meadowville.

After eleven consecutive wins, five with Piggott as his rider, Nijinsky was beaten in his last two races. Experts later suggested that O'Brien perhaps ran the horse a little too often. The Prix de L'Arc de Triomphe was his eighth major outing of the season and Nijinsky was obviously jaded. Certainly O'Brien's later Derby winners ran far less frequently. After a second place in the Champion Stakes, Nijinsky was retired. He had won a then record £282,359 in prize money.

THE TEAM

Nijinsky

He was bred by Edgar P. Taylor in Ontario, Canada. His sire, Northern Dancer, had won the Kentucky Derby in record time. On his retirement Nijinsky was bought by a syndicate; there were thirty-two shares, at $170,000 each, which made his stud value at over $5.5 million. He stood at Clayborne Farm. His first crop of foals included Green Dancer, and he also sired Ile de Bourbon. He was voted Horse of the Year in 1970.

Nijinsky's Record

Two-Year-Old

Erne Maiden Stakes	Curragh	L. Ward	1st
Railway Stakes	Curragh	L. Ward	1st
Anglesey Stakes	Curragh	L. Ward	1st
Beresford Stakes	Curragh	L. Ward	1st
Dewhurst Stakes	Newmarket	L. Piggott	1st

Three-Year-Old

Gladness Stakes	Curragh	L. Ward	1st
2000 Guineas	Newmarket	L. Piggott	1st
Derby	Epsom	L. Piggott	1st
Irish Sweeps Derby	Leopardstown	L. Ward	1st
KGVI & QEII Diamond Stakes	Ascot	L. Piggott	1st
St Leger	Doncaster	L. Piggott	1st
Prix de L'Arc de Triomphe (2nd to Sassafras)	Longchamps	L. Piggott	2nd
Champion Stakes (2nd to Lorenzaccio)	Newmarket	L. Piggott	2nd

Lester Piggott

Born on 5 November 1935 in Berkshire, Lester Piggott was apprenticed to his father Keith and rode his first winner at the age of twelve. He became first jockey to Noel Murless in 1954 and for the next twelve years they had a string of classic successes. In 1966 he rode Vincent O'Brien's Valoris to victory in the Oaks, which led to a split between Piggott and Murless. In 1967 Piggott turned freelance. He has been champion jockey eleven times. On 15 September 1984 he won the St Leger, breaking the nineteenth-century record of Frank Buckle to become the first jockey to win twenty-eight classics. He retired at the end of the 1985 season to take up training.

Piggott's English Classic Victories

Derby	St Leger
1954 Never Say Die	1960 St Paddy
1957 Crepello	1961 Aurelius
1960 St Paddy	1967 Ribocco
1968 Sir Ivor	1968 Ribero
1970 Nijinsky	1970 Nijinsky
1972 Roberto	1971 Athens Wood
1976 Empery	1972 Boucher
1977 The Minstrel	1984 Commanche Run
1983 Teenoso	

	1000 Guineas
	1970 Humble Duty
Oaks	1981 Fairy Footsteps
1957 Carozza	
1959 Petite Etoile	2000 Guineas
1966 Valoris	1957 Crepello
1975 Juliette Marny	1968 Sir Ivor
1981 Blue Wind	1970 Nijinsky
1984 Circus Plume	1985 Shadeed

Nijinsky announces himself as the outstanding two-year-old of 1969 with this easy win in the Dewhurst Stakes at Newmarket

Vincent O'Brien

A renowned gambler, Vincent O'Brien was born in Churchtown, County Cork, on 9 April 1917. His father Dan was a small-time farmer who raced a few jumpers, and Vincent was one of eight children. He started training in 1944, mostly National Hunt. He was still an amateur jockey at that time. In 1951 he moved to Ballydoyle where he still trains. In the same year he married an Australian, Jacqueline Witternoom, who became a respected racehorse photographer. As well as his flat-racing successes, O'Brien won the Grand National on three occasions – with Early Mist, Quare Times and Royal Tan – the Champion Hurdle three times with Hatton's Grace, and the Cheltenham Gold Cup four times, including three successive years with Cottage Rake.

O'Brien's Major Flat-Race Winners

1953

Irish Sweeps Derby	Chamier

1957

St Leger	Ballymoss
Irish Sweeps Derby	Ballymoss

1958

Arc de Triomphe	Ballymoss
KGVI & QEII	Ballymoss

1959

Irish 2000 Guineas	El Toro
Irish St Leger	Barclay

1962

Derby	Larkspur

1964

Irish Oaks	Ancasta

1965

Oaks	Long Look
Irish Oaks	Aurabella

1966

Oaks	Valoris
1000 Guineas	Glad Rags
Irish 1000 Guineas	Valoris
Irish St Leger	White Gloves

1968

Derby	Sir Ivor
2000 Guineas	Sir Ivor
Washington Int'nal	Sir Ivor

1969

Irish Oaks	Gaia
Irish St Leger	Reindeer

1970

Derby	Nijinsky
St Leger	Nijinsky
2000 Guineas	Nijinsky
KGVI & QEII	Nijinsky
Irish Sweeps Derby	Nijinsky

1972

Derby	Roberto
St Leger	Boucher

1975

Irish St Leger	Caucasus

1976

Irish St Leger	Meneval

1977

Arc de Triomphe	Alleged
Derby	The Minstrel
KGVI & QEII	The Minstrel
Irish 1000 Guineas	Lady Capulet
Irish Sweeps Derby	The Minstrel
Irish St Leger	Transworld

1978

Arc de Triomphe	Alleged
Irish 2000 Guineas	Jaazeiro

1979

Irish 1000 Guineas	Godetia
Irish Oaks	Godetia

1980

Irish St Leger	Gonzales

1981

Irish 2000 Guineas	Kings Lake

1982

Derby	Golden Fleece

1983

2000 Guineas	Lomond
French Derby	Caerleon

1984

2000 Guineas	El Gran Señor

Brazil World Cup Team, 1970

For the third time in four tournaments Brazil won the World Cup in 1970 and retained the Jules Rimet trophy for all time. From an objective point of view the success of Brazil, with a team solely committed to attack and with a defence which was decidedly porous, was a splendid deed in a grey footballing world. Creative football, rather than the negative wingless 'catanaccio', was the order, rather than expectancy, during the next four years.

Their triumph was all the more remarkable because they arrived at Mexico City with a new manager, the skilled left winger in their 1958 and 1962 victories, Mario Zagalo. In March 1970, Joao Saldanha was sacked following his country's defeat by Argentina, and, silly man, for daring to drop Pele for the next game against Chile.

Once the finals had started the Guadalajara group pivoted on the match between Brazil and England, the holders. It was each team's second match. In a temperature of 98 degrees, the game was played at studious walking pace. Brazil clearly missed Gerson, their general, but it was only a remarkable save by Banks from a bouncing header from Pele that kept the scores level at half time. After fourteen minutes of the second half, Tostao held off three defenders, found Pele, who dummied for Jairzinho to score. Hurst and Lee missed chances, as did Ball and, finally and decisively, Astle.

Playing with Rivelino as the withdrawn left winger, Brazil had beaten Czechoslovakia in their opening game. They had arrived in Mexico with only three defeats in their last twenty-one games, but Zagalo needed to sort out his priorities. Petras gave the Czechs a thirteenth minute lead, but goals from Rivelino – a bending free kick – from Pele and two from Jairzinho, brought a memorable victory. The match, however, will be remembered for Pele's attempt to chip Viktor, the Czech keeper, from inside his own half, the ball narrowly missing the upright leaving Viktor stranded.

Pele's marvellous dummy fools Uruguayan keeper Mazurkwicz, but the ball ran tantalizingly past the post once Pele reclaimed possession

Jairzinho, who scored in every match

Virtually secure for the quarter finals, Brazil won only 3–2 against Rumania, for whom Dumitrache was a skilled centre forward. Pele and Jairzinho put Brazil 2–0 ahead, Rumania pulled a goal back, Pele added a third, and further defensive mistakes almost set up a Rumanian comeback.

In the quarter finals Brazil beat Peru in an error-ridden match in Guadalajara. Two goals down to Tostao and Rivelino, Peru's black striker Gallardo, formerly with AC Milan, kept Peru within range after Felix, Brazil's dreadful keeper, had made another error. Tostao restored the two-goal margin, Cubillas pulled another back, but a fine individual flourish from Jairzinho was decisive.

Uruguay were Brazil's opponents in the semi final, but the Italy–West Germany match took the pressure away from Pele's team. The European match was both a classic of excitement and a comedy of errors, with Rivera settling a seven-goal thriller well into extra time.

In Guadalajara against Uruguay, Felix was the benefactor supreme again when he misjudged a Sunday-morning-park shot from Cubilla. However, Brazil always managed to find not only a man for a crisis, but a new star too – Clodoaldo, who equalized just before half-time. Redemption for Felix came with a stunning save from Cubilla, but Brazil were well clear after Jairzinho's customary goal and Rivelino's last-minute effort.

The final was a much easier affair. Italians claimed exhaustion after their semi final, but their tactics, especially and surprisingly in defence, played into Brazil's hands. The Italians placed two players on Pele, but failed to stop Jairzinho from drifting in from the right wing and left Carlos Alberto, the captain and right back, to roam as an overlapping winger.

Pele connected with Rivelino's cross to put Brazil ahead after eighteen minutes. But the usual frailty in defence left Boninsegna with a clear path to goal and not until Gerson's left footer from 20 yards after sixty-six minutes were Brazil back in control. Pele then set up Jairzinho to score – he scored in every match in the finals – and Carlos Alberto smashed in the fourth three minutes from time.

Open, expressive attacking football had triumphed over sterility.

BRAZIL'S WORLD CUP RECORD, 1970

Group 11 Qualifying Matches

v. Colombia (a)	won 2–0 (Tostao 2)
v. Venezuela (a)	won 5–0 (Tostao 3, Pele 2)
v. Paraguay (a)	won 3–0 (Edu 2, Jairzinho)
v. Colombia (h)	won 6–2 (Jairzinho 2, Pele, Tostao, Edu, Rildo)
v. Venezuela (h)	won 6–0 (Tostao 3, Pele 2, Jairzinho)
v. Paraguay (h)	won 1–0 (Pele)

	P	W	D	L	F	A	Pts
Brazil	6	6	0	0	23	2	12
Paraguay	6	4	0	2	6	5	8
Colombia	6	1	1	4	7	12	3
Venezuela	6	0	1	5	1	18	1

Group Matches in Mexico

Group C (all Brazil's matches played in Guadalajara)

3 June v. Czechoslovakia	won 4–1 (Jairzinho 2, Rivelino, Pele)
7 June v. England	won 1–0 (Jairzinho)
10 June v. Rumania	won 3–2 (Pele 2, Jairzinho)

	P	W	D	L	F	A	Pts
Brazil	3	3	0	0	8	3	6
England	3	2	0	1	2	1	4
Rumania	3	1	0	2	4	5	2
Czech	3	0	0	3	2	7	0

Quarter Final

At Guadalajara
14 June v. Peru   won 4–2 (Tostao 2, Rivelino, Jairzinho)

Semi final

At Guadalajara
17 June v. Uruguay   won 3–1 (Clodoaldo, Jairzinho, Rivelino)

Final

At Mexico City
21 June v. Italy   won 4–1 (Pele, Gerson, Jairzinho, Carlos Alberto)

Team

Felix; Carlos Alberto, Brito, Piazza, Everaldo; Gerson, Clodoaldo; Jairzinho, Tostao, Pele, Rivelino.

PLAYERS IN THE FINAL STAGES

	Number of Matches	*Goals scored*
Brito	6	
Carlos Alberto	6	1
Clodoaldo	6	1
Edu	1 (as substitute)	
Everaldo	5	
Felix	6	
Fontana	1	
Gerson	4	1
Jairzinho	6	7
Marco Antonio	2 (1 as substitute)	
Paulo Cesar	4 (2 as substitute)	
Pele	6	4
Piazza	2	
Rivelino	5	3
Roberto	2 (both as substitute)	
Silva	4	
Tostao	6	2

The British Lions, 1971

The 1971 Lions may not quite have had an unblemished record, but they were pioneers – a team which went to New Zealand and returned three months later as the first British team to have won a series there. It was a tour that was brilliantly planned, brilliantly modified when the need arose and brilliantly executed. The credit was shared by a united party.

Much of what happened in New Zealand was the direct result of the forethought of the management, Doug Smith and Carwyn James. Throughout the British season they had closely watched all the likely candidates and had decided that the reserves would have to be particularly strong.

The management then chose as captain John Dawes who had just led the Welsh team to the Grand Slam in the international championship. The basis of success was built around the Welsh

team but the Lions were fortunate that talented individuals emerged from the other countries.

Although the Lions had structured their team around the Welsh Grand Slam unit, the emphasis and style were very similar to the most successful club side in the land – London Welsh. Dawes, who was never given the credit his talents deserved, perhaps because he didn't live in Wales at the time, was captain of London Welsh. A firm believer in open rugby and the counter-attack, he was himself quite the best passer of a ball in the modern era. Dawes's club colleagues included the back-row man, Mervyn Davies, the world's outstanding No. 8, and John Taylor, a devastating flanker especially on the attack. Gerald Davies, on the right wing, and J. P. R. Williams, at full back, were also quite simply the best in the world. The two

Forward domination was one of the key factors in the successful 1971 British Lions strategy. From the left, Gordon Brown, Ian McLauchlan, Derek Quinnell, Mervyn Davies and John Taylor shield No. 9 Gareth Edwards from all but Ian Kirkpatrick (far right) during the Third Test at Wellington

A typical Gareth Edwards charge sets up a try for Peter Dixon in the final Test at Auckland. Lions flanker John Taylor (second from right) backs up

locks, Mike Roberts, and the replacement, Geoff Evans, were vital members of the party, Roberts spending as much time as makeshift prop as he did in his normal position.

The other Welsh stars were the half backs, Gareth Edwards, whose duels with Sid Going were always of the highest quality, and his partner Barry John, who scored 191 points on tour, almost twice as many as the previous record in New Zealand by a tourist. Ireland provided the incomparable McBride and Gibson, England's major contributions to the cause came from Duckham, Dixon and Pullin, whilst McLauchlan and Brown upheld the finest Scottish traditions.

The role played by the midweek 'gin and tonic' side was a credit to the party. They consistently produced winning rugby which eased the pressures on the Saturday Test team. Bob Hiller, who scored over 100 points on the Lions tour in 1968, repeated the achievement in 1971 and yet didn't play in a Test on either tour. His midweek XV with starring roles from Biggar, Spencer, Rea, Lewis, Hopkins, Laidlaw and Slattery meant that there were two XVs in the party which acted as one.

Not even an early hiccup in Australia could disturb the Lions. In their opening game they were beaten 15–11 by Queensland before scraping home 14–12 against New South Wales. Smith blamed the travel problems and also queried refereeing interpretations which allowed Queensland (16–5) and New South Wales (19–5) to be awarded an almost ridiculous number of penalties. 'We will win the series in New Zealand 2-1 with one drawn,' said the manager.

A seven-try performance against the strong Waikato side was the first inkling the confident New Zealanders had that this team had to be respected. John Bevan's four tries out of the nine collected against Wellington the following weekend confirmed rumours. Otago were beaten by a Lions team for the first time since 1950, then David Duckham scored six tries against Buller.

After 'Wait till you get to Waikato' and 'Wait till you get to Wellington', it became 'Wait till you get to Canterbury'. The Ranfurly Shield holders were a tough bunch and an afternoon of general mayhem ensued. Canterbury were a disgrace; but they also found themselves against the first Lions team ready to trade back any nonsense thrown in their direction. Carmichael, McLoughlin and Hipwell were so badly injured that they never played again on tour. The management thanked their lucky stars that they withdrew Barry John on the eve of the match. The Lions left the field with most of them solemnly pointing to the scoreboard.

'Wait till you get to the Tests' was the next bleat. At Dunedin the Lions administered the first traumatic shock to New Zealand rugby. A charge-down by McLauchlan was prelude to the only try of the match. The All Blacks had been held, somehow, up front, the backs had defended heroically and John's kicking had done the rest.

The tour had almost gone too well and, not surprisingly, the honeymoon was over by the Second Test – hard work would have to be done. A fine All Black performance saw them notch five tries at Christchurch (although the penalty try was fortuitous). New Zealand, wounded, were all square, their convincing performance epitomized by a magnificent 50-yard try from Kirkpatrick. It was now that the 'gin and tonic' lads played their part. The four wins after the Second Test were a stabilizing influence as they headed for the third international at Wellington.

The Lions liked Wellington – they had scored 47 points there against Wellington and another 27 against the Universities. Dawes's shrewd decision to play with the wind paid dividends. After eighteen minutes they were 13 points up. Incisive tries from Gerald Davies and John, and a drop goal and two conversions from John, put the Lions out of sight. The All Blacks managed only a try from Mains, and the Lions were ahead 2–1.

The Fourth and final Test at Auckland was a triumph of team work and pursuit of a target. They even managed to provide Doug Smith with the score draw (14–14) for his forecast coupon. From 8–0 down the Lions pulled back to 8–8. At 11–11 J. P. R. Williams dropped a magnificent goal from 45 yards to make the score 14–11. The hoots of laughter from the 'gin and tonics' were not nervous giggles; in training the previous day Williams had essayed some drop goal attempts from half the distance – none of them had left the turf.

Mains's equalizing penalty only delayed the celebrations, which were not over even after Quantas flight no. 530 had landed at Heathrow at 9.20 p.m. on 16 August. It was the sort of tour in which Barry John could happily thumb a lift back to the training ground after being sent on a run because Carwyn James knew that he could rely on him in a crisis. Smith, the diplomat, had mixed discipline with tolerance.

Coaching, dedication, teamwork, enthusiasm and flair had won the day. The Lions had blown through New Zealand almost as strongly as Harold Macmillan's wind of change through the continent of Africa.

THE TOUR PARTY

Full Backs

R.B. Hiller (Harlequins and England), J.P.R. Williams (London Welsh and Wales)

Threequarters

D.J. Duckham (Coventry and England), A.G. Biggar (London Scottish and Scotland), T.G.R. Davies (London Welsh and Wales), J.C. Bevan (Cardiff College of Education and Wales), A.J. Lewis (Ebbw Vale and Wales), J.S. Spencer (Headingley and England), C.W.W. Rea (Headingley and Scotland), S.J. Dawes (London Welsh and Wales)

Half Backs

C.M.H. Gibson (NIFC and Ireland), B. John (Cardiff and Wales), G.O. Edwards (Cardiff and Wales), R. Hopkins (Maesteg and Wales)

Forwards

T.M. Davies (London Welsh and Wales), P.J. Dixon (Harlequins and England), J. Taylor (London Welsh and Wales), J.F. Slattery (University College, Dublin, and Ireland), M.L. Hipwell (Terenure College and Ireland), D.L. Quinnell (Llanelli), R.J. Arneil* (Leicester and Scotland), W.D. Thomas (Llanelli and Wales), W.J. McBride (Ballymena and Ireland), M.G. Roberts (London Welsh and Wales), G.L. Brown (West of Scotland and Scotland), T.G. Evans* (London Welsh and Wales), A.B. Carmichael (West of Scotland and Scotland), R.J. McLoughlin (Blackrock College and Ireland), J. McLauchlan (Jordanhill College and Scotland), J.F. Lynch (St Mary's College and Ireland), C.B. Stevens* (Penzance, Harlequins and England), J.V. Pullin (Bristol and England), F.A.L. Laidlaw (Melrose and Scotland)

* Replacement

Manager: Dr D.W.C. Smith
Assistant Manager: C.R. James

THE LIONS *v.* NEW ZEALAND, 1971

	First Test	*Second Test*	*Third Test*	*Fourth Test*
Williams	FB	FB	FB	FB (1DG)
T.G.R. Davies	RW	RW (2T)	RW (1T)	RW
Dawes	C	C	C	C
Gibson	C	C	C	C
Bevan	LW			
Duckham		LW	LW	LW
John	FH (2DG)	FH (1DG, 1PG)	FH (1T, 2C, 1PG)	FH (1C, 2PG)
Edwards	SH	SH	SH	SH
Hopkins	SH (substitute)			
Lynch	P	P	P	P
Pullin	H	H	H	H
McLauchlan	P (1T)	P	P	P
McBride	L	L	L	L
Thomas	L	L		
Brown			L	L
Taylor	F	F	F	F
T.M. Davies	No. 8	No. 8	No. 8	No. 8
Dixon	F	F		F (1T)
Quinnell			F	
Score:	9–3	12–22	13–3	14–14

TOUR RECORD

12 May (Brisbane)

Queensland	15 (2DG, 3PG)
British Isles	11 (1T, 1C, 2PG)

15 May (Sydney)

New South Wales	12 (4PG)
British Isles	14 (2T, 1C, 2PG)

22 May (Pukekohe)

Counties and Thames Valley	3 (1PG)
British Isles	25 (3T, 2C, 1DG, 3PG)

26 May (Wanganui)

King Country and Wanganui	9 (2T, 1PG)
British Isles	22 (3T, 2C, 3PG)

29 May (Waikato)

Waikato	14 (1T, 1C, 1DG, 2PG)
British Isles	35 (7T, 4C, 1DG, 1PG)

2 June (Auckland)

Maoris	12 (4PG)
British Isles	23 (1T, 1C, 6PG)

5 June (Wellington)

Wellington	9 (1DG)
British Isles	47 (9T, 7C, 2PG)

9 June (Timaru)

South and Mid Canterbury, North Otago	6 (2 PG)
British Isles	25 (5T, 2C, 2PG)

12 June (Dunedin)

Otago	9 (1T, 1DG, 1PG)
British Isles	21 (3T, 3C, 1DG, 1PG)

17 June (Greymouth)

West Coast, Bullar	6 (1T, 1PG)
British Isles	38 (8T, 6C, 1PG)

19 June (Christchurch)

Canterbury	3 (1PG)
British Isles	14 (2T, 1C, 2PG)

22 June (Blenheim)

Marlborough and Nelson Bays	12 (4T)
British Isles	31 (7T, 5C)

26 June (Dunedin)

New Zealand	3 (1 PG)
British Isles	9 (1T, 2PG)

30 June (Invercargill)

Southland	3 (1PG)
British Isles	25 (5T, 5C)

3 July (New Plymouth)

Taranaki	9 (2T, 1PG)
British Isles	14 (1T, 1C, 2DG, 1PG)

6 July (Wellington)

NZ Universities	6 (2T)
British Isles	27 (3T, 3C, 1DG, 3PG)

10 July (Christchurch)

New Zealand	22 (5T, 2C, 1PG)
British Isles	12 (2T, 1DG, 1PG)

14 July (Masterton)

Wairarapa Bush	6 (1T, 1PG)
British Isles	27 (7T, 3C)

17 July (Napier)

Hawkes Bay	6 (1DG, 1PG)
British Isles	25 (4T, 2C, 1DG, 2PG)

21 July (Gisborne)

Poverty Bay and East Coast	12 (1T, 3PG)
British Isles	18 (3T, 2DG, 1PG)

24 July (Auckland)

Auckland	12 (1DG, 3PG)
British Isles	19 (2T, 2C, 3PG)

31 July (Wellington)

New Zealand	3 (1T)
British Isles	13 (2T, 2C, 1DG)

4 August (Palmerston North)

Manawatu Horowhenua	6 (1DG, 1PG)
British Isles	39 (8T, 3C, 3PG)

7 August (Whangarei)

North Auckland	5 (1T, 1C)
British Isles	11 (3T, 1C)

10 August (Tauranga)

Bay of Plenty	14 (3T, 1C, 1PG)
British Isles	20 (2T, 1C, 1DG, 3PG)

14 August (Auckland)

New Zealand	14 (2T, 1C, 2PG)
British Isles	14 (1T, 1C, 1DG, 2PG)

Scorers

	Appearances	Tests	Tries	Conversions	Drop Goals	Penalty Goals	Points
B. John	17	4	7	31	8	26	191 (record)
R. Hiller	11		2	25	2	16	110
J.C. Bevan	14	1	18				54
D. Duckham	16	3	11				33
T.G.R. Davies	10	4	10				30
A.G. Biggar	10		9				27
C.M.H. Gibson	16	4	5	1	1	1	23
S.J. Dawes	19	4	5		1		18
J.P.R. Williams	15	4	2	2	1	1	16
J. Taylor	15	4	4				12
J.S. Spencer	10		4				12
T.M. Davies	13	4	3				9
G.O. Edwards	16	4	3				9
P.J. Dixon	15	3	2				6
C.W.W. Rea	9		2				6
A.J. Lewis	19		2				6
R. Hopkins	10	1	1				3
R.J. McLoughlin	6		1				3
A.B. Carmichael	6		1				3
J. McLauchlan	16	4	1				3
D.L. Quinnell	10	1	1				3
T.G. Evans	6		1				3
J.V. Pullin	16	4					
J.F. Lynch	15	4					
G.L. Brown	14	2					
W.J. McBride	15	4					
W.D. Thomas	15	3					
F.A.L. Laidlaw	11	3					
M.G. Roberts	11						
M.L. Hipwell	6						
J.F. Slattery	13						
C.B. Stevens	6						
R.J. Arneil	5						

Princess Anne and Doublet, 1971

In 1971 Arsenal won the 'Double', John Dawes led both Wales and the British Lions to record achievements, England regained the Ashes, and David Bedford was running to packed houses at the Crystal Palace. But, come the end of the year, three polls had elected a new heroine as their Sports Personality of the Year – H R H Princess Anne for her achievement in winning the European Championship on Doublet. Television viewers (BBC Sports Personality), newspaper readers (*Daily Express*), and the knowing press (Sports Writers) were unanimous in their decision.

Princess Anne had added another dimension to the family love for horses. The Queen Mother (a National Hunt owner with over three hundred winners), the Queen (a leading owner on the flat in 1956), Prince Philip (world carriage and pairs champion) and Prince Charles (polo) were steeped in equestrian activities.

Princess Anne, like Lucinda Green, came to the three-day-event via the Pony Club. One of her most successful partners in those days was a pony called High Jinks.

Princess Anne and Doublet soar over the water jump at Badminton

Princess Anne and Doublet during their dressage test, Hickstead, 1973

The partnership with Doublet encompassed just two years internationally. The pair competed at Badminton for the first time in 1971 and finished fifth. Later that year the European Championships were held at Burghley, the imposing and beautiful home of the former Olympic 400-metres hurdles champion, the Marquess of Exeter. Princess Anne and Doublet won the individual gold for Britain and were part of the team which won the gold. Observers were deeply impressed by a rider who had created time to achieve perfection, despite having to attend functions and being pursued by a hounding press.

Olympic selection for the Munich Games followed in 1972. Doublet, however, developed leg trouble which forced him to be withdrawn not only from Munich but from all competition during the remainder of the year. Back in training the following year with the Princess in the saddle, Doublet smashed a leg in Windsor Great Park and had to be destroyed.

Her next quality horse Goodwill almost compensated for that day of despair and disappointment. Goodwill provided the Princess with her best Badminton placing (fourth in 1974), they were runners-up to Lucinda Prior-Palmer in the European Championships in 1975, and were selected for the Montreal Games of 1976. At the Olympics the pair finished twenty-fourth after a crashing fall on the cross-country section.

The Montreal Games were to be the last major equestrian event for the Princess. Marriage (in 1973 to the Olympic gold medallist and 1971 team-mate Mark Phillips), a family and development of their home at Gatcombe Park took priority. Mark and Anne now organize a major event at Gatcombe Park which, in only a couple of years, has become an important venue on the equestrian calendar.

When Mary Peters won the BBC Sports Personality of the Year award in 1972 she thanked the previous household for 'looking after the trophy and keeping it clean'. Had Doublet been fit in 1972, the royal family might have kept the trophy on the mantlepiece for another year. At that time Princess Anne and Doublet were quite simply the best in the world.

THE TEAM

Doublet was a chestnut gelding by the Argentinian-born thoroughbred Doubtless II. He was bred by Her Majesty the Queen in 1963, originally as a polo pony, but grew too big, eventually standing at 16.2 hands. Princess Anne started riding Doublet for the Queen in 1969. Their first success together was at the Windsor Horse Trials that year. The following year Princess Anne was given Doublet as a Christmas present.

THEIR RECORD

Princess Anne's Medals

European Championships, 1971
Individual Gold (on Doublet)
Team Gold (on Doublet)
European Championships, 1975
Individual Silver (on Goodwill)

European Championships, 1971

Individual

1	H R H Princess Anne (GB) Doublet
2	Deborah West (GB) Baccarat
3	Stewart Stevens (GB) Classic Chips

Team

1	Great Britain
2	USSR
3	Ireland

Liverpool Football Club, 1973–84

It has been said time and time again that the Football League is the strongest league in the world. More recently there may be better claims from the Bundesliga and, most certainly, the Italian League, but, day in, day out, with its crippling forty-two fixtures to a season, plus two major cup competitions, the sustained pressures on players and the resources of the successful clubs mean that only the very best survive. Then, of course, success means Europe.

Liverpool on the field of play have been the epitome of all that is good in British football. Their success has been unequalled and their club has been built on solid basic principles. Moreover, they have continued their traditions and standards of excellence in a city whose recent social and economic problems are well chronicled.

Liverpool have won the Football League championship on a record fifteen occasions. Between 1973 and 1985 they have only once finished outside the first two in the championship – in 1980–81, when even their fifth place was augmented by wins in the European Cup and Milk Cup. In October 1984, when they were having to make adjustments to a team ravaged by injuries and transfers they had slipped to eighteenth in the League. Amidst cries of 'Liverpool have gone', they climbed to the runners-up position behind Everton, the club a mile away on the other side of Stanley Park. Quietly, they reached the European Cup final.

Domestic honours have been allied to success in Europe. In many ways the record of Liverpool is as formidable as that of Real Madrid and their unparalleled domination of the European Cup in its early years. Real won the Cup in its first five years, from 1956 to 1960, and again in 1966. It took nineteen long years for them to annexe their next trophy. Between 1973 and 1985 Liverpool won the European Cup on four occasions and reached the final in 1985. But during the same period they were also successful in winning the UEFA Cup, a competition laced with fine teams, in both 1973 and 1976. These further successes indicated an extra resilience and an ability to master continental teams, who use different tactics, in unfamiliar surroundings, and supported by distinctly inhospitable audiences.

When the run of successes encompasses such a period of time, no Liverpool team stands out. Disagreements and pub talk abound. People have their own views, their own favourites, their own remedies. The success of Liverpool FC is as much the success of the management as the players. The theme has always been that of simplicity and continuity.

In this respect Liverpool have had three marvellous managers. Totally different in character, their aims have been

Tommy Smith (turning away, bottom right) *fires his header past Kneib in the Borussia goal. It was Liverpool's second goal in their 3–1 triumph in the 1977 European Cup final*

broadly to follow the same philosophy. They have had to nurture hundreds of players under their command, established internationals, loyal club men, eccentrics and even failures. Bill Shankly, Bob Paisley and Joe Fagan have been the three managers who have guided the fortunes of Liverpool FC. Under their influence, no club in the world has maintained such a level of excellence and consistency. It seems a difficult act for Kenny Dalglish to follow.

MANAGERS

Bill Shankly

Shankly enjoyed a seventeen-year playing career that started at Carlisle before Preston bought him for £500 in 1933. Altogether he played 312 League games and scored 13 goals. He won an FA Cup winners' medal in 1938, having gained a runners-up medal the previous year. He played for Scotland five times. He finished playing in 1949, and on 22 March that year returned to Carlisle as manager. There, Shankly had an undistinguished managerial career, and subsequently at Grimsby, Workington and Huddersfield. It was while in charge at the latter club, he spotted the talents of a straggly, bespectacled youngster – Denis Law. Shankly moved to Liverpool in December, 1959, officially taking over on 14 December. The club's first game with 'Shanks' in charge was a 4–0 home defeat by Cardiff City. Shankly had no say in the selection of the team that day but he did for the away game with Charlton on Boxing Day – Charlton won 3–0.

Liverpool stories about the sayings of Shankly are legendary – so much so that he probably wasn't responsible for most of them. He did, however, say to Tommy Docherty, when handing over the No. 4 shirt to him at Preston, 'No need to worry about anything, Tom. It'll run round the park on its own.' He stirred local rivalry when agreeing that there were two great teams in Liverpool – 'Aye, Liverpool and Liverpool Reserves.' But he always denied that, on his wedding anniversary, he took his wife to watch Rochdale Reserves, claiming that he would never have got married in the football season in the first place.

Shankly's First Team

19 December 1959 v. Cardiff City (h) lost 0–4, attendance 27,291
Team: Slater, Molyneux, Moran, Wheller, White, Campbell, Morris, Hunt, Hickson, Melia, A'Court

Shankly's Last Team

4 May 1974 v. Newcastle United (Wembley Stadium – FA Cup Final) won 3–0, attendance 100,000
Team: Clemence, Smith, Thompson, Hughes, Lindsay, Hall, Callaghan, Cormack, Keegan, Toshack, Heighway

Shankly's Record

League

Season	P	W	D	L	F	A	Pts	Pos.	Div.
1959–60	21	11	5	5	46	30	27	3rd	2
1960–61	42	21	10	11	87	58	52	3rd	2
1961–62	42	27	8	7	99	43	62	Champs	2
1962–63	42	17	10	15	71	59	44	8th	1
1963–64	42	26	5	11	92	45	57	Champs	1
1964–65	42	17	10	15	67	73	44	7th	1
1965–66	42	26	9	7	79	34	61	Champs	1
1966–67	42	19	13	10	64	47	51	5th	1
1967–68	42	22	11	9	71	40	55	3rd	1
1968–69	42	25	11	6	63	24	61	2nd	1
1969–70	42	20	11	11	65	42	51	5th	1
1970–71	42	17	17	8	42	24	51	5th	1
1971–72	42	24	9	9	64	30	57	3rd	1
1972–73	42	25	10	7	72	42	60	Champs	1
1973–74	42	22	13	7	52	31	57	2nd	1

Other Honours

1964–65	FA Cup (winners)
	Charity Shield (joint winners)
1965–66	European Cup Winners' Cup (runners-up)
	Charity Shield (joint winners)
1966–67	Charity Shield (winners)
1968–69	Central League (champions)
1969–70	Central League (champions)
1970–71	FA Cup (runners-up)
	Central League (champions)
1972–73	UEFA Cup (winners)
	Central League (champions)
	Manager of the Year
1973–74	FA Cup (winners)
	Central League (champions)

Bob Paisley

Paisley served Liverpool for over forty years. He first joined them during the war after winning an FA Amateur Cup winners' medal with Bishop Auckland in 1939. He made his Liverpool debut in 1946, the same day as Billy Liddell, and was a member of their championship winning team in 1946–47. He succeeded Shankly as Liverpool manager in 1974 and his record in British football as a manager is unparalleled.

Paisley's First Team

10 August 1974 v. Leeds United (Wembley Stadium – Charity Shield) won on penalties after 1–1, attendance 67,000
Team: Clemence, Smith, Lindsay, Thompson, Cormack, Hughes, Keegan, Hall, Heighway, Boersma, Callaghan

Paisley's Last Team

14 May 1983 v. Watford (a) lost 1–2, attendance 27,148
Team: Grobbelaar, Neal, Kennedy, Lawrenson, Thompson, Hansen, Dalglish, Lee, Hodgson, Johnston, Souness (substitute: Nicol)

Paisley's Record

League

Season	P	W	D	L	F	A	Pts	Pos.	Div.
1974–75	42	20	11	11	60	39	51	2nd	1
1975–76	42	23	14	5	66	31	60	Champs	1
1976–77	42	23	11	8	62	33	57	Champs	1
1977–78	42	24	9	9	65	34	57	2nd	1
1978–79	42	30	8	4	85	16	68	Champs	1
1979–80	42	25	10	7	81	30	60	Champs	1
1980–81	42	17	17	8	62	46	51	5th	1
1981–82	42	26	9	7	80	32	87	Champs	1
1982–83	42	24	10	8	87	37	82	Champs	1

Other Honours

1974–75	Charity Shield (winners)
	Central League (champions)
1975–76	UEFA Cup (winners)
	Central League (champions)
	Manager of the Year

1976–77	FA Cup (runners-up)
	European Cup (winners)
	European Super Cup (winners)
	Charity Shield (winners)
	Central League (champions)
	Manager of the Year
1977–78	Football League Cup (runners-up)
	European Cup (winners)
	Charity Shield (joint winners)
1978–79	Central League (champions)
	Manager of the Year
1979–80	Charity Shield (winners)
	Central League (champions)
	Manager of the Year
1980–81	Football League Cup (winners)
	European Cup (winners)
	Charity Shield (winners)
	Central League (champions)
1981–82	Football League Cup (winners)
	Central League (champions)
	Manager of the Year
1982–83	Milk Cup (winners)
	Charity Shield (winners)
	Manager of the Year

Joe Fagan

A centre half in his playing days, Joe, although born in Liverpool, started his playing career with Manchester City before the war. He stayed at Maine Road until 1953 and was their captain for a period in the postwar years. After leaving City he went to Bradford Park Avenue but played only three games for them. Fagan's first managerial post was with the non-League Lancashire side Nelson, but he was tempted to

Anfield as assistant trainer in 1958. He subsequently became first-team trainer, assistant manager to Bob Paisley, and then manager in 1983. Resigned in May 1985.

Fagan's First Team

20 August 1983 *v.* Manchester United (Wembley Stadium – Charity Shield) lost 0–2, attendance 92,000
Team: Grobbelaar, Neal, Kennedy, Lawrenson, Thompson, Hansen, Dalglish, Lee, Rush, Robinson, Souness (substitutes: Johnston, Hodgson)

Fagan's Last Team

29 May 1985 *v.* Juventus (Brussels – European Cup final) lost 0–1, attendance 60,000
Team: Grobbelaar, Neal, Lawrenson, Hansen, Beglin, Nicol, Dalglish, Wark, Whelan, Walsh, Rush (substitutes: Gillespie, Johnston)

Fagan's Record

League

Season	P	W	D	L	F	A	Pts	Pos.	Div.
1983–84	42	22	14	6	73	32	80	Champs	1
1984–85	42	22	11	9	68	35	77	2nd	1

Other Honours

1983–84	Milk Cup (winners)
	European Cup (winners)
	Central League (champions)
1984–85	European Cup (runners-up)
	Central League (champions)

Kenny Dalglish's delicate chip beats Bruges' keeper Birger Jensen for the only goal of the 1978 European Cup final

1976–77

Round 1

1st leg *v.* Crusaders (h)	won 2–0	Neal (pen.), Toshack
2nd leg *v.* Crusaders (a)	won 5–0	Johnson (2), Keegan, McDermott, Heighway

Round 2

1st leg *v.* Trabzonspor (a)	lost 0–1	
2nd leg *v.* Trabzonspor (h)	won 3–0	Heighway, Johnson, Keegan

Quarter final

1st leg *v.* St Etienne (a)	lost 0–1	
2nd leg *v.* St Etienne (h)	won 3–1	Keegan, Kennedy, Fairclough

Semi final

1st leg *v.* FC Zürich (a)	won 3–1	Neal (2, 1 pen.), Heighway
2nd leg *v.* FC Zürich (h)	won 3–0	Case (2), Keegan

Final

v. B. Mönchengladbach (Rome)	won 3–1	McDermott, Smith, Neal (pen.)

1977–78

Round 2

1st leg v. Dynamo Dresden (h)	won 5–1	Case (2), Hansen, Neal (pen.), Kennedy
2nd leg *v.* Dynamo Dresden (a)	lost 1–2	Heighway

Quarter final

1st leg *v.* Benfica (a)	won 2–1	Case, Hughes
2nd leg *v.* Benfica (h)	won 4–1	Callaghan, Dalglish, McDermott, Neal

Semi final

1st leg *v.* B. Mönchengladbach (a)	lost 1–2	Johnson
2nd leg *v.* B. Mönchengladbach (h)	won 3–0	Kennedy, Dalglish, Case

Final

v. FC Bruges (Wembley)	won 1–0	Dalglish

1980–81

Round 1

1st leg *v.* OPS Oulu (a)	drew 1–1	McDermott
2nd leg *v.* OPS Oulu (h)	won 10–0	Souness (3, 1 pen.), Fairclough (2), McDermott (3), Lee, R. Kennedy

Round 2

1st leg *v.* Aberdeen (a)	won 1–0	McDermott
2nd leg *v.* Aberdeen (h)	won 4–0	Miller (o.g.), Neal, Dalglish, Hansen

Quarter final

1st leg *v.* CSKA Sofia (h)	won 5–1	Souness (3), Lee, McDermott
2nd leg *v.* CSKA Sofia (a)	won 1–0	Johnson

Semi final

1st leg *v.* Bayern Munich (h)	drew 0–0	
2nd leg *v.* Bayern Munich (a)	drew 1–1	R. Kennedy
(won on away-goals rule)		

Final

v. Real Madrid (Paris)	won 1–0	A. Kennedy

1983–84

Round 1

1st leg *v.* Odense BK (a)	won 1–0	Dalglish
2nd leg *v.* Odense BK (h)	won 5–0	Robinson (2), Dalglish (2), Clausen (o.g.)

Round 2

1st leg *v.* Athletic Bilbao (h)	drew 0–0	
2nd leg *v.* Athletic Bilbao (a)	won 1–0	Rush

Quarter final

1st leg *v.* Benfica (h)	won 1–0	Rush
2nd leg *v.* Benfica (a)	won 4–1	Whelan (2), Johnston, Rush

Semi final

1st leg *v.* Dynamo Bucharest (h)	won 1–0	Lee
2nd leg *v.* Dynamo Bucharest (a)	won 2–1	Rush (2)

Final

v. AS Roma (Rome)	drew 1–1	Neal
(won 4–2 on penalties)		

Liverpool retain the European Cup, 1978

Red Rum, Don McCain and Noel Le Mare, 1973–77

'The greatest horse of Aintree' was how BBC commentator Peter Bromley described Red Rum after his third win in the Grand National in 1977. Red Rum had previously won the race in 1973 and 1974, and finished as runner-up in 1975 and 1976. He cleared a total of 150 fences, among them some of the most feared in the world, without a mistake.

The partnership of horse, trainer and owner was unique, the story of how they came together unconventional. Red Rum was born in 1965, bred by Martin McEnery by Quorum out of Mared. The bay gelding's first owner was Mrs Lurline Brotherton, who had also owned the 1950 Grand National winner Freebooter. Red Rum was trained by Bobby Renton at Ripon and was Renton's last winner before the trainer died in the mid-seventies. It was in August 1972 when Red Rum was bought at the Doncaster Sales by Don McCain. His price was 6000 guineas and his new owner was Noel Le Mare.

Up to that point Red Rum's career had not been very distinguished. He had won three flat races, three hurdles and five chases. Lester Piggott had ridden him on the flat.

His new trainer, Don McCain, had been a National Hunt jockey. He had started racing in 1952 but had little success; his height was a disadvantage. In 1969 he took out a trainer's licence, but for the most part could only attract broken-down horses to his yard at Southport. To supplement his income, he used to drive a taxi. This he developed into a successful business, and he subsequently started a second-hand-car business also. He now has a British Leyland dealership at Upper Aughton Road, Southport. His compact stable yard is at the rear of the showrooms.

It was in his days as a taxi driver that he met Noel Le Mare, by now a local industrialist. Brought up in poverty in Liverpool, Le Mare used to sell newspapers on street corners. He eventually became a millionaire as chairman of the Norwest-Holst construction empire based on Merseyside. He was a regular customer of Don McCain, taxi driver, and as both men loved horses they were naturally a frequent topic of conversation on their journeys together. Le Mare revealed to McCain that he had always had three ambitions in life: to be a millionaire; to marry a beautiful woman; and to own the winner of the Grand National. The first two he had achieved, and in 1972 he asked McCain to help him achieve the third.

The change to the sea air of Southport turned Red Rum into a new horse. He loved training on the sands at Birkdale and enjoyed the sea as well. With McCain, Red Rum won sixteen chases including his three Grand Nationals. One of his best performances was in the 1973 Hennessy Gold Cup when he finished second to Red Candle despite conceding 14 lb.

Red Rum was all set to compete in his sixth Grand National in 1978 but bruised a heel shortly before the race. The week leading up to the race was filled with 'will he', 'won't he' speculation. In the end he was withdrawn at about 7 p.m. on the eve of the race. He was immediately retired.

After his retirement he remained a celebrity and is still in big demand to attend functions. He even switched on the Blackpool illuminations one year. He has been turned into a limited company – the first horse to have done so. His manure sold for a small fortune and a limited edition of a miniature statuette of him sold out within hours of going on sale. Sadly, his home town of Southport has shunned the great horse. A statue, but only in miniature form, was erected after much wrangling in local council.

Ivor Herbert, who wrote the definitive book on Red Rum, says, 'Bred wrong, sold cheap, handled by five trainers, ridden by over two dozen jockeys, moved from Ireland to Leicestershire to Yorkshire to Lancashire, racing from a two-year-old into his 11th season and over 100 races – most of them hard ones, Red Rum has achieved his triumphs against all the odds, without advantages, and very often, in spite of people.

'Red Rum is like the man who makes it from rags: he is a survivor.'

RED RUM, DON McCAIN AND NOEL LE MARE'S GRAND NATIONALS

1973

		Weight
1	Red Rum	10–5
2	Crisp	12–0
3	L'Escargot	12–0

Red Rum won by half a length and 25 lengths. Brian Fletcher was aboard, and the horse started as 9–1 joint favourite. Crisp 'died' in the final 50 yards, but both horses beat Reynoldstown's thirty-eight-year-old record for the race by over 18 seconds. Rummie's record was 9 minutes 1.90 seconds.

1974

		Weight
1	Red Rum	12–0
2	L'Escargot	11–13
3	Charles Dickens	10–0

Fletcher was on Red Rum again; this time they started at 11–1 and won by 7 lengths and a short head. It was the first double victory since Reynoldstown. Red Rum won the Scottish Grand National the same year, the first horse to win both races in the same year. A statue was erected at Ayr racecourse to commemorate the event.

Billy Ellison, Red Rum's stable lad, takes the Grand National winner for a training run on Southport Sands

1975

		Weight
1	L'Escargot	11–3
2	Red Rum	12–0
3	Spanish Steps	10–3

Fletcher yet again in the saddle.

1976

		Weight
1	Rag Trade	10–12
2	Red Rum	11–10
3	Eyecatcher	10–7

Tommy Stack rode him in the National for the first time, after a stable dispute with Fletcher.

1977

		Weight
1	Red Rum	11–8
2	Churchtown Boy	10–0
3	Eyecatcher	10–1

With Stack aboard again, Red Rum won at 9–1, by 25 lengths and 6 lengths, thus becoming the first horse to win the race three times. He was thirteen at the time.

The British Lions, 1974

The triumphant tour of South Africa by Willie John McBride and his 1974 Lions is already part of history. It was a tour, like so many others, which had its roots in apprehension when the team left. There had been a ragged domestic season, three of the finest backs of the modern era – Gibson, Duckham and Gerald Davies – were not available for business reasons, and the moral question of whether the Lions should leave their own shores was being aired at the highest level.

The Lions flew to Africa hoping to return with some shred of honour. The 1971 party had been the first to win a series in New Zealand but several of that memorable combination had now stepped aside. McBride was leading his men on an unpromising mission. The Springboks had not lost to the Lions since the pioneer team of the previous century. They also had the advantage, and a considerable one, of playing at home where, because of climate and altitude, conditions are unique; another factor was that the South Africans, starved of international sport through their misguided politicians, were an anxious nation, desperate to succeed.

Yet it soon became clear that either the Springboks had gone soft or, more likely, were made to look soft. Records tumbled – the Lions scored the most points (729), most tries (107) and most Test points (79) ever in South Africa. The 28–9 rout in the second international was the heaviest defeat ever suffered by South Africa.

Individuals had their moments. Andy Irvine's 156 points were a new record there, as were J. J. Williams's four Test tries. Alan Old's 37 points against South West Districts was another. The damage inflicted at Mossel Bay against the South West Districts could have filled a pamphlet – 97–0 with sixteen tries, six by J. J. Williams. And the contribution of the Scotland lock, Gordon Brown, with eight tries was the most by a touring forward in South Africa.

But the real memories were of a great captain, Willie John McBride; of a team spirit, welded from four widely differing countries, that brooked no thought of failure; of an outstanding pack of forwards; and of many fine performers behind the scrum, with the four Welshmen – Edwards, Bennett and the two Williamses – much to the fore. The Springboks graciously conceded that Edwards and McLauchlan were the best, in their positions, to have visited their country.

The Springbok choices for the Test matches indicated alarm and concern in the country on the state of their national sport. The selectors then disintegrated into outright panic. Mind you, it is easy to offer remedies when one side is vastly superior; solutions take a little longer. For the First Test the Springboks correctly chose seven of the Western Province team which had performed so capably a week earlier against the Lions. The Test pitch was a quagmire, there was never a hope of a try but the Lions won the match up front, and presented Bennett with the

Lions left winger J.J. Williams delights the local population with the first try in the 26–9 rout of South Africa in the Third Test at Port Elizabeth

opportunity to kick three penalties and Edwards to seal the match with a fine drop goal.

For the Second Test in Pretoria the Springboks made eight changes – too many for a side that had been also bogged down in the Cape Town mud through no fault of their own. The result was a disaster, the Lions running in five tries in what was South Africa's heaviest defeat ever. J. J. Williams scored two tries, Bennett a brilliant 50-yard effort, and Slattery was outstanding in a marvellous front eight. If Bennett, who had five stitches inserted in a cut ankle after scoring his try, had been in kicking form the score could have reached 40 points.

The Springbok selectors revealed further uncertainties by making eleven changes for the third and decisive Test at Port Elizabeth. The Lions made one, covering the problem of Bennett's bad ankle by bringing in another kicker, Irvine. Bennett took to the less painful experience of dropping two goals, J. J. Williams helped himself to another two tries, and the Springboks, only 3–0 down at half time, trudged off to the changing rooms glancing back at the sight of McBride being chaired around the ground. It was South Africa's second worst defeat.

Taking the game as a whole, a draw was a fair result to the final Test at Ellis Park, Johannesburg. The Springboks were less changed than before but they had reached the bottom of the barrel. They gave their best performance of the series; the Lions forwards, jaded by now, were well held. With the score at 13–13 and the Lions searching desperately to maintain a 100 per cent record, the vast majority of those present thought that Slattery had scored in the closing minutes but the referee, unsighted and blameless, awarded otherwise. The Lions were prevented from making it an all-conquering tour but they were unbeaten, and there were doubts about a try awarded to Uttley earlier in the game.

As befits a man of McBride's character, the Lions trained hard. They played hard too. On one of their few days off – a week in the Kruger Park – they arrived in two planes. One was full of personnel, the other plane carried refreshments. Twenty-four hours later the 'drinks' plane was dispatched back to Johannesburg to refill.

McBride epitomized the qualities needed to succeed on a tour – strength, fortitude and endurance. Yet all were heroes, in a greater or lesser degree, in such a collective effort. British rugby will long savour the deeds of McBride and his men. Whether their successors digested and learned from their exploits, however, is, in the succeeding years, rather doubtful. And that is a shame.

THE TOUR PARTY

Full Backs
A.R. Irvine (Heriot's FP and Scotland), J.P.R. Williams (London Welsh and Wales)

Threequarters
T.O. Grace (St Mary's College, Dublin, and Ireland), C.F.W. Rees (London Welsh and Wales), W.C.C. Steele (Bedford, RAF and Scotland), J.J. Williams (Llanelli and Wales), A.J. Morley* (Bristol and England), R.T.E. Bergiers (Llanelli and Wales), G.W. Evans (Coventry and England), I.R. McGeechan (Headingley and Scotland), R.A. Milliken (Bangor and Ireland)

Half Backs
P. Bennett (Llanelli and Wales), A.G.B. Old (Leicester and England), C.M.H. Gibson* (NIFC and Ireland), G.O. Edwards (Cardiff and Wales), J.J. Moloney (St Mary's College, Dublin, and Ireland)

Forwards
T.M. Davies (Swansea and Wales), A.G. Ripley (Rosslyn Park and England), T.P. David (Llanelli and Wales), S.A. McKinney (Dungannon and Ireland), A. Neary (Broughton Park), J.F. Slattery (Blackrock College and Ireland), G.L. Brown (West of Scotland and Scotland), W.J. McBride (Ballymena and Ireland), C.W. Ralston (Richmond and England), R.M. Uttley (Gosforth and England), M.A. Burton (Gloucester and England), A.B. Carmichael (West of Scotland and Scotland), F.C. Cotton (Coventry and England), J. McLauchlan (Jordanhill and Scotland), K.W. Kennedy (London Irish and Ireland), R.W. Windsor (Pontypool and Wales)

Manager: A.G. Thomas

Assistant Manager: S. Millar

* Replacement

THE LIONS *v.* SOUTH AFRICA, 1974

	First Test	Second Test	Third Test	Fourth Test
J.P.R. Williams	FB	FB	FB	FB
Steele	RW			
McGeechan	C	C (1DG)	C	C
Milliken	C	C (1T)	C	C
J.J. Williams	LW	LW (2T)	LW (2T)	LW
Bennett	FH (3PG)	FH (1T, 1C, 1PG)	FH (2DG)	FH (1C)
Edwards	SH (1DG)	SH	SH	SH
Cotton	P	P	P	P
Windsor	H	H	H	H
McLauchlan	P	P	P	P
McBride	L	L	L	L
Brown	L	L (1T)	L (1T)	
Uttley	F	F	F	F (1T)
Davies	No. 8	No. 8	No. 8	No. 8
Slattery	F	F	F	F
Irvine			RW (1C, 2PG)	RW (1T, 1PG)
Score:	12–3	28–9	26–9	13–13

15 May (Potchefstroom)

| Western Transvaal | 13 (2T, 1C, 1PG) |
| British Isles | 59 (9T, 7C, 3PG) |

18 May (Windhoek)

| South West Africa | 16 (2T, 1C, 2PG) |
| British Isles | 23 (3T, 1C, 3PG) |

22 May (Wellington)

| Boland | 6 (2PG) |
| British Isles | 33 (5T, 2C, 3PG) |

25 May (Port Elizabeth)

| Eastern Province | 14 (3T, 1C) |
| British Isles | 28 (3T, 2C, 4PG) |

29 May (Mossel Bay)

| South Western Districts | 0 |
| British Isles | 97 (16T, 15C, 1PG) |

1 June (Cape Town)

| Western Province | 8 (2T) |
| British Isles | 17 (2T, 3PG) |

4 June (Cape Town – Goodwood)

| Proteas | 6 (1PG, 1DG) |
| British Isles | 37 (5T, 1C, 5PG) |

8 June (Cape Town)

| South Africa | 3 (1DG) |
| British Isles | 12 (3PG), 1DG |

11 June (Cape Town)

| Southern Universities | 4 (1T) |
| British Isles | 26 (4T, 2C, 2PG) |

15 June (Johannesburg)

| Transvaal | 15 (3PG, 2DG) |
| British Isles | 23 (3T, 1C, 3PG) |

18 June (Salisbury)

| Rhodesia | 6 (2PG) |
| British Isles | 42 (6T, 3C, 3PG, 1DG) |

22 June (Pretoria)

| South Africa | 9 (2PG, 1DG) |
| British Isles | 28 (5T, 1C, 1PG, 1DG) |

27 June (Johannesburg)

| Quaggas | 16 (1T, 4PG) |
| British Isles | 20 (3T, 1C, 2PG) |

29 June (Bloemfontein)

| Orange Free State | 9 (2PG, 1DG) |
| British Isles | 11 (2T, 1PG) |

3 July (Kimberley)

| Griqualand West | 16 (2T, 1C, 2PG) |
| British Isles | 69 (12T, 9C, 1PG) |

6 July (Pretoria)

| Northern Transvaal | 12 (4PG) |
| British Isles | 16 (2T, 1C, 2PG) |

9 July (East London)

| Leopards | 10 (1T, 2PG) |
| British Isles | 56 (10T, 5C, 2PG) |

13 July (Port Elizabeth)

| South Africa | 9 (3PG) |
| British Isles | 26 (3T, 1C, 2PG, 2DG) |

17 July (East London)

| Border | 6 (2PG) |
| British Isles | 26 (3T, 1C, 4PG) |

20 July (Durban)

| Natal | 6 (2PG) |
| British Isles | 34 (4T, 3C, 4PG) |

23 July (Springs)

| Eastern Transvaal | 10 (1T, 2PG) |
| British Isles | 33 (5T, 2C, 3PG) |

27 July (Johannesburg)

| South Africa | 13 (1T, 3PG) |
| British Isles | 13 (2T, 1C, 1PG) |

Scorers

	Games*	Tries	Conversions	Penalty Goals	Drop Goals	Points
Irvine	15	5	26	27	1	156
Bennett	11	1	15	21	2	103
Old	4	1	17	7		59
Grace	11	13				52
J.J. Williams	12	12				48
Brown	12	8				32
Edwards	15	7			1	31
Steele	9	7				28
Milliken	13	6				24
Slattery	12	6				24
Davies	12	5				20
Ripley	9	5				20
David	9	5				20
Evans	8	4				16
J.P.R. Williams	15	3				12
Rees	6	3				12
Moloney	8	3				12
Gibson	7	2	1			10
Bergiers	10	2				8
Uttley	16	2				8
Neary	8	2				8
Kennedy	10	2				8
McGeechan	14	1			1	7
Morley	2	1				4
McBride	13	1				4
McKinney	8			1		3

* includes appearances as replacements

The following played but did not score any points: Ralston (13), Burton (8), Cotton (14), McLauchlan (13), Carmichael (10) and Windsor (12).

United States 4 x 100-Metres Medley Relay Team, 1976

The world record for the medley relay which had been set at the Munich Olympics in 1972 had not been broken by the time the Games were held again, in Montreal in 1976. Inspired by Mark Spitz the Americans had clocked a time of 3 minutes 48.16 seconds in 1972.

In the heats of the Montreal Olympics the Americans fielded a team which consisted of Peter Rocca, Chris Woo, Joe Bottom and Jack Babashoff. They broke the world record with a time of 3 minutes 47.28 seconds.

For the final, the Americans changed the entire team. In came John Naber, John Hencken, Matt Vogel and Jim Montgomery. They won the gold medal in a time of 3 minutes 42.22 seconds – a new world record. Canada were second in 3.45.94 and West Germany third in 3.47.29. There were no excuses to be made about withdrawals either; the black African nations and Taiwan are not at the forefront of international swimming. The domination of the Americans was total It is the only country where a reserve squad can break a world record, then be stood down for a better team.

THE TEAMS

The Heats

Peter Rocca

He took the Olympic silver medal in both the 100- and 200-metres backstroke behind Naber in 1976. His time for the 100 metres was four hundredths of a second outside the previous world record, and his 200-metres time bettered the previous world record, but his performances were eclipsed by Naber.

Chris Woo

He was eighth and last in the final of the 100-metres breaststroke in 1976.

Joe Bottom

He was sixth in the 100-metres freestyle in 1976. In the medley relay he swam the butterfly leg, having won the silver medal in the individual butterfly event.

Jack Babashoff

He won the silver medal in the 100-metres freestyle in 1976. His sister, Shirley Babashoff, won two golds and six silver medals at the Montreal Olympics.

The Final (22 July 1976)

John Naber

In 1976 he was the gold medallist in the 100- and 200-metres backstroke, both in new world record times, ending the seven-year winning run of the famous East German Roland Matthes. He was also a member of the winning 4 x 200-metres freestyle relay team. Weighing 195 lb and 6 feet 6 inches tall, Naber won four gold medals in the 1976 Games, each in a world record time; his backstroke times were not bettered at the 1980 Moscow Olympics.

John Hencken

Born in 1954, he is a graduate of Stanford University. He was gold medallist in the 100-metres and 200-metres breaststroke at the 1972 Olympics at Munich. He retained his 100-metres title at Montreal and gained a silver behind David Wilkie in the 200-metres.

Matt Vogel

Gold medallist in the 100-metres butterfly at the Montreal Olympics. He came from Fort Wayne, Indiana, and returned to the University of Tennessee only to find that he couldn't cope with the pressure of being an Olympic champion. He dropped out and found himself a job as a supermarket attendant.

Jim Montgomery

In Montreal he won the 100-metres freestyle in 49.99 seconds, the first time of under 50 seconds recorded for the race, beating his old time of 50.59. He had lowered that to 50.39 in the semi final. He gained the bronze in the 200-metres freestyle behind Bruce Furniss and Naber, and left the 400 metres to others. He won gold in the 4 x 200-metres freestyle.

John Naber begins the backstroke leg in the Montreal Olympic final

Oxford Boat Race Crews, 1976–85

Oxford's problem in winning ten consecutive boat races could well be boredom. During training in the icy depths of Oxfordshire, the fact that they are overwhelming favourites might lead to arrogance and an overcasual approach. Cambridge, although in a certain amount of disarray, have twice broken existing course records while trailing behind the Dark Blues.

Part of the reason for Oxford's extraordinary domination can be attributed to their coach, Daniel Topolski, who was in the losing crew in 1973; 'weighing only 11 stone, I got my blue before the days of the dreadnoughts.' He has maintained a varied and rigorous training programme, instilling a continuing discipline when slackness could have crept in. In the week before the race the crew lives in a rambling house near Barnes Common rather than the more salubrious setting of the Richmond Hill Hotel. Oxford have now become victims of their own success – the guilt and embarrassment of defeat will be difficult to digest, when that day eventually arrives.

THE BOAT RACE, 1976–85

1976

Oxford broke the course record. Their time was 16 minutes 58 seconds – they won by 22 seconds – the first time the race was won in under 17 minutes. They were the heaviest crew in the history of the race, averaging over 14 stone, and in Stephen Plunkett, at 16 stone 3 lb, they had the heaviest oarsman to have rowed in the race. David Beak, the bowman, became the first man to row the race wearing a sun hat. Isis won the reserve race also in record time. Oxford won the toss and chose the Surrey side of the river.

The Crew

		Weight
Bow	*D.R.H. Beak	13–6
2	*G.S. Innes	13–10
3	A.D. Edwards	14–0
4	*R.S. Mason	14–6
5	S.G.H. Plunkett	16–3
6	N.C. Brown	14–6
7	A.J. Wiggins	13–5
Stroke	*A.G.H. Baird	12–10
Cox	*J.N. Calvert	9–4
	Average weight:	14–0½

1977

Oxford won by seven lengths, their biggest winning margin since 1898, in a time of 19 minutes 53 seconds. Their cox was Colin Moynihan, later MP for Lewisham East. He was to cox the 1984 eights crew in Los Angeles. Oxford won the toss and chose Surrey.

The Crew

		Weight
Bow	P.S.T. Wright	12–11
2	G.E. Vardey	12–10
3	M.M. Moran	14–4
4	*R.S. Mason	14–8
5	*C.J.N. Money-Coutts	15–2
6	A. Shealy	14–6
7	*A.J. Wiggins	13–3
Stroke	A.G. Michelmore	12–3
Cox	C.B. Moynihan	7–9
	Average weight:	13–9½

1978

In only their second hat trick since 1911, Oxford finished alone when Cambridge became the sixth crew to sink. But up to Barnes Bridge it was one of the best races for twenty-five years. Oxford broke the records for the mile post and Hammersmith, and were 10 seconds up when Cambridge sank. Their time was 18 minutes 54 seconds. Goldie won the best reserve race ever seen. Oxford won the toss and chose Surrey.

The Crew

		Weight
Bow	T.J. Sutton	14–2
2	R.A. Crockford	13–2
3	J.R. Crawford	14–0
4	N.B. Rankov	14–3
5	*M.M. Moran	14–2
6	*A.W. Shealy	14–2
7	J.W. Wood	12–10
Stroke	*A.G. Michelmore	12–3
Cox	J. Fail	7–13
	Average weight:	13–8¼

1979

Oxford's time of 20 minutes 33 seconds was the slowest since 1963, but they still won by 3.5 lengths. Cambridge suffered the misfortune of losing John Woodhouse on the morning of the race through illness. Goldie won the reserve race in the slowest race ever – it was 94 seconds slower than the previous slowest. Oxford won the toss for the fifth successive year and chose Surrey.

The Crew

		Weight
Bow	P.J. Head	12–4
2	*R.A. Crockford	13–4
3	R.J. Moore	13–3
4	*N.B. Rankov	14–5
5	*J.R. Crawford	14–0
6	C.J. Mahoney	13–4
7	*A.J. Wiggins	13–4
Stroke	M.J. Diserens	12–9
Cox	C.P. Berners-Lee	7–9
	Average weight:	13–4

1980

In a race in which the lead changed many times, Oxford won by 7 feet – a canvas – in a time of 19 minutes 20 seconds. They finished with just seven oarsmen, the bow, Francis, having collapsed in exhaustion. He was taken to Royal Middlesex Hospital but was released later that night. Their coach, Daniel Topolski, took his place in the boat for the 'row in'. Oxford won the toss and chose Surrey again.

The Crew

		Weight
Bow	S.R. Francis	13–12
2	N.A. Conington	13–0
3	M.D. Andrews	14–0½
4	J.L. Bland	13–11
5	*N.B. Rankov	14–8
6	*C.J. Mahoney	15–6
7	T.C.M. Barry	13–4½
Stroke	*M.J. Diserens	12–13
Cox	J.S. Mead	8–3½
	Average weight:	13–8½

1981

With arguably their best crew ever Oxford won by eight lengths in a time of 18 minutes 11 seconds. Not counting sinkings, it was Oxford's best win since 1898 when the official result was an 'easy' win to Oxford. Oxford's cox Sue Brown made history by becoming the first woman to compete in the race, and Boris Rankov became the first don. He also became the first oarsman from a women's college to take part. He was at St Hugh's (Sue Brown was at a men's college). Rankov also became one of eleven men to win four boat races. Cambridge won the toss for the first time since 1974 and chose Surrey.

The Crew

		Weight
Bow	*P.J. Head	12–6
2	*N.A. Conington	12–10
3	R.P. Yonge	14–4
4	R.P. Emerton	13–1
5	*N.B. Rankov	14–5
6	*C.J. Mahoney	13–8
7	*M.D. Andrews	14–1
Stroke	J.L. Bland	14–1
Cox	Sue Brown	6–8
	Average weight:	13–8

1982

Oxford won by 3.25 lengths in a time of 18 minutes 21 seconds. Their average weight was 10 lb heavier than Cambridge's, the biggest weight difference for twenty-seven years. Rankov became the first man to win five boat races. The Oxford crews by now had fourteen boat race and Isis victories to their credit. Oxford won the toss and chose Surrey.

The Crew

		Weight
Bow	*N.A. Conington	12–10
2	G.R.N. Holland	13–2
3	H.E. Clay	14–2
4	R.P. Emerton	13–1
5	*N.B. Rankov	14–12
6	S.J.L. Foster	13–11
7	A.K. Kirkpatrick	14–8
Stroke	R.C. Clay	13–6
Cox	*Sue Brown	6–11
	Average weight:	13–13⅞

Sue Brown verbally assaulting the Oxford crew, as they pass under Hammersmith Bridge on their way to success in 1981

Oxford's lead in the 1978 race is marginal as the crews pass Hammersmith Bridge. Moments later Cambridge sank

1983

Oxford won by 4.5 lengths in 19 minutes 7 seconds. Their crew contained a World Championship silver medallist (Bland), two world junior bronze medallists and four blues with ten Boat Race wins between them. The crew also contained a pair of twins – the Evans brothers – and was the heaviest to row in the race. The reserve race saw two female coxswains for the first time. Oxford won the toss and chose Surrey.

The Crew

		Weight
Bow	W.J. Lang	14–13
2	*H.E. Clay	14–6
3	*H.P. Yonge	14–8
4	G.R.D. Jones	14–5
5	*N.B. Rankov	15–5
6	J.M. Evans	14–6
7	W.M. Evans	14–6
Stroke	*J.L. Bland	14–4
Cox	S.E. Higgins	8–0
	Average weight:	14–8½

1984

Oxford won by 3.75 lengths in a record time of 16 minutes 45 seconds. It is the first time this century that Oxford has won nine races in succession. Cambridge was also inside the old record time by one second. The Race was run on the Sunday after the Cambridge boat was damaged on the Saturday twenty minutes before the start of the race. Oxford had four internationals in their line-up and averaged 11 lb per man heavier than Cambridge. Their crew consisted of two Australians, two Canadians and an American cox. Oxford won the toss and chose Surrey.

The Crew

		Weight
Bow	*R.C. Clay	13–0
2	C.L.B. Long	12–4
3	J.A.G.H. Stewart	14–7
4	D.M. Rose	15–2½
5	*W.M. Evans	14–5
6	*G.R.D. Jones	14–0½
7	*W.J. Lang	14–0½
Stroke	*J.M. Evans	13–10
Cox	S.R. Lesser	8–1
	Average weight:	13–12½

1985

Oxford's time of 17 minutes 11 seconds was the third fastest winning time in the race's history. They won by 4.75 lengths (13 seconds). Their stroke, Fran Reininger, a Pan-Am Games gold medallist, was greeted by a topless Kiss-O-Gram girl at the end of the race. B.M. Philp became the first man to win Blues for both universities, having moved from Cambridge. It was the ninth race to be sponsored by Ladbroke Hotels. Cambridge won the toss and chose Surrey.

The Crew

		Weight
Bow	G. Cartledge	13–6
2	C.L. Richmond	12–1
3	*B.M. Philp	15–0
4	A.M.S. Thomas	13–1
5	P.M. Hare	15–3
6	*G.R.D. Jones	14–1
7	*W.J. Lang	14–3
Stroke	F.M. Reininger	14–6
Cox	*S.R. Lesser	8–4
	Average weight:	13–4

* Blues.

East Germany 4 x 100-Metres Medley Relay Team, 1976

When the 1972 Olympics were scheduled for Munich, the ideal platform was created for the 'other half' of Germany, the communist East, to parade their increasing sporting prowess. The East had always thought that Olympics were the ideal shop window in which to advertise their wares. So, for East Germany, Munich would be a register of their progress since the two countries went their separate ways in 1964.

In 1972 in the Munich *Sportshalle*, the East German results in the swimming pool were a shambles, particularly in the women's events, in which they failed to win a single gold medal. That fine backstroker Roland Matthes saved the men's team from similar embarrassment and although the East beat the West by twenty golds to thirteen in all events, there was much reorganization and restructuring of the swimming administration and coaching to be done.

Four years later, the East Germans won no fewer than eleven of the thirteen gold medals in the women's swimming events. The dominant Americans, who had just reached the number one ratings after having been themselves dominated by the Australians, were caught cold. They even refused to shake hands after medal ceremonies.

In his book, *The Complete Book of the Olympics*, David Wallechinsky suggests that there were two major factors in this change. At the World Championships in 1973 at Belgrade, the East German women appeared in new skintight lycra swimming suits. These soon became universal. The protesters were cut short when it was discovered that the suits were made in West Germany, by Mr Adi Dassler's company, and were available to the Western world. But the more significant factor was the emphasis placed on sports science. The East Germans claimed that while the Russians and Americans were intent on landing people on the moon and designing nuclear weapons, it was they themselves who were testing athletes for performance and nutritional needs. When the German athletes were accused of taking steroids, they countered by showing a programme of weight-training schedules which, they said, explained their muscular development.

A month before the Olympics, the East German women smashed several world records at their National Championships. No heed was taken by the rest of the world. Everything, including wind-assisted times, were used as excuses to dismiss the performances. So, it must have delighted coach Professor Rudolf Schramme when the best of the East German performances was in the first event – the 4 x 100-metres medley relay. Before the Games the world record was the property of the Dynamo Berlin SC with a time of 4 minutes 13.41 seconds. The National team of Ulrike Richter, Hannelore Anke, Andrea Pollack and Kornelia Ender obliterated that time with a new record of 4:07.95. The silver medal was won by the Americans, who were virtually half the pool away, in 4:14.55. The record was to last until the East Germans themselves beat it in a solo swim at the Moscow Olympics.

Kornelia Ender parades the controversial swimsuit which brought forth American complaints, until it was discovered that the swimsuit was available in Western stores

THE TEAM

Kornelia Ender

Born at Plauen on 25 October 1958, she won three silvers as a thirteen-year-old in the Munich Olympics. A year later she beat Shane Gould's 100-metres freestyle world record and, between then and the 1976 Olympics, she broke the record on nine more occasions. The medley gold was one of four golds at Montreal: she won the 100-metres freestyle, then, on the same evening, she won the 100-metres butterfly at 7.48 p.m. and the 200-metres freestyle only twenty-seven minutes later. She won eight Olympic medals and was the first female swimmer to win four golds at one Olympics. Just before Montreal she married Olympic champion and world backstroke record holder Roland Matthes. They are now divorced.

Ulrike Richter

She swam the backstroke leg of the medley relay at Montreal. She entered the Olympics as a nine times world record holder and left as Olympic champion. Aged seventeen in 1976, she came from Dynamo Dresden SC. In 1975 she won the 200-metres backstroke at the World Championships in Cali, Colombia.

Hannelore Anke

An eighteen-year-old from the Wismut SC in Aue, Hannelore went on to win the 100-metres breaststroke at Montreal, breaking the world record in her heat and in the semi final.

Andrea Pollack

Born 8 May 1961 at Schwerin, she was a member of the Dynamo Berlin SC which were the world record holders before the Games. At Montreal she was beaten by Kornelia Ender in the 100-metres butterfly, but won the 200-metres. She was the only swimmer to remain in the team when the East Germans broke the medley relay world record in Moscow.

Each member of the team recorded the fastest time for her own leg. Professor Schramme's team in Montreal won every gold medal except those in the 200-metres breaststroke, which was won by Marina Koshevaia of the Soviet Union in a new world record time of 2 minutes 33.35 seconds, and the 4 x 100-metres freestyle, which the Americans won by just seven tenths of a second in another world record.

EAST GERMANY'S RECORD IN THE SWIMMING AND DIVING IN MONTREAL

Swimming

100-metres freestyle	1 Kornelia Ender (world record)
	2 Petra Priemer
200-metres freestyle	1 Kornelia Ender (world record)
400-metres freestyle	1 Petra Thumer (world record)
800-metres freestyle	1 Petra Thumer (Olympic record)
100-metres backstroke	1 Ulrike Richter (Olympic record)
	2 Birgit Treiber
200-metres backstroke	1 Ulrike Richter (Olympic record)
	2 Birgit Treiber
100-metres breaststroke	1 Hannelore Anke
	(world record in heat and in semi final)
200-metres breaststroke	4 Hannelore Anke
100-metres butterfly	1 Kornelia Ender
	(equalled world record)
	2 Andrea Pollack
200-metres butterfly	1 Andrea Pollack (Olympic record)
	2 Ulrike Tauber
	3 Rosemarie Gabriel (Kother)
400-metres individual medley	1 Ulrike Tauber (world record)
4 x 100-metres freestyle	2 (Ender, Primer, Pollack, Hempel)
4 x 100-metres medley	1 (Richter, Anke, Pollack, Ender – world record)

Diving

Springboard	2 Christa Kohler

United States Ice Hockey Team, 1980

Swept along on an astonishing tide of national hysteria which overspilled onto a world television audience, the 1980 United States Olympic ice hockey team demonstrated at Lake Placid how to write a typical Hollywood script which included a series of victories after coming from behind, an East–West confrontation of epic proportions and a final twist.

The good guys of the tournament were the Americans. Seeded only seventh out of the twelve teams, they looked to have no chance. David Wallechinsky wrote in *The Complete Book of the Olympics*: 'America was undergoing an identity crisis. It seemed as though nothing was going right. There was a crippling inflation rate at home. The hostages in Iran seemed to have given up hope of leaving Tehran. The Russians had invaded Afghanistan. When Jimmy Carter pulled American teams out of the Summer Olympics in Moscow, Americans were left with just the Winter Games to regain a sense of pride.'

Then the baddies arrived in the shape of the Russians. Their politicians had blandly dismissed the atrocities in the mountains around Kabul. And just because the United States would not go to the Summer Games in Moscow, why should they withdraw from Lake Placid? After all, sport is a fine platform.

But what made it worse was that the Russians were embarrassingly good. In the Olympics from 1956 onwards they had played forty-five games, won thirty-nine, drawn two and lost four. And they had just beaten (with their so-called amateur side) the pride of the National Professional Hockey League. Three days before the tournament the Russians beat the United States 10–3.

The teams were split into two groups, with the first two teams in each group going through to the medal play-off. Russia was in one group, the Americans were in the other.

The United States squad was built around the University of Minnesota team. Nine of the twenty-man squad attended the university, as did the coach, Herbie Brooks. With an average team age of twenty-two, Brooks decided they needed experience, so he lined up a series of sixty-three matches, culminating in the 10–3 drubbing by the Russians. It had hardly seemed worthwhile.

In their opening game against Sweden they barely got out of trouble. Trailing 2–1 with a minute to go, Brooks pulled off his keeper Jim Craig and substituted an outfield player. Bill Baker slammed in an equalizing shot with just 27 seconds left to play. Next came one of the favourites, Czechoslovakia. Again, the United States let in an early goal, but it was 2–2 at the end of the first period. The Americans then ran riot to win 7–3, capturing the attention of the television audience.

Against Norway the pattern continued with the loss of an early goal, then a recovery to win 5–1. The Rumanians, although an Eastern Bloc country, are not a strong ice hockey nation; their team provided target practice for the American forwards, who were growing in confidence. The USA won 7–2. Against West Germany in the last group match they again fell behind in typical fashion, presenting the visitors with 2 goals

American and Russian players performing Torvill and Dean impersonations during the most amazing ice hockey match in Olympic history, at Lake Placid in 1980

Mass celebrations after the win over the Soviet Union

before winning 4–2. The nation was now prepared for sleepless nights.

The United States and Sweden from one group and the Soviet Union and Finland from the other made up what was described as the 'medal round'. Top of the league took the gold and so on. The USA drew 2–2 with Sweden and the Russians won 4–2 against Finland.

On 22 February the motley crew of college boys went out to face the Russians, the best team in the world, amateur or professional. Predictably, the Soviets went a goal up through Vladimir Krutov. Buzz Schneider equalized, Russia scored again, and Mark Johnson brought the scores level at 2–2. Johnson scored his second goal to level the game again after Alexander Maltsev had given the Russians a 3–2 interval lead. Halfway through the final period Mike Eruzione put the United States into the lead for the first time and that, amazingly, was how the scoreline remained. Jim Craig, who, it is reported, made thirty-nine saves during the game, fought off a seemingly endless barrage of attacks by the frenzied Russians. Back in the dressing room they sang 'God Bless America', although most of them did not know the words. Coach Brooks took himself off to the lavatory.

As the years pass memories grow vague. Ask most people and they will say that the United States won the gold medal that night. Wrong. Two evenings later Finland formed the opposition in the final round-robin match. They, too, were in the running for a medal. Had the Americans lost, they would have taken the bronze and handed the gold to the Russians.

Finland scored first and led 2–1 after two periods. With the customary deficit, the Americans began to organize themselves again. Mark Johnson equalized, Phil Verchota added a third, before Rob McClanahan scored what the Americans delightfully call the 'insurance' goal. Captain Mike Eruzione received the gold medal on behalf of the team, but then insisted on the rest of the squad joining him on the dais. President Carter then invited them to the White House.

Just as quickly the team disbanded. Some became professional, some continued with their studies, and some even drifted out of the limelight. But, just for a few weeks, everyone could recall the names – Mike Eruzione, Jim Craig the goalkeeper, Dave Christian (whose father and uncle were in the winning team at the 1960 Olympics), Ken Morrow, Mark Johnson top goalscorer, Bill Baker, Bob Suter, Neal Broten, Mark Wells, Buzz Schneider, Eric Strobel, John Harrington, Michael Ramsey, John O'Callaghan, David Silk, Steve Christoff, Mark Pavelich, Robert McClanahan, Phil Verchota.

When the names are forgotten one remark will linger on. Before the start of the first match, coach Herbie Brooks said, 'Gentlemen, you do not have the talent to win on talent alone.'

Jayne Torvill and Christopher Dean, 1981–84

When being interviewed after winning the 1984 BBC Sports Personality of the Year award, Christopher Dean said, 'When the team prize went, I thought we had no chance. After all, we are hardly individuals.'

European, world and Olympic ice dance champions, Jayne Torvill and Christopher Dean are quite the most outstanding skaters of the modern era. In a sport known for its individuals, they are, with the Protopopovs, the ice pairs skaters, the only team, or pairing, worth remembering. Their blend of fluency, technical expertise and artistic refinement has brought a new interpretation to the ice dance programme.

Their initial problem was with the calendar. With an Olympic Games every fourth year, many champions have been lucky enough to peak in an Olympic year. Jayne and Chris became world champions in 1981 and so had to wait three years, staving off challenges, changing sequences and setting new standards, before being able to challenge for the gold medal at the 1984 Winter Olympics in the Yugoslavian mountain centre of Sarajevo.

At the start of their careers, in 1975, their first trainer was Janet Sawbridge. Both Jayne and Chris were training at the Nottingham rink and both, after some success with other partners, needed a change. They made a verbal agreement on a one-month trial, then extended it to two months.

Jayne, the daughter of a newsagent, began skating at the age of nine. She attended Clifton Hall Grammar School and then worked as an insurance clerk before taking up ice skating full time. Like Chris, she was a much better individual skater than initially given credit for, but she first made her mark not in the ice dance but in the ice pairs competitions. With her partner, Michael Hutchinson, she won the 1970 British junior title, and the next year, largely through a lack of depth in the event, the pair were British senior champions.

Christopher began skating at the age of ten. An electrician's son, his first involvement in skating came when he was trying to find something after school to occupy him. He was given a pair of skates for Christmas and was encouraged by his mother to take up an evening hobby.

Shortly after, he broke his leg but couldn't wait to return to the Nottingham ice rink. He has always been an ice dance specialist. In 1974 he won the British Junior Ice Dance Championship with Sandra Elson. (Now Sandra Horvath, she is married to a Hungarian businessman and spends most of her time abroad.)

Experts claimed that the set pattern rendition of the Paso Doble which Jayne Torvill and Christopher Dean performed at the 1984 Olympics was superior to their free dance routine

Torvill and Dean's dramatic exit from amateur life – the end of Bolero

What happened to the one- or two-month trial period is now history. In their very first competition in Bristol, Torvill and Dean finished second. In 1976 they won three major events on the British calendar; the Sheffield Trophy, the Northern Championship, and the St Gervais title. By 1978 they were British champions for the first time.

Betty Calloway, a British trainer of overseas champions, had already noticed some outstanding potential in her own country. The nation, too, had become aware of ice skating through the exploits of John Curry and his successor, Robin Cousins.

As British champions in 1978, Jayne and Chris were invited to the major championships. In the European they finished in ninth place, and eleventh in the World Championships. By 1980 they had improved to fifth at the Olympics at Lake Placid, and fourth at the World Championships. Betty Calloway had coached the Hungarians, Andras Sallay and Krisztina Regoczy, to a win in the 1980 World Championships, and as part of the same 'stable' Torvill and Dean were able to gauge their own progress.

Torvill and Dean succeeded Sallay and Regoczy as world champions in 1981 when they won the title at Hartford, Connecticut; they were also European champions that year. The next Olympics, however, were three years away.

For the first time they had attracted sponsors. The Sports Aid Foundation donated £8000 and the Nottingham City Council took a calculated risk and gave £42,000 over a three-year period; there were some who thought that perhaps the money might have been appropriated elsewhere. Up to that time Chris had been a policeman with the local Nottingham force, and their training sessions had to be fitted in either at the crack of dawn or late at night to fit in with Jayne's nine-to-five job, Chris's late shifts and the few precious moments when the Nottingham ice rink was deserted. The grant gave them the opportunity to accept the kind offer to use the West German training centre, a superb rink at Oberstorf, near Garmisch.

In the three years before the Winter Olympics at Sarajevo, Jayne and Chris won every major championship bar one, the 1983 European. (While practising, Chris fell, bringing Jayne down heavily on her shoulder. They wisely decided not to risk further injury.)

Maintaining their progress towards Sarajevo meant constant adjustments to their routines. The three free-dance programmes brought maximum marks in most of the major championships. Preferring not to employ their own choreographer, they chose to skate to 'Mack and Mabel' in 1982.

The following year, after watching Michael Crawford in 'Barnum' at the London Palladium, they chose the theme song from the show. Michael Crawford himself taught them the routine. And in 1984, Olympic year, Jayne and Chris unwrapped Ravel's 'Bolero' and gave the music almost more publicity than Bo Derek had managed in the film *10*. They were thorough too. The costumes for 'Bolero' took six months to design.

Meanwhile the set-pattern marks continued to improve. By the time they had given their rendition of the 'Paso Doble' at the Olympics, experts rated their performance as superior to that of the 'Bolero'. The judges had been caught up in a plethora of maximum sixes. Jayne Torvill and Christopher Dean were so far in advance of the rest of the world that the European, World, and finally, the goal – the Olympic gold medal – came their way with utter domination.

The concept that they have brought to skating is best summed up by those who know these matters, Britain's former World ice dance champion Courtney Jones, and world and Olympic champion, John Curry. Jones explained, 'They have pushed out the frontiers farther and farther. They have opened a new era, if only the rest of the world can grasp what they do.' Curry echoed the sentiments: 'People don't realize that because they are a team, they are still fine skaters in their own right. Good enough to have been champions. Their subtleties are lost on those who don't know.'

THEIR RECORD

World Champions   1981, 1982, 1983, 1984
European Champions   1981, 1982, 1984
Olympic Champions   1984

Total Number of Maximum Points Awarded

British Championships
1981   7
European Championships
1982   11
1984   11
World Championships
1982   5
1983   9
1984   11
Olympic Games
1984   19

Martina Navratilova and Pam Shriver, 1981–85

Whilst Martina Navratilova has spent most of the 1980s compiling a singles record of near invincibility, her partnership with Pam Shriver in the women's doubles has taken lower billing. That is until it dawned upon people that the Navratilova–Shriver partnership had not lost a match for three years in the most prestigious set of events – those that go to make up the Grand Slam.

Pam Shriver is the lesser known of the two, if that description fits a player who has, for long spells, been ranked number three in the world. She was one of the first of a succession of 'child prodigies' and now a member of an increasing group of players who, because of the demands of the game, suffer severe injuries and even illness.

She was born in Baltimore on 4 July 1962 – Independence Day. Initially, the early publicity was for others, like Tracy Austin; Pam, although the same age, was thankfully not subjected to so much pressure. However, that changed when, at the 1978 US Open, she reached the final when barely sixteen years of age. She beat the Australians Kerry Reid and Lesley Hunt, and then put out Martina 7–6, 7–6, before being beaten in two close sets 7–5, 6–4, by Chris Evert.

Then came the almost inevitable injuries. With Tracy Austin it was back trouble. Pam 'went' in the shoulder (the next phenomenon, Andrea Jaeger, had a nervous breakdown at eighteen). On several occasions Pam has had to take an enforced rest from the game due to tendonitis in the right shoulder.

Martina and Pam first teamed up in doubles in 1981. They entered eleven tournaments and won nine. Most encouraging was their first major victory, in the United Airlines Tournament of Champions, when they beat Rosie Casals and Wendy Turnbull in the final 6–1, 7–6. Their opponents were acknowledged doubles experts. One of the two defeats was in the final of the Australian Open when Jordan and Smith took revenge for their Wimbledon defeat. In 1982 they lost their Grand Slam match, when, in the US Open, Barbara Potter and Sharon Walsh surprised them (and themselves) by winning in the semi final.

Martina Navratilova entered 1985 having earned $9.4 million in prizemoney from the sport. At the start of her doubles partnership with Pam Shriver, however, she was experiencing a certain amount of self-doubt. Her American naturalization papers were delayed and publicity stories about her and writer and guide Rita Mae Brown were unfair, unkind and probably wrong. She had slipped from world number 1 in 1978 and 1979 to number 4 in 1980 and number 3 in 1981. These were admittedly singles rankings but they give an indication of her attitude at the time. Early in 1981 Martina was whitewashed by Chris Lloyd at Amelia Island in Florida and her career seemed to be on a helter-skelter to nowhere.

Martina had won doubles titles before, but she needed a secure partner. Before 1981 she had won seven doubles championships in Grand Slam events with four different partners. After pairing up with Pam Shriver in 1981, Martina won only the 1982 French Championship with another partner – Anne Smith.

Like McEnroe and unlike Connors, Martina prefers to play doubles rather than rest on singles victories. With the nonstop pressure of singles, Martina needs a break. Pam Shriver, with the history of shoulder trouble, agrees that it is wise to curtail singles events.

At present the pair are working at achieving a happy medium between major tournament play in singles and doubles, coupled with physical and mental breaks from the game. Just how long they will remain at the top is probably up to them. There are no rivals in sight, despite their first defeat in 110 matches when Kathy Jordan and Liz Smyllie beat them at Wimbledon in 1985.

GRAND SLAM WINS

1981	Wimbledon	beat	Jordan and Smith	6–3, 7–6
1982	Wimbledon	beat	Jordan and Smith	6–4, 6–1
	Australian	beat	Kohde and Pfaff	6–4, 6–2
1983	Wimbledon	beat	Casals and Turnbull	6–2, 6–2
	US Open	beat	Fairbank and Reynolds	6–7, 6–1, 6–3
	Australian	beat	Hobbs and Turnbull	6–4, 6–7, 6–2
1984	Wimbledon	beat	Jordan and Smith	6–3, 6–4
	French	beat	Mandlikova and Kohde	5–7, 6–3, 6–2
	US Open	beat	Hobbs and Turnbull	6–2, 6–4
	Australian	beat	Kohde and Sukova	6–3, 6–4
1985	French	beat	Kohde and Sukova	4–6, 6–2, 6–2

Martina Navratilova (left) *and Pam Shriver with the 1984 Wimbledon Doubles trophy*

Australia Rugby League Team, 1982

At the end of September 1982 a twenty-eight man squad of Australian Rugby League players – the Kangaroos – left Sydney for a tour of Britain and France. The choices were not automatic and the tourists left amid cries of selection critics. When they returned, unbeaten, after a fifteen-match tour of Britain and a further seven games in France, they presented a picture of invincibility. In two months they had achieved a new dimension of fitness, skill and tactical awareness which won them acclaim from rugby circles – both League and Union alike – as the best touring side ever.

The 1982 Kangaroos became the first touring party from any country to win all their games in Britain. They scored ninety-seven tries to seven in Britain and in France their tally was sixty-nine to two. They were the first to win all three tests in Britain, Alarmingly, some of the highest scores were made against the top club sides – the current League champions Leigh (44–4), top of the table Leeds (31–4), and Hull Kingston Rovers (30–10). They beat Great Britain 40–4, 27–6 and 32–8, conceding just one try to Hull's Steve Evans. Only Wigan, Bradford Northern and Hull limited the free-running scoring machine.

The Kangaroos relied on a foundation of experience of previous British tours with Ray Price (loose forward), Rod Reddy (second row), Craig Young (prop) and Steve Rogers (centre). Manager Frank Stanton introduced centre Mal Meninga, at 16 stones and well over 6 feet tall, back-row forward Wayne Pearce, scrum half Peter Sterling, stand-off Brett Kenny, and full back Greg Brentnall. All quickly, and embarrassingly for Britain, established themselves immediately as world class.

The captain was a controversial selection when the team left Australia. Max Krilich had made only a limited number of appearances as hooker, and although the Manly captain was often beaten for possession in the tight, he was the springboard of the Australian tactical plan and maintained a discipline from which only the unruly prop, Les Boyd, deviated.

As with all successful touring sides, the reserve squad would have done credit to any other country. Leading try scorer John Ribot couldn't get into the Test team.

Painfully, the Rugby League are learning the lesson. On 4 May 1985 Wigan beat Hull 28–24 in what was described as the best Challenge Cup final of all time. Sterling, Muggleton and Kenny were on the field and eleven of the chosen squad of thirty were not eligible for Great Britain selection. Ten tries were shared in an afternoon which brought the game world acclaim. Detractors will complain that the overseas players stifle home-grown talent but, in the short term, the introduction of players and, more importantly, coaches with different tactical awareness of the game will broaden interest in the sport. Amateur Rugby League is flourishing and there seems less point in taking a risk on an unproven Union 'name' player when the amateur leagues are providing the basic grounding for the future.

The domination of the southern hemisphere is still total, but after the 1985 Challenge Cup final, when the home-spun talent stood up well in comparison with overseas stars, the British game is benefiting. However, the problem is highlighted when the comparison is with a player like Ray Price, whose dedication is so total that he would go for an eight-mile run each morning, then join the remainder of the team and begin training.

THE TEAM

Chris Anderson	(winger, Canterbury Bankstown)
Kerry Bousted	(winger, Eastern Suburbs)
Les Boyd	(second row, Manly-Warringah)
Ray·Brown	(hooker, Manly-Warringah)
Greg Brentnall	(full back, Canterbury Bankstown)
Greg Conescu	(hooker, Northern Suburbs)
Steve Ella	(centre/stand-off, Parramatta)
Eric Grothe	(winger, Parramatta)
Rohan Hancock	(second row/prop, Toowoomba, Wattles)
Brett Kenny	(stand-off/centre, Parramatta)
Max Krilich	(captain, hooker, Manly-Warringah)
Wally Lewis	(vice-captain, stand-off/loose forward, Fortitude Valley, Brisbane)
Mal Meninga	(centre, Southern Suburbs)
Gene Miles	(centre, Wynnum-Manly)
Steve Mortimer	(scrum half, Canterbury Bankstown)
Rod Morris	(prop, Wynnum-Manly)
John Muggleton	(second row, Parramatta)
Mark Murray	(scrum half/stand-off, Fortitude Valley)
Donny McKinnon	(prop, North Sydney)
Paul McCabe	(second row/loose forward, Manly-Warringah)
Wayne Pearce	(loose forward, Balmain)
John Ribot	(winger, Manly-Warringah)
Rod Reddy	(second row, St George, Sydney)
Steve Rogers	(centre, Cronulla-Sutherland)
Ian Schubert	(utility player, Eastern Suburbs)
Peter Sterling	(scrum half, Parramatta)
Ray Price	(loose forward, Parramatta)
Craig Young	(prop, St George, Sydney)

Australian winger Eric Grothe brushes aside a tentative tackle to set up yet another Australian attack during the one-sided series with Britain in 1982

THEIR RECORD

		In Britain	In France
Played		15	7
Won		15	7
Drew		0	0
Lost		0	0
For	– tries	97	69
	– goals	66	42
	– points	423	291
Against	– tries	7	2
	– goals	29	7
	– points	80	20

In Britain	
Hull KR	30–10
Wigan	13–9
Barrow	29–2
St Helens	32–0
Leeds	31–4
Wales	37–7
First Test	40–4
Leigh	44–4
Bradford N.	13–6
Cumbria	41–2
Fulham	22–5
Hull	13–7
Second Test	27–6
Widnes	19–6
Third Test	32–8

In France	
Roanne	65–0
First Test	15–4
Sélection Aquitaine	67–2
French U-24	42–3
Catalans de France	53–2
Sélection Mid-Pyrénées-Rouergue	26–0
Second Test	23–9

Australia II, 1983

At 5.21 p.m. on 26 September 1983 the crew of *Australia II* ended one tradition and started another. The America's Cup, the '100 Guinea Cup', which had remained in the New York Yacht Club since 1851, had a new home in Perth, Western Australia.

Australia II was the twenty-fifth challenger for the America's Cup in the 132 years of the event – the Blue Riband of all yachting races. If ever a cup was properly named, it was the America's Cup, for it had not left their shores in all those 132 years and the United States had, on average, conceded just one race every three series.

During the months of July, August and September, just what the Australians had to overcome was quite astonishing. The political manoeuvring, the protests, the all-night vigils to guard their boat, to say nothing of actually having to win the races, would have tried the patience of any crew. But the Australians, who challenged under the auspices of the Royal Perth Yacht Club, had the characters, and the character, to beat the Americans at whatever game they wished to play.

There were three central personalities in the challenge of *Australia II* – Ben Lexcen, the boat's designer, Alan Bond, the owner, and John Bertrand, the skipper. Of the three, Lexcen was probably the most charismatic. He was also, in many ways, the man on whom the whole issue pivoted.

Lexcen had invented a revolutionary keel. It immediately aroused suspicion. The Americans said that it contravened the rules of 12-Metre racing. Lexcen fuelled these arguments by declaring that the keel would not be revealed until the event was over. The Americans hired the sort of photographer who takes holiday snaps of Joan Collins, Jackie Onassis and Brigitte Bardot. It was as though the Loch Ness monster had appeared in the harbour of Newport, Rhode Island.

Such is the popularity of the America's Cup that for the first time an elimination series of considerable substance was held. Seven boats began the challenge for the right to meet the American yacht that was to defend the trophy. Of those seven, three would be eliminated and the other four would go forward into a second series of races. There would then be a best of seven races final between the top two yachts from the second series.

In the first series *Australia II* was so dominant that the Americans were genuinely worried. The discussions about the validity of the keel were, perhaps, prompted by an awareness that for the first time a genuine challenger was upon them. In sixteen races the Australians lost only once and that was when they conceded a race to Canada after crew member Scott McAllister broke his arm whilst repairing a broken mast crane. McAllister, whose arm was badly lacerated, was found to be unconscious.

The British boat, *Victory '83*, masterminded by Peter de Savary, who spent £6,000,000 on his challenge, and crewed by a variety of Olympic medallists headed by double gold winner Rodney Pattison, joined *Azzura*, the Italian yacht, and *Canada I* in the second series.

There was one surprise in the second series – *Victory* beat *Australia* by 2 minutes 50 seconds in one of the series of races.

Australia made the other seven races a procession, and with *Victory '83*, now skippered by Pattison instead of Phil Crebbin, qualified easily for the elimination final.

Sadly but predictably, *Victory* failed to disrupt the Australians' shrewd planning, although by winning the first of seven races by 13 seconds, they at least offered a challenge. *Australia* reeled off the next four races with a minimum winning margin of 2 minutes 20 seconds. They had won forty-eight of fifty-four races and most of the defeats were conceded after equipment had broken or when new tactics were being tried.

Meanwhile the Americans had held their own trials, with *Liberty* gaining selection from *Defender* and *Courageous*. In a series of qualifying races *Liberty* was marginally the best.

In the final challenge for the cup itself, *Liberty* took a 3–1 lead. The elimination series had temporarily taken its toll on *Australia*'s resources, although her victory in the third race by over three minutes hinted at her full potential. *Australia*'s win in the fifth race meant that, for the first time since 1934, there would be a sixth race. And when *Australia* took that too, there was a seventh race for the first time.

The final race was a classic. With never more than 30 seconds between the yachts either way, *Australia* took the lead on the fifth leg. Radio and television programmes dropped their schedules and went live to the course. Dennis Connor, who skippered *Liberty*, put in no fewer than sixteen desperate tacks. When that failed, he tried to put Bertrand into the spectators' flotilla.

The winning margin was 49 seconds. The America's Cup belonged to Australia, Newport belonged to Australia, and virtually the whole of America belonged to Australia. Lexcen revealed the keel.

The 'Auld Mug' – the '100 Ton Cup' as it was originally known – was so much a part of American heritage that it had been bolted to the floor of the New York Yacht Club by a 4-foot bolt. The Australians were so thorough that they had made a gold spanner with which to unscrew the bolt. Before they had a chance to use the spanner, the Americans unscrewed it and presented the cup to *Australia II*. It was about the only time that they had succeeded in outsmarting them.

THE TEAM

John Bertrand

The thirty-seven-year-old skipper of *Australia II*. A silver medallist at the 1976 Olympics in the Finn class, he sailed in his first America's Cup in 1970.

Alan Bond

British-born multimillionaire, who had, by the time he was twenty-six, made and lost £1 million. This was his fourth challenge for the America's Cup.

Ben Lexcen

The forty-seven-year-old designer. He changed his name from Bob Miller by deed poll. Brought up in Newcastle, New South Wales, he left school at fourteen and 'survived'. Formerly a boilermaker, he fell from the top of a mast in 1960 and while in hospital, decided to make a career from designing boats. His definition of a good sailor is someone who, 'when he capsizes his boat, has the presence to try and keep his smokes and matches dry!'

THE AMERICA'S CUP CHALLENGE, 1983

The Defender
Liberty (USA)

The Challengers
Advance (Australia)
Australia II (Australia)
Azzura (Italy)
Canada I (Canada)
Challenge XII (Australia)
France III (France)
Victory '83 (Great Britain)

The controversial keel is unveiled

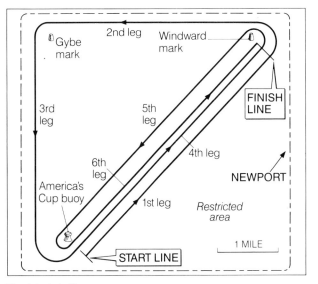
The America's Cup course

First Series

	Races	Won	Lost
Australia II	16	15	1
Victory '83	16	10	6
Azzura	16	9	7
Canada I	16	9	7

Eliminated: *Advance, Challenger XII, France III*

Second Series

Australia II	8	7	1
Victory '83	8	6	2
Azzura	8	3	5
Canada I	8	0	8

Elimination Final

		Winning margin
Race 1	*Victory '83*	13 seconds
Race 2	*Australia II*	4 minutes 43 seconds
Race 3	*Australia II*	3 minutes 40 seconds
Race 4	*Australia II*	2 minutes 20 seconds
Race 5	*Australia II*	3 minutes 19 seconds

Final

		Winning margin
Race 1	*Liberty*	1 minute 13 seconds
Race 2	*Liberty*	1 minute 28 seconds
Race 3	*Australia II*	3 minutes 22 seconds
Race 4	*Liberty*	3 minutes 37 seconds
Race 5	*Australia II*	2 minutes 24 seconds
Race 6	*Australia II*	3 minutes 32 seconds
Race 7	*Australia II*	3 minutes 49 seconds

Australia II (left) leads Liberty *over the final few miles of the seventh and deciding race of the 1983 America's Cup at Newport, Rhode Island*

McLaren, 1984

Niki Lauda (left) and Alain Prost achieved unparalleled domination of world motor racing in 1984 thanks, in no small measure, to the back-up mechanics in their splendid Marlboro-McLaren team

Never before had one team dominated Formula 1 racing in the way McLaren did in 1984. Before the final Grand Prix of the year – at Estoril in Portugal – they had already clinched the constructor's title, and both their drivers, Niki Lauda and Alain Prost, were locked together at the top of the drivers' championship with Prost only 3½ points behind his team-mate.

To win the title Prost had to finish at least third even if Lauda failed to complete the seventy laps. During practice he did enough to secure a place on the front row of the grid alongside Nelson Piquet's Brabham. Lauda, however, had a series of problems and only qualified for a place on the sixth row.

Prost's charge away from the line was not as quick as Keke Rosberg's from the second row and, for eight laps, the little Frenchman followed the Williams as it slid desperately around the circuit clinging determinedly to the lead. By the time Prost squeezed through and accelerated away from the field, Lauda had picked off two of the men in front of him. He had moved up to seventh by lap 19 as Prost continued his brilliantly fast drive

in front, seeking to become the first Frenchman ever to take the World Championship.

Back in the group of cars trailing Prost, Lauda was well aware that Prost would not surrender his lead through driving error and he also appreciated that the reliability of the McLaren made a retirement for technical reasons unlikely. He therefore had to finish second to win his third championship. Slipping into third place on lap 33, Lauda found the Englishman Nigel Mansell ahead of him. Mansell, in a Lotus, was grimly determined to do well after a season of disappointments. He held off Lauda until lap 51, then found his brakes failing and quietly slid into the pits. Lauda, after a brilliant drive, had made up nine places in fifty-one laps, taking more risks than normal to force his way through, but once he was in second place he returned to his usual immaculate style. Prost, realizing from pit signals that Lauda, against all odds, had now achieved his objective, also started to concentrate on finishing. His 52-second lead over Lauda had dwindled to 13.42 seconds by the flag and his hopes of the championship had vanished. Lauda was champion again by a mere half point.

On the podium Prost forced back the tears, only breaking into a smile when Lauda whispered, 'Next year we'll be even stronger.' Lauda's celebrations were completed by the arrival of his wife Marlene who had not been to a Grand Prix for seven years. 'I hate it,' she said, 'and I hate it even more now than before.' She was referring to the horrific accident at Nurburgring in 1976 which had nearly cost Lauda his life. His comeback was complete. His reputation as one of the living legends of world sport was assured.

Prost's disappointment was expertly disguised. 'Niki deserved it,' he said, making no mention of the fact that he had won seven Grands Prix that season to Lauda's five. But overall it was a triumph for the superb skills of the McLaren team.

For Ron Dennis, team manager, it was the culmination of an ambition. The final piece of the complicated jigsaw that constitutes a Formula 1 team had fallen into place at the end of the previous season when he had signed Prost (who had just left Renault after finishing second in the championship to Piquet) to partner Lauda instead of Britain's John Watson. Two superb drivers in an excellent car, powered by a T A G–Porsche turbo engine and designed by an engineering genius – John Barnard.

THE TEAM

John Barnard

John Barnard on the surface has little of Ron Dennis's total dedication to motor racing. He lives with his wife and two daughters close to the McLaren factory in Woking so that he can go home to lunch each day, and his most quoted comment is: 'Basically motor racing is a rotten life which leaves you very little time for friends.' But Barnard's genius is unquestioned. He introduced the revolutionary use of composite materials, notably carbon fibre, to car design. He designed the now widely copied 'coke bottle' look to cars to reduce drag and produced a reliable winning car only months after being presented with a new power unit – the T A G–Porsche turbo. Barnard accomplished the task with style and notable success. But he still has little time for turbo engines in Grand Prix racing. 'They are nasty things that have destroyed the sport.'

Ron Dennis

Ron Dennis, the team manager, has been involved with racing throughout his working life. In 1966, at the age of eighteen, he worked for the Cooper–Maserati team owned by Jochen Rindt and after four years began his own team, racing Brabham cars in Formula 2. In 1980 he moved to the new McLaren team originally started by the New Zealander Bruce McLaren in 1963. Dennis expects consistently high standards of preparation from the staff. His perfectionist demands prompted him to team up with designer John Barnard in 1979 and they have been together as a working partnership ever since. Following the 1984 championship success, Dennis immediately looked forward to 1985. 'Our objective,' he said, 'is to win every race.'

Niki Lauda

Born in Vienna in February 1949, Lauda first competed in a Grand Prix in 1971 in Austria driving a March. Three years later, having joined Ferrari, he secured his first win, in Spain, and the following year was world champion. His terrible accident at the Nurburgring in 1976 left him scarred from burns, but, after a priest had given him the last rites, he made a miraculous recovery, returning to racing two months later to defend his

championship lead which was under threat from James Hunt. In the last Grand Prix of the season at Mount Fuji in Japan he retired from the race when he decided the rain-soaked track was too dangerous. Hunt clinched the title with a fourth place. For his decision to pull out Lauda was branded a 'coward' by the Ferrari aficionados. But Lauda was back as champion the following year. He then left Ferrari to drive for Brabham. But financial pressures on his airline business provoked a sudden decision to retire in 1979. 'I wasn't enjoying racing so I quit,' he said at the time. By 1982 he was back testing the McLaren at Donington Park. 'I wanted to prove everyone wrong when they said a comeback was impossible.' His 1984 championship victory – the third of his distinguished and frequently stormy career – is sufficient proof. By the end of the 1984 season he had contested more Grands Prix than anyone except Graham Hill, held the record for the greatest number of championship points and secured more pole positions than anyone except Clark and Fangio. Lauda's reaction when told of his record-breaking exploits was 'That's boring.' He gives away all his trophies to his local garage man, who in return for displaying them has given Lauda free car-washes for life. 'That's a good deal,' says Lauda. 'Most of the trophies are so ugly anyway.'

Bruce McLaren

Born in 1937, Bruce McLaren was killed while testing one of his Can–Am cars at Goodwood in 1970. An Auckland engineering student, he was awarded a motor-racing scholarship in 1957 by the New Zealand Grand Prix Association and set sail for England. His first season in England, in 1958, saw him team up with Jack Brabham at Cooper. He mostly drove Formula 2 and was runner-up in the European Formula 2 Championship. He had his first Formula 1 Grand Prix race that season, finishing twelfth in the Moroccan Grand Prix. His first Formula 1 Grand Prix success came in 1959 when he won the US Grand Prix; aged twenty-two years 104 days, he was the second youngest winner of a Formula 1 Grand Prix. In 1963 he formed Bruce McLaren Motor Racing Limited to design and build his own cars. His first Formula 1 car made its Grand Prix debut in 1966 at Monaco, and in 1968 it had its first win in the Belgian Grand Prix with Bruce driving. By the end of the 1984 season the car had enjoyed forty-two Grand Prix wins. McLaren himself had started in exactly 100 Grands Prix.

Bruce McLaren's Grand Prix Wins as a Driver

1959 United States (Cooper)
1960 Argentine (Cooper)
1962 Monaco (Cooper)
1968 Belgian (McLaren)
He also won the 1966 Le Mans Twenty-Four Hour race with Chris Amon.

Bruce McLaren's World Championship Placings

1959	6th	1965	9th
1960	2nd	1966	16th
1961	8th	1967	14th
1962	3rd	1968	5th
1963	6th	1969	3rd
1964	7th	1970	14th

Alain Prost

Prost was born in St Chamond in France in February 1955. At the end of 1984, when he was renowned as one of the greatest drivers in the world, he had only been in Formula 1 for four years. He made his debut for McLaren in Argentina in 1980, moved to Renault for the following season and won in France. After he had finished second in the 1983 championship, pipped at the post by Piquet, he left Renault following a disagreement

Niki Lauda wins the 1984 British Grand Prix

and was snapped up by McLaren. The 1984 season proved to be a monumental success for the team although a disappointment for Prost personally in that he failed by the narrowest of margins to become the first Frenchman to win the title. But his narrow failure earned him immense popularity in his home country. 'The French,' says Prost, 'do not like winners, they like glorious losers, like Joan of Arc.'

MARLBORO–McLAREN, 1984

Of the sixteen races that make up the World Championship, Marlboro–McLaren won twelve. They only failed to gain points for their drivers in two races: the Dallas Grand Prix and the Belgian Grand Prix. Prost equalled Jim Clark's record of seven Grand Prix wins in a season; it was also the greatest number of wins by a driver not winning the title. Apart from Lauda and Prost, the only other drivers to win races were Michele Alboreto (Ferrari), Nelson Piquet (Brabham), and Keke Rosberg (Williams). The 1984 Portuguese Grand Prix was the 250th race in which McLaren had competed.

Drivers' Championship, 1984

			Points
1	Lauda	(Marlboro–McLaren)	72
2	Prost	(Marlboro–McLaren)	71.5
3	De Angelis	(Lotus)	34
4	Alboreto	(Ferrari)	30.5
5	Piquet	(Brabham)	29
6	Arnoux	(Ferrari)	27

Constructors' Championship, 1984

		Points
1	Marlboro–McLaren	143.5
2	Ferrari	57.5
3	Lotus	47
4	Brabham	38
5	Renault	34
6	Williams	25.5

1984 Race by Race

Grand Prix	Prost	Lauda
Brazilian	1st	
South Africa	2nd	1st
Belgian		
San Marino	1st	
French	7th	1st
Monaco	1st	
Canadian	3rd	2nd
Detroit	5th	
Dallas		
British		1st
German	1st	2nd
Austrian		2nd
Dutch	1st	2nd
Italian		1st
European	1st	4th
Portuguese	1st	2nd

West Indies Cricket Team, 1984

'Blackwash' screamed the banner headlines when the West Indies thrashed England five matches to nil in the 1984 Test series in England. The West Indies had been forged into a tremendously competitive unit by Clive Lloyd of Guyana, a player with over a hundred Test caps in a career stretching back to the time Gary Sobers led the side, and captain on a record number of occasions.

In his line-up he had a remarkable array of talent: the best Test opening partnership in the Barbardians Gordon Greenidge and Desmond Haynes, arguably the greatest batsman since Bradman in Viv Richards, and the fastest trio of bowlers the world had ever seen in Malcolm Marshall (small but strong and deceptively, viciously fast), Michael Holding (lithe and athletic with a whippy action) and Joel Garner (massively built, he was over 6 feet 7 inches tall and his pace off the pitch matched that of Marshall). In support, Lloyd in his Test side had a promising wicketkeeper-batsman in Jeffrey Dujon, the steadiness of Larry Gomes at number three, the off spin and brilliant fielding of Roger Harper, and the support bowling of Eldine Baptiste.

Against them England fielded a somewhat lightweight side led by the inexperienced captain David Gower. Nevertheless, the team could hardly have predicted that by the end of the summer they would be the holders of a completely unwanted record – that of the first England team to be beaten five-nil in a Test series at home.

The series could not have started worse for England. At Edgbaston, Garner and Holding reduced them to 49 for 4 on the first morning; it was also the end of Andy Lloyd's season when Marshall's thunderbolt thudded into his head, damaging an eye. England never recovered, and when the batting assault was launched by the West Indies, first by Richards and Gomes, and then by Lloyd and Gomes, the match was beyond their grasp. Richards's 117 was a typical display of power and timing; Gomes's 143 was a delightful exhibition of quiet, unhurried strokeplay. The West Indies, already well in command at 455 for 8, decided to continue. Baptiste and Holding threw the bat at the ball to add 150 in 29 overs for the ninth wicket. Lloyd always pushed home his advantage. Not surprisingly, England wilted in their second innings as Garner took 5 wickets.

The second Test at Lord's demonstrated the West Indies' talent for wrenching the advantage from their opponents. After England had batted quite well but without really threatening to make enough runs, the West Indies collapsed to Ian Botham (8 for 103) to concede a first-innings lead. England, inspired by 110 from Lamb and 81 from Botham, set the West Indies 342 to win in less than a day. That the West Indies lost their first wicket in their second innings for 7 that day is now forgotten. Greenidge played one of the greatest Test innings of all time and, supported by Gomes, saw the West Indies home by 9 wickets. Off 242 balls Greenidge made 214 not out, with twenty-nine 4s and two 6s – the best by a Caribbean batsman at Lord's. Greenidge, spurred on by claims that he was losing his touch as an opening bat, played superbly well, gloriously taking the attack to Willis and Botham and dealing with the change bowlers with impunity. Those who were at Lord's that

Another salvo from the feared West Indian fast bowling attack. Here the 6-foot 8-inch Joel Garner fires another bouncer past the unfortunate Graeme Fowler during the West Indies' 5–0 trouncing of England in 1984

afternoon or were watching on television will never forget one of the most glorious innings of all time.

At Headingley another century by Allan Lamb prevented a complete rout by Holding, Garner and the rapidly improving Harper. The West Indies in turn owed much to the little Guyanian Larry Gomes, who, as the star names Greenidge, Haynes, Richards and Lloyd fell comparatively cheaply, made his way calmly and coolly to 104 not out. But it was a century which in the end owed much to the bravery of Malcolm Marshall. He came in to bat with a broken thumb and stayed long enough for Gomes to complete a deserved century; he also clipped a one-handed boundary himself. Inspired by Gomes's batting display, Marshall took the new ball and proceeded to rip through the England batting, taking 7 for 53. The target of 128 was never defensible against the West Indies bowling, although they did, in the end, lose 2 wickets.

Old Trafford was the scene for the next instalment. The West Indies collapsed to 70 for 4 before Dujon joined the opener Greenidge. Dujon had always looked a player of immense promise and classical style, but had yet to prove it on this tour.

With Greenidge, he added 197 in 69 overs. Greenidge, disciplining himself compared with the extravagances of Lord's, but still reaching a double century – 223 in almost ten hours – was partnered, after Dujon had gone for a marvellous 101, by nightwatchman Winston Davis, replacing the injured Marshall. On the second day Davis stayed to make 77 and ruin England's hope of gleaning anything from the match. England, in fact, collapsed in their first innings, although Lamb hit his third consecutive 100. England followed on but found the developing Harper's off spin too much for them. In a subtle display of control he took 6 for 57.

The many thousands of West Indies supporters in England that summer demanded their 'Blackwash' to be completed at the Oval. But it was a low-scoring game – 60 from Lloyd enabled his team to creep up to 190 in their first innings. England failed to gain the lead, however, as Marshall, with 5 wickets, blasted his way through the batting. In the West Indies second innings it was the turn of Haynes to display his undoubted talent with an effortless 125 to set England 375 to win – a target that was always beyond them as Holding, spurred on by a chance remark from a spectator in the crowd who had never seen him bowl off his full run, returned his best figures of the series (5 for 43) to earn the West Indies another comfortable victory.

Like all great sides, the West Indies had world-class players in abundance and a number of support players who would have starred in most other Test sides. Richards, as always, grabbed the limelight with his glittering 100 at Edgbaston and numerous cameo knocks. Even greater contributions came from Gordon Greenidge, with his two double centuries, and from the calm, efficient accumulator, Larry Gomes. While the bowling was never less than penetrative, Marshall, Holding and Garner were frequently irresistible. But it is worth noting that – again, like all great sides – there was tremendous spirit in the team, enough to extricate themselves from trouble on occasions. Holding's batting in support of Gomes at Leeds, the sudden burst of blistering pace by the injured Marshall at the same match which set up the comfortable win, the batting of Dujon and Davis at Old Trafford when few others could stay with the great Greenidge; and Desmond Haynes's timely century at the Oval. For a team to produce such performances regularly requires great talent and spirit and excellent leadership. Lloyd's contribution as captain of this great side should never be underestimated.

WEST INDIES TEST RECORD, 1984

On 21 March 1984 West Indies drew the second Test with Australia at Port-of-Spain. On 27 December 1984 they drew with Australia in the fourth Test at Melbourne. In between they played eleven Tests and won them all. Their full record was as follows:

v. Australia

Third Test (Bridgetown)	won by 10 wickets
Fourth Test (St John's)	won by innings and 36 runs
Fifth Test (Kingston)	won by 10 wickets

v. England

First Test (Birmingham)	won by innings and 180 runs
Second Test (Lord's)	won by 9 wickets
Third Test (Leeds)	won by 8 wickets
Fourth Test (Manchester)	won by innings and 64 runs
Fifth Test (Oval)	won by 172 runs

v. Australia

First Test (Perth)	won by innings and 112 runs
Second Test (Brisbane)	won by 8 wickets
Third Test (Adelaide)	won by 191 runs

During that eleven-match run they used fifteen players. The averages of the players during that period were as follows:

	M	I	No	Runs	Hs	Avge	100	Ct	Wkts	Runs	Avge	5wI	10wM	Best
E.A.E. Baptist	8	9	1	218	87*	27.25	0	2	14	420	30.00	0	0	3–31
W.W. Davis	1	1	0	77	77	77.00	0	1	2	77	38.50	0	0	2–71
P.J. Dujon	11	13	0	525	139	40.38	2	44(1)						
J. Garner	11	12	3	80	17	8.89	0	6	56	1168	20.86	2	0	5–55
L.A. Gomes	8	13	5	729	143	91.13	4	2	0	1		0	0	
C.G. Greenidge	11	17	3	978	223	69.86	3	9						
R.A. Harper	9	11	1	177	39*	17.70	0	16	24	595	24.79	1	0	6–57
D.L. Haynes	11	18	2	621	145	38.81	2	7						
M.A. Holding	9	10	2	163	69	20.38	0	5	40	763	19.08	2	0	6–21
C.H. Lloyd	11	13	1	587	114	48.92	1	16						
M.D. Marshall	10	11	0	169	57	15.36	0	7	65	1092	16.80	8	1	7–53
I.V.A. Richards	11	15	2	497	178	38.23	2	8	0	18		0	0	
R.B. Richardson	6	8	1	439	154	62.71	3	10						
M.A. Small	1	1	1	3	3*		0	0	3	78	26.00	0	0	3–40
C.A. Walsh	3	3	1	9	9*	4.50	0	0	8	213	26.62	0	0	3–55

* Not out.